*Reading the Bible
in the Global Village:
Cape Town*

Society of Biblical Literature

Global Perspectives on Biblical Scholarship

Number 3

Reading the Bible in the Global Village:
Cape Town

Reading the Bible in the Global Village: Cape Town

Justin S. Ukpong
Musa W. Dube
Gerald O. West
Alpheus Masoga
Norman K. Gottwald
Jeremy Punt
Tinyiko S. Maluleke
Vincent L. Wimbush

Society of Biblical Literature
Atlanta

READING THE BIBLE IN THE GLOBAL VILLAGE:
CAPE TOWN

Copyright © 2002 by the Society of Biblical Literature

All rights reserved.

No part of this work may be reproduced or transmitted in any form or by any means, electronic or mechanical, including photocopying and recording, or by means of any information storage or retrieval system, except as may be expressly permitted by the 1976 Copyright Act or in writing from the publisher. Requests for permission should be addressed in writing to the Rights and Permissions Department, Society of Biblical Literature, 825 Houston Mill Road, Suite 350, Atlanta, GA 30329, USA.

Library of Congress Cataloging-in-Publication Data

Reading the Bible in the global village : Cape Town / Justin S. Ukpong ... [et al.].
    p. cm. — (Global perspectives on biblical scholarship ; no. 3)
"The 2000 SBL International Meeting in Cape Town, South Africa."—Pref.
  Includes bibliographical references.
  ISBN 1-58983-025-3 (pbk. : alk. paper)
  1. Bible—Criticism, interpretation, etc.—Africa, Sub-Saharan—Congresses. I. Ukpong, Justin S. II. Series.
BS511.3 .R43 2002b
220.6'096—dc21   2002006306

This book is printed on recycled, acid-free paper.

02 03 04 05 06 07 08 09 — 5 4 3 2 1

MANUFACTURED IN THE UNITED STATES OF AMERICA

Contents

Preface
  Kent Harold Richards 7

Chapter 1: Reading the Bible in a Global Village:
  Issues and Challenges from African Readings
  Justin S. Ukpong 9

Chapter 2: Villagizing, Globalizing, and Biblical Studies
  Musa W. Dube 41

Chapter 3: Unpacking the Package That Is the Bible
  in African Biblical Scholarship
  Gerald O. West 65

Chapter 4: Redefining Power: Reading the Bible in Africa
  from the Peripheral and Central Positions
  Alpheus Masoga 95

Chapter 5: The Role of Biblical Politics in Contextual
  Theologies
  Norman K. Gottwald 111

Chapter 6: Towards a Postcolonial Reading of Freedom
  in Paul
  Jeremy Punt 125

Chapter 7: What If We Are Mistaken about Bible and
  Christianity in Africa?
  Tinyiko S. Maluleke 151

Chapter 8: Response
  Vincent L. Wimbush 173

Notes. 179
References. 199
Contributors 219

Preface

Kent Harold Richards

The Society of Biblical Literature annual International Meeting outside North America, launched in 1983, has provided an opportunity for Biblical scholars from around the world to share their research and to explore emerging methods, tools, and approaches to Biblical scholarship with colleagues in the global village. This volume is the second to be published by the SBL in its Global Perspectives on Biblical Scholarship series under the title "Reading the Bible in the Global Village." These volumes provide access to some of the fruits of the SBL International Meetings for those who are unable to participate in person.

This volume originated in the 2000 SBL International Meeting in Cape Town, South Africa. The eight scholars whose essays are presented here all either come from Africa or have very strong interests in and commitments to African Biblical scholarship. Taken together, their work provides a good overview of and introduction to the issues, themes, theories, and practices that are characteristic of the best contemporary Biblical study in Africa. Vincent Wimbush observes in his response to these essays that they are "historic and fascinating and most important as a harbinger of a radical epistemic challenge" to Biblical scholarship.

Justin S. Ukpong delivered the opening plenary address to the 2000 SBL International Meeting, to which Musa W. Dube offered a probing and spirited response. Both Ukpong and

Dube have extended and enriched their oral presentations in the essays presented here. The exchange between them provides a stimulating examination of both the possibilities and the limitations of the idea of a global village as related to the reading and interpretation of the Bible in Africa.

Gerald O. West and Alpheus Masoga focus explicitly on some of the important theories and practices that characterize contemporary African Biblical scholarship; in different ways they stress both the distinction and the relationships between "trained" and "ordinary" readers of the Bible. Norman Gottwald cautions about the dangers of simplistic readings and naïve appropriations of the political themes and images of the Old Testament in contextual theologies. Jeremy Punt contributes a sophisticated rereading of Paul's discussion of freedom in the context of postcolonial and post-Apartheid South Africa. Tinyiko Maluleke stresses the importance of understanding clearly the complex nature of Christianity in Africa as it provides a context for Biblical interpretation.

In his concluding essay, Vincent Wimbush observes that the voices heard here, taken together, contribute significantly to a "de-centering and de-stabilization of the discourse" about Biblical scholarship, despite the limitations of the volume's size and scope. In speaking of the challenge to Biblical scholarship represented here, he asserts that the challenge is more than methodological:

> ... it has to do more pointedly with what one can know and how one can know it. I think this collection of essays points to a radical challenge for certain scholars about what it is that they claim to know, what it is that they can know, what are or ought to be their practices in relation to that complex abbreviation "Bible."

Chapter 1

Reading the Bible in a Global Village: Issues and Challenges from African Readings

Justin S. Ukpong

Introduction

Up to about the middle of the twentieth century, biblical criticism as an academic discipline was taught in an undifferentiated manner throughout the world including Africa (Hartin 1992). However, with the entry of Africa and the rest of the Third World around the middle of the twentieth century as actors in the scene, the hitherto "untroubled waters" of classical biblical pedagogy, to use the phrase of Cain Hope Felder (1994), underwent a sea change and things are not likely to be the same again (at least in Africa). In academic biblical pedagogy and discourse in Africa today, there is a big departure from what was hitherto considered normal: African ways of reading the Bible are being taught alongside classical methods in academic institutions; the Bible is being studied against the background of African contexts, and African contextual issues form the agenda for reading the Bible; Africans, hitherto objects, are being constructed into *subjects* of biblical interpretation; African conceptual frame of reference is competing with that of the West (hitherto considered universal and normal) as a methodological tool of exegetical practices; the ordinary people's approach to the Bible is informing scholarly reading practices; critical reading masses are being nurtured at the grassroots, and the hitherto muted voices of the ordinary people are coming alive in academic biblical discourses.

The Bible is being democratized by the academy in Africa. This is tantamount to questioning what, from another perspective, Fernando Segovia (1999) calls "the methodological and theoretical consensus" in the discipline. Put differently, a protest movement is taking place for the reorientation of biblical interpretation within the academy. At bottom, it is about reclaiming the status of the Bible as word of God and classic, a guide to moral and spiritual life as well as an ancient literature worth attention beyond its time. Academic readings of the Bible in Africa therefore bring up issues that pose a challenge within the global scene of biblical scholarship. Here I must make a distinction between the classical Western biblical scholarship practiced in Africa, and the African version. The observable difference lies in the latter's concern to link the biblical text with the realities of African contexts, and the methodological implications that this entails. This paper is concerned with the latter. I must also add that African biblical scholars have been trained in one or other of the Western exegetical methodologies, and that the rise of the African version owes to the realized inadequacy of these methodologies in answering typically African questions (for example, see Tutu 1978, 336; Pobee 1985–86, 22–29; Abogunrin 1980, 18–29; Wambutda 1980, 34; Boesak 1982; Mosala 1989; West 1992, 3–13; West 1993).

Elsewhere, I have identified and analyzed, in terms of background, mode of discourse and interpretive interest, the different models of biblical interpretation in Africa as: *comparative* studies, *evaluative* studies, *Africa-in-the-Bible* studies, *feminist/womanist* hermeneutics, *liberation* hermeneutics, *Black theology* and *inculturation hermeneutics* (Ukpong 1999a). I have also discussed the developments that have taken place till the present showing that in the period covering the 1990s, biblical studies in Africa became much more assertive and proactive daring to make an original contribution with the introduction of two new orientations (Ukpong, 1999b). One is the orientation that recognizes the *ordinary African readers* (the poor, the marginalized, non-biblical experts) and *ordinary African women* as important partners in academic Bible reading, and seeks to integrate their perspectives in the process of academic interpretation of the Bible. This is exemplified in Gerald West's *contextual Bible study* (West 1993) and Musa Dube's *feminist hermeneutics* (Dube 1996) modes of reading. The other is the orientation which, in addition to recognizing the role of the ordinary readers, articulates and emphasizes the use of the African conceptual frame of reference in the interpretation process. This is exemplified in my *inculturation hermeneutics* mode of reading (Ukpong 1995, 3–14). Thus, the African context is seen as providing the critical resources for biblical interpretation and as being the *subject* of interpretation.

Through these analyses have crystallized some methodological issues that may be considered as basic to the presuppositions, conceptualizations and practices of contemporary African biblical hermeneutics. My intention in this paper is to discuss these issues in relation to the classical Western tradition of biblical interpretation within the context of the concept of global village. They include: the meaning of *exegesis and hermeneutics*, the issue of the Bible as *sacred classic*, the issues of *contextual* hermeneutics and *engaged* hermeneutics, the idea of *ordinary people* as *subjects* of interpretation, and the idea of *reading with* ordinary readers. It must however quickly be added that these are collective issues; they are not all featured in every model of African reading of the Bible. And since the models in which they are embedded are many and varied, to make the discussion concrete, I shall discuss these issues in relation to one of the models—the *inculturation hermeneutics* model. I have chosen this model because of its inclusive methodology and its openness to a broad spectrum of contextual questions, and because these issues are well represented and articulated in it. I shall start with a brief introduction of inculturation hermeneutics. I shall next discuss these theoretical issues as they relate to classical Western exegesis, and then African readings in relation to classical Western readings. The aim is not so much to propose a resolution to the problems raised here as to create a critical consciousness about them.

Inculturation Hermeneutics

Inculturation hermeneutics is a contextual hermeneutic methodology that seeks to make any community of ordinary people and their social-cultural context the *subject* of interpretation of the Bible through the use of the conceptual frame of reference of the people and the involvement of the ordinary people in the interpretation process. It involves a commitment to the world of the ordinary people and their historical life experience, and interaction between ordinary readers and ordinary ways of reading the Bible on the one hand, and academic readers and academic ways of reading on the other. The goal is social-cultural transformation focusing on a variety of human situations and issues. It exhibits the following among its distinctive characteristics: a *holistic approach to culture*, use of *African conceptual frame of reference for interpretation*, awareness of *functional conditioning* in the process of reading, seeing the *meaning of a text as a function of the interaction* between the text in its context and the present context (Ukpong 1995, 5–10).

Holistic Approach to Culture

The idea of culture is a conceptual construct generally agreed to be a tool for clarifying identity and difference in the human community. Its definition is today a highly contested terrain that I do not wish to tread here. For our purpose, it is sufficient to note that culture is seen holistically in inculturation hermeneutics—not just as signifying practices (Storey 1998, 2) but also as the totality of the way of life of a human community. Thus the way of viewing reality and the activities of any given human community whether they be social, political, economic, religious, leisure activities, the arts, textual productions, reading practices, etc., all belong in the realm of culture. Besides, culture is seen as having two dimensions—secular/material and sacred/religious—that impact upon each other in an interlacing manner that makes any discourse within one dimension impinge upon the other. Within this conspectus, therefore, no issue may be seen as purely secular or purely religious. Every issue has both a secular as well as a religious dimension to it. Culture is also the medium for interpreting the world, for self-expression and self-understanding. It emerges through human interaction within a community (it is not a matter of external and ingenious human contrivance and manipulation), and is dynamic and open-ended. The holistic understating of culture recognizes the importance and the contribution of the ordinary and commonplace in the production of knowledge. It bypasses the ideological separation of the popular from the elite, the traditional from the modern in cultures, accepting all as legitimate objects of inquiry (Mukerji and Schudson 1991, 2). This understanding of culture makes it possible to raise, within the ambit of inculturation hermeneutics, a variety of issues—justice issues of gender, race, social, economic, political, andreligious oppression as well as issues of indigenous cultural identity, customs and practices.

The Use of an African Conceptual Frame of Reference

A very important feature of inculturation hermeneutics is its emphasis on using an African conceptual frame of reference in interpreting the Bible in Africa rather than using another conceptual frame for interpretation and applying the result in the African context. Every reading activity entails three elements that function together. These are the *reading practice* that is used, the *reading method* that is used, and the *conceptual frame of reference* on which both the reading method and practice are grounded.

Reading practices involve the use of reading methods. No readers read the Bible without using some method whether scientific or unscientific, albeit unconsciously, even if they are untrained Bible readers.[1] However, the reading operation itself is not just the *application* of a reading method to read a text; it involves the *implementation* of the regime of the method in a particular way directed by particular interests and concerns of both the method and the readers (Patte 1995, 59). Readers, most often unconsciously, go to texts with some questions in mind reflecting the interests they have unconsciously imbibed over the years as well as some expectations derived from their pre-understandings, and are influenced by their status in society, denominational affiliation, gender, etc. in the way they understand texts. Thus different readers may use the same method of reading but arrive at different results. It is at this level that we locate the differences we find, for example, in feminist readings as opposed to androcentric male readings, readings by the poor as opposed to readings by the materially comfortable, readings by those in power as opposed to readings by those under power, readings by the elite as opposed to readings by the lower class, even though all these may be using the same methods.

A *reading method* embodies a procedure along with a conceptual apparatus with its particular set of cultural (political, social, economic, etc.) and interpretive interests. It comprises theoretical assumptions about the meaning of texts, the nature and purpose of reading, and the world of the reader. It is a child of a particular culture and is founded on a particular conceptual frame of reference. (Every method therefore needs to be critiqued to discover its basic assumptions and interpretive interests.) The historical critical method, for example, is a child of the culture of the Enlightenment and the industrial revolution. It is informed by the interest to search for historical truth devoid of the intervention of human or divine authority which is one of the ideals of the Enlightenment. In its positivistic form, it involves bracketing out the presence of the supernatural in the Bible. Inculturation hermeneutics is informed by the ideals of African culture. It seeks to make the message of the Bible come alive in contemporary contexts, and is strongly affirmative of the presence of the supernatural in the Bible.

A *conceptual frame of reference* is a mental apparatus. It refers to the type of understanding of the universe that informs the reading, that is, the mind-set that is at work in the reading operation. It comprises a particular set of world-view, values, disvalues, and basic assumptions about reality. It forms the basic foundation of any reading method, informs the method and the reading practice in which the method is used, and is acquired imperceptibly through the use of the method. It is, at bottom, the grid through which the biblical text is read. (It is important then to critique every reading method to discover the conceptual frame of reference that informs it.) Classical Western reading methods and practices are informed by the Western conceptual frame of reference while inculturation hermeneutics is informed by the African conceptual frame of reference. The difference between the two is significant. For example, within the African conceptual frame of reference, the reality of the interaction between the supernatural and natural worlds, the spirit world and the world of physical human existence, and the interconnectedness of all these, are taken for granted while that is not the case in the Western conceptual frame of reference. Other characteristics of the Western conceptual frame of reference include dualism, individualism, historicism, and intellectualism while a unitive view of reality, emphasis on community, and pragmatic outlook are among what mark the African conceptual frame of reference (see Talbot 1923, 140; Tempels 1959, 25; Lienhardt 1961, 28; Mbiti 1970, 97; Anyanwu 1981, 90–93; Ikenga-Metuh 1981, 52).

In any reading practice, the conceptual frame of reference used may be that of the reader's cultural community or of another (Bailey 1998, 78; Fish 1980; Iser 1978; Tompkins 1980). One practice in academic Bible reading in Africa today is the use of the Western conceptual frame of reference to read a text and then apply the result to the African context. When, for example, Africans *uncritically* use the historical critical method which is informed by the Western conceptual frame of reference, they are using another cultural community's conceptual grid to read.[2] An important aspect of inculturation hermeneutics is the use, in the interpretation process, of the conceptual frame of reference of the community within which interpretation is done. Thus in inculturation hermeneutics, texts are not appropriated with a foreign conceptual frame of reference and then applied to the African context; rather, African conceptual frame of reference is used in appropriating the text. Historical tools are used critically and made to function within the African conceptual frame of reference. In that way the African people and their contexts are made the *subject* of the interpretation.

Functional Conditioning of Readers

In inculturation hermeneutics the role of the personal conditioning of the readers in reading practices is recognized, and it is required that these be articulated and used critically. "Personal conditioning" has to do with how the subjectivity of the reader is constructed, and involves world view, gender, and factors that are *economic, religious, social, political,* and *racial*. Every form of conditioning has both positive and negative effects depending on whether or not they constitute liberative or oppressive practices. For example, with regard to gender differentiation, male dominated readings of certain texts of the Bible have often produced results that are oppressive of women, or that are not sympathetic to women's cause, while feminist hermeneutics has led to new and liberative readings of such texts. Also, biases and predetermined positions such as racial prejudice, the religious confession of the readers, etc., may produce oppressive readings, but they could also be used to subvert such readings. The conditioning works like lenses through which readings are filtered; it gives colors to the reading. No reader or reading community is free from it. This makes reading practices somewhat subjective, but that subjectivity is transcended by recognizing these conditions and using them creatively, and by reflecting in a community. Inculturation hermeneutics emphasizes the need to be critically aware of these personal conditions, and to articulate and use them critically and positively in the interpretation process.

Location of Meaning in a Text

In inculturation hermeneutics, the meaning of a text is seen as a function of the interaction between the text studied in its social-historical context on the one hand, and the social-cultural context of the readers on the other. The purpose of interpretation is to appropriate a text's meaning in a contemporary social-cultural context. Biblical texts are seen as rooted in their historical contexts yet as plurivalent, capable of speaking to different situations and contexts across time and space (see Croatto 1987, 19). Thus the hermeneutic process involves four poles that interplay: the *text*, the *context* of the text, the *reading community*, and the *context* of the reading community. Meaning is understood as *produced* in the process of a *community* of ordinary readers within their *social-cultural context* reading *the text* against its *social-historical context*. Both the contemporary social-cultural context and the social-historical context of the text are analyzed to establish a meaningful relationship between them.

Because there are many levels, ramifications, and dimensions to the historical context of any text, the contemporary context is analyzed first to identify the specific issue(s) to be reflected upon in the reading. Thus methodological priority is given to the context of the readers (Mosala 1989, 123–25). This enables the readers to establish a focus for the historical research, and to clarify for themselves the sort of questions to put to the text. The validity of readings is judged by their faithfulness to the ethical demands of the gospels which include love of neighbor, respect for one another, etc.

Inculturation hermeneutics therefore involves interpreting a text in terms of the present but not in isolation from the past. It recognizes that though given in specific historical past contexts, the biblical message transcends the particularity of its context and becomes part of our world today and can therefore speak to the present. Simply put, then, within the context of inculturation hermeneutics, interpreting a text means putting it in interaction between its historical-social context and our own context and making it address and question our context (see Wimbush 1985, 19).

African Readings and Western Readings: Issues and Challenges

The preceding discussion outlines in broad strokes what inculturation hermeneutics stands for, and sets the stage for a discussion of the issues that arise from African readings of the Bible when they are considered in relation to classical Western readings.

The Meaning of Exegesis and Hermeneutics

Within the framework of inculturation hermeneutics, the classical opposition, which one encounters in some authors of the historical critical method, between *exegesis* as an objective, historical exercise concerned with the task of reconstructing the past and the recovery of the intention of the author, and *hermeneutics* as a subjective, contextual exercise concerned with the application of the meaning of the text so recovered to the present context, does not obtain. For, since the past can only be reached and communicated through our situatedness in the present, the meaning we get of the past is not a meaning of what happened in the past *pure and simple*, but of what happened in the past filtered through the present; that is, the meaning that we, from the present standpoint, are able to make of the past. Hence we do not "recover" the intention of the author of a biblical text *pure and simple*. What we achieve in the historical exercise is making meaning of (reconstructing) the past with the insights (tools and wisdom) of our present situatedness. (This is hardly "recovering" the past *as it was*.) This means that the present is a determining factor in making meaning of texts. Thus in inculturation hermeneutics, the past collapses into the present, and exegesis fuses with hermeneutics. The past is not ignored, it is indeed regarded as important, but is seen as reached only through the eyes of the present; the present is thus given due recognition as a conditioning for understanding the past.

The Bible as a Sacred Classic

In classical Western scholarship, among some authors, scientific, academic readings of the Bible are expected to be devoid of faith biases. The Bible is considered purely as an ancient literary work of art, and therefore purely an object of critical enquiry.

On the contrary, academic readings of the Bible in Africa issue from a commitment to the Christian faith. The Bible is seen both as a sacred text and as a classic. As a sacred text the Bible is the word of God in human language which implies that human culture with its world-view, values and disvalues is intertwined with the word of God. In inculturation hermeneutics, emphasis is placed on ethical reading in the light of the basic human and biblical values of love and justice, peace and inclusiveness, such that exclusive and oppressive texts are viewed as a challenge to the readers with respect to these values rather than as a basis for action. Interpreting the Bible means unleashing the liberating message of God to be experienced as good news in the concrete to nourish as well as challenge life within the society. The Bible is also regarded as classical literature to be investigated as any other literature, and read using techniques from secular literary practices. It is thus amenable to critical scrutiny and scholarly debate. The combined sacred and classical characters of the Bible make it a "living" book that is open to critical investigation. African exegesis in general seeks to hold these two ideals in creative tension.

The Contextual Character of African Reading

For want of a better term and in contradistinction to African readings, I designate classical Western Bible reading methodologies that were common until recently as *intellectualist*, by which I mean that they *professedly* seek objective truth as interpretive interest, and *profess* to employ a universal perspective. A major concern is *knowledge* of the meaning of the biblical text through the use of methods of investigation established by the academy. Their conclusions are expected to have a universal applicability. By contrast, however, African readings are *existential and pragmatic* in nature. They lay no claim to universality of perspective and are interested in contemporary and existential questions in relation to the biblical message. The results of their investigations are considered valid for the contexts concerned but with possible validity for other contexts. They are concerned with the meaning of the biblical text not in an intellectualist but in an existential sense. They are explicitly *contextual* in character, and this refers to the following:

(1) The readings are done *from a certain standpoint or perspective*. African readings of the Bible are explicitly perspectival; they do not claim to issue from a universal standpoint. This stems from the fact that in physical terms we, as human beings, can only stand at one location at a time when viewing things. Similarly, in epistemological terms, the human mind does not perceive reality from a universal but from a particular perspective. It is always limited to a certain perspective that provides the "angle of vision" for understanding. Biblical interpretation practices in Africa are based on this simple experience and therefore do not claim to be universal. They therefore explicitly state the context of their interpretation, that is, the location from which the interpretation takes place.

(2) The readings do not claim to appropriate the totality of the meaning of the texts read. This is based on the theory that in any given reading only *a certain aspect or certain aspects of a text* get appropriated. By virtue of the limitation of our human nature, it is not possible to appropriate all aspects of a text at once; only a certain aspect is accessible to us in any reading process depending on our standpoint. In other words, a text has more aspects, dimensions and perspectives than we see and appropriate in any given reading (Patte 1999, 37–65). As a corollary, the more perspectival readings of a text we are aware of, the more dimensions of the text are disclosed to us, and the better off we are in appreciating it.

(3) The readings are done in relation to some context outside the Bible itself. Human knowledge does not take place in a vacuum but always in relation to other things in the external

world. New things are known through a process of relating them to things we already know. Making meaning of a biblical text involves relating the text to some empirical experience we have in the world outside the Bible. Thus the meaning we have is contextual: it is produced through relating the text with something else that we already know. This may happen implicitly or explicitly.

(4) The readings are mediated through a particular *conceptual frame of reference* derived from the world-view and the social-cultural context of a particular cultural community. This informs and shapes the exegetical methodology and the reading practice and acts as a grid for making meaning of the text.

Based on these considerations, every reading is regarded as contextual; and readings that claim to be universal remain suspect, and are seen as attempt to universalize the particular. African readings therefore do not claim to be universal, they are explicitly contextual and particular. However, such particular readings are not exclusivist or closed, but are open to "conversation" with other forms of reading.

Engaged Hermeneutics

Academic readings of the Bible in the West preclude involvement in concrete situations and are expected to be a matter of dialogue within the academic community only. On the contrary however, academic Bible readings in Africa are inserted within the dynamics of the ordinary people's committed action and seek to articulate the people's experience of their life in Christ as well as provide insights for reflecting on such experience. They are life-centered readings. They seek to appropriate the biblical message not in abstract theoretical terms but within the context of concrete human situations. The goal is not merely to acquire knowledge about the Bible but to facilitate the living of the Christian faith in concrete life situations and provide answers to questions of practical life concerns from the perspectives of the questioners. The focus, for example, is not on God in an abstract way or on God who relates to people in a vague general way, but on God who relates to people in their specific social-cultural and historical contexts. Academic readers are not mere armchair theoreticians but active pastoral agents who are involved in the life of the people. In this way the word of God is not presented as mere theory but is made to find expression in the concrete aspects of the people's life of commitment to action. Thus, ideally, from this perspective, academic Bible reading is seen to be inadequate if it is not inserted within the dynamics of a people's committed action.

The People and Their Context as the Subject of Interpretation

The Bible has often been referred to as a "site of struggle" in contemporary Third World biblical hermeneutics, and the question often arises as to "whose Bible" (whose understanding of the Bible) is to be privileged. In a particular sense the Bible is the site of struggle for control and legitimization between the ordinary people, the church, and the academy. In classical Western readings, the epistemological privilege is given to the academy, for it is only the interpretations of trained experts who follow certain laid down procedures of the academy that are regarded as valid within the academy. Non-expert interpretations of the ordinary people are regarded as uninformed and therefore inconsequential for ascertaining the true meaning of the biblical text. There is, therefore, no dialogue with ordinary readings of the Bible. Church interpretations are equally discountenanced for being dogmatic and unscientific.

On the contrary, however, in inculturation hermeneutics, there is concern to make African peoples, identified social-culturally as groups and defined in terms of their common identities and concrete historical social life situations, the *subject* of interpretation of the Bible. This means more than that these people do read the Bible. It means primarily that they use their social-cultural resources as critical tools of reading; that they read from their social-cultural perspective and world view, and with a conceptual apparatus that is informed by their culture; that they read with the consciousness and confidence of being in control of the interpretation; that they do not allow already learned meanings of the text to control their reading but seek to discover new meanings through a new subjectivity that they clarify for themselves; that the readings emerge from the community and not from individual theologians working in isolation from the community. These people read in concert with trained readers to produce critical readings. Thus the primacy of the reading activity is located not among individual theologians working in isolation but in concert with communities of ordinary people.

As a general category the term "ordinary people" refers to a social class, the common people in contradistinction to the elite. In most of Africa they live by the world-view provided by their traditional cultures, they are poor and marginalized, they suffer economic, social and political disadvantage, and are found in both rural and urban areas. They are not trained in the theological sciences, and are generally illiterate, semi-literate or functionally illiterate. However, they have a high sense of self-worth and would not be compromised because of their low social status. Scars of struggle for survival mark their lives. Even though in most cases they live below the subsistence level, they never give up on living (one rarely finds cases of suicide among them). They are "incurably" religious. All these, in different ways, constitute their conditioning in reading. Preference for their insights and life experience as a conditioning in reading does not mean exclusion of the elite; rather it means inviting the elite to be converted to the perspective of the poor and to learn from the experience of the poor in reading the Bible.

Reading "with" the People

Within the Western academy, Bible readings are done by trained persons generally working in isolation. However, an important feature of inculturation hermeneutics and some other Bible reading practices in Africa is that trained readers read "with" the ordinary people (see West 1993a, 8–9). Reading "with" means that the reading agenda is that of the community and not that of the trained readers. The trained readers do not direct or control the reading process or seek to "teach" to the community the meaning of the text they have already known. Rather, they read as part of the community, and facilitate an interactive process that leads to the community producing a critical meaning of the text. It is a collaborative reading process that transforms and enlarges the subjectivity of the readers through hearing and appropriating the text with people whose personal experiences and insights are different from one's own. It implies the recognition and affirmation of the otherness and personal worth of the others (see Patte 1995, 25, 33 n. 21; Spivak 1988, 295). Through such a process the academic reader accesses the resources of popular readings of the Bible, and academic scholarship is informed and enriched by resources outside its own circle, while the ordinary readers acquire the perspective of critical reading.

Reading "with" ordinary readers also entails reading "from" their perspective; this in turn implies many things. First is that the community reflects on its context in interaction with the text set in its social historical context using the appropriate conceptual frame of reference. Second is that the trained readers know and share the cultural perspectives of the community; that they situate themselves within the community. It would be impossible for them to use the resources of the people's culture for reading if they do not possess adequate knowledge of and competence in it. Elsewhere I have referred to this as meaning that the trained readers should be "insiders" in the culture (Ukpong 1995, 5), that is, people with adequate knowledge of and competence in the culture. They do not have to be indigenous to the culture. Knowledge of other cultural perspectives and of other methods of reading is indispensable because these function as a point of reference for self-criticism. Third is that as a matter of priority, questions are put to the text from the perspectives of the most disadvantaged characters (generally whose voices are not "heard" or are passive) in the text. Questions are also posed from the perspectives of the other characters to complement these. A fourth implication which flows from the above is the concern to bring out the "voices" of the unimportant characters which may sometimes be present only thematically in the text.

Globalization: Concept and Practice

To situate the above discussion within the discourse of global village, I shall first discuss globalization. I make a distinction between *globalization* and the *global village* concept. I see both as related but not exactly the same thing. Only globalization practiced in an interactive two-way direction leads to the situation of global village. I further distinguish two ways of looking at globalization. One is the fact that today through modern means of communication, what happens in one part of the globe easily becomes common knowledge in other parts with incredible speed, and we have therefore become more and more aware of being interconnected in a common world. This is a given, an indisputable fact. It is the object of analysis in theories of globalization. It is, however, not the focus of the discussion here. At issue here also is not whether or not this situation has advantages. It certainly has, but it also has damaging effects. The other way of looking at globalization is to ask what this contemporary phenomenon means in terms of power relations in the world, and the processes that have brought it about. This is the aspect of globalization that this paper seeks to address.

The term "globalization" is supposed to have been first used in its verb form "globalize" in 1959 (Waters 1995, 2), but it is only in late the 1990s that the globalization debate really flourished. However, the reality this phenomenon represents is considered as dating back much earlier. According to Jonathan Friedman (1994, 18–19), it started with intercultural trade that first appeared in the late Bronze Age. In José Míguez Bonino's reading (1999, 18–21), the Tower of Babel story of Genesis 11:1-9 reflects a historical attempt at Empire building in the late Bronze Age that failed due to God's intervention. Though he does not use the term globalization to describe this event, in my reading, the story reflects an attempt at globalization that did not succeed but which is interpreted in the narrative as having been thwarted by God. According to Immanuel Wallerstein (1974; 1980; 1989) globalization started with the Western European explorations to the outside world in the fifteenth century. In the succeeding centuries, Western European merchants established trade with far away territories that were not ruled from one political capital, especially the Baltic lands and the new world, thus creating a world-economy that was not contiguous with any single political territory. This, accordingly, created its own geographical divisions of core, periphery and semi-periphery (Wallerstein 1979, 37–48). According to Peter Beyer (1994, 14), the contemporary globalization phenomenon is a feature of late twentieth century, and the development of globalization as a social-scientific theoretical theme dates only to the 1970s and 1980s. While the Bronze age and fifteenth century dating of this phenomenon does point to its long existence, generally it is the phenomenon as it manifests itself in late twentieth century that is at issue and with which I am concerned here.

Globalization as it exists today comprises a variety of highly complex phenomena that affect all facets of human existence in the world (see Mittleman 2000, 6; Tabb 1999, 1; Giddens 1990, 64; Cvetkovich and Kellner 1997, 11). At its core is the integration into world systems of national political, economic, cultural and even demographic forces in a homogenizing trend, through the global extension of Western cultural systems into the way of life of other nations. Peter Beyer (1974, 8–9) has argued that even though the various globalizing social structures originate in the West, globalization should not be seen as an extension of Western cultural systems to other cultures or as a homogenizing force because Western culture also gets relativized in the process. But it is to be noted that this relativization is only a necessary by-product of the extension of Western culture to other regions. No culture that expands and interacts with other cultures can be expected to remain the same and unchanged nor can the other cultures involved in the interaction. Besides, in the process there has arisen from the peripheral cultures a resistance to the homogenizing trend such that while the contexts in which these cultures exist have changed (they have been relativized), they still maintain their identities however transformed. In other words, globalization has to be seen as the extension of Western power through the globe that has evoked the resistance of the host cultures and the relativization of both the host cultures and globalizing culture. Again Beyer observes that the problem about globalization "is one of power," the issue of who controls change in the world; however, he sees a paradox in this in that the process "encourages relativization of particular identities as a way of gaining control over systemic power" (1974, 3). Beyer is right that globalization is about power, but the paradox he identifies does not really make a difference. In a system where a strong partner (the West) interacts with a weak one (Third World), it is predictable that the strong one will always gain control of the system's power in spite of any relativization.

Globalization is experienced in various aspects of contemporary life. *Economically* we experience it through transnational corporations that extend their business interests across the globe, and through such Western controlled institutions as the International Monetary Fund (IMF) and the World Bank that monitor and shape the course of world economy, deciding on the economic measures and conditions to be implemented in the Third World countries for the "health" of the "world" economy. What is scarcely adverted to and much less questioned is that these measures are based on Western perspectives and patterns of living, which are assumed to be of universal applicability, and this masks the fact that the trumpeted "health of world economy" actually translates to the health of Western economy. *Politically* we experience globalization through the breakdown of the Soviet Bloc and the homogenization of the political system in the world through the extension of the democratic forces of the West. It is symbolized in the democratic pursuits of such institutions as the United Nations, the Organization of African Unity, the European Union, and other regional governmental organizations. *Socially* we experience it in rapid change, as the compression of time and distance through the modern means of communication, particularly the Internet: that we can, from the comfort of our living rooms anywhere in the world, watch certain events like the Olympics as they take place. We also experience it in the presence, in our neighborhoods through migration, of peoples and cultures hitherto far away. Thus people of differentiated cultures who were hitherto spatially distant are today living in spatial proximity. In cities like New York, London and Frankfurt it is possible to find people of nearly every nationality and culture in the world. This creates a sense of the world shrinking and becoming more and more "a single place" (Robertson 1987, 43). *Within the academy* we experience it in the giving of epistemological privilege to the Western mode of intellectual production; to be accepted within the academy, scholars from other cultures must do things the way they are done in the West. Accepted rules and techniques of scholarly production, now regarded as normative and universal, follow Western patterns of thought and practices with little or no consideration for cultural differences.

As mentioned above, analysis of globalization only started to flourish in the late 1990s. But within this short time, a large body of literature has built up making the topic to overshadow post-modernism (which was popular in the 1980s) in importance. The mass of literature, however, reveals a wide spectrum of positions from those that acclaim it as the way to progress (e.g. Beyer 1974; Meyer 1980; Marber 1988) to those that see and critique it as another form of the spread of Western cultural dominance over the globe (e.g. Brecher and Costello 1994; Sassen 1998; Dallmayr 1998). Most often, the positions diverge according to the side of the Atlantic (North or South) with which the author pitches camp. Invariably, globalization is regarded as a blessing when viewed from a Western (North Atlantic) perspective. Peter Marber (1988, 5) has enumerated its benefits to include improvements to human life in what he calls the "backward countries" such as "increased rates of literacy, daily caloric intake, and life expectancy," and the "narrowing gap" between the West and the "backward countries" (one is inclined to ask what, in real terms, constitutes the narrowing of the gap). He advocates integration of economies as opposed to "inward-looking protectionism" as the true road to economic progress. For him, globalization is synonymous with progress; to be against it, therefore, is to be against progress. Clearly, the idea of progress here betrays modernistic thinking and masks the vital issues connected with globalization.

From a Third World perspective, however, there are many things wrong with globalization (in the second sense indicated above) as currently experienced in the Third World. In spite of Western protestations to the contrary (Cvetkovich and Kellner 1997, 13; Schreiter 1998, 11), globalization is experienced in the Third World as a totalizing influence of a Western central capital culture integrating into itself hitherto diverse cultural systems all over the globe. It is experienced as cultural capitalism that leaves in its wake massive impoverishment of the Third World in every respect. Most pro-Northern analyses of it are seen in the Third World as a problematization of the global system constructed around a subtle ideology of dominance that seeks to mask the exploitation of the poor nations of the South by their rich Big Northern neighbors, and the inequalities that exist between them. Thus, from a South Atlantic perspective, globalization as it exists today is Western imperialism in disguise, at best, a new invasion of non-Western cultures by Western power interests. Cvetkovich and Kellner (1997, 11) have rightly said that "globalization by and large means the hegemony of transnational cultural industries, largely American." Similarly, according to Fred Dallmayr (1998, 1), globalization "involves to a large extent the spreading or dissemination of modern Western forms of life around the globe." And as Malcolm Waters (1995, 3) states the matter:

> Globalization is the direct consequence of the expansion of European culture across the planet via settlement, colonization and cultural mimesis. It is also bound up intrinsically with the pattern of capitalist development as it has ramified through political and cultural arenas. However, it does not

imply that every corner of the planet must become Westernized and capitalist but rather that *every set of social arrangements must establish its position in relation to the capitalist West* [emphasis added] . . . it must relativize itself.

At the economic level the IMF represents an example of an impoverishing instrument of globalization. In the 1980s, the IMF introduced into the Third World economic system the Economic Structural Adjustment Program (ESAP). Among other things, the program involves the devaluation of national currencies, removal of government subsidies on essential commodities like fuel, introduction of certain features of the consumer market culture like sales tax, etc. In all of Africa, there is no country whose economy has not gone worse, with phenomenal rise in unemployment, loss of the purchasing power of the local currency, etc. at the introduction of ESAP. At the social-cultural level let us look at Marshall McLuhan's realized dream of a global village—people in different parts of the globe watching, for example, the Olympics, the Wimbledon, the now popular Elian's case, the democratic elections in South Africa or Nigeria in the comfort of their living rooms (see Cvetkovich and Kellner 1997, 7). Malcolm Waters' (1995, xi) reference to Tasmania, a remote place in Australia where one feels part of the globe through the Internet is another good example. The contention here is not that these are in themselves bad. Rather the problem arises when we probe into the inner structure of their social-cultural implications. The pertinent questions are: how many people, indigenous to Nigeria and Tasmania, have access to the Internet? And so whose "village" are we talking about—the village of a few elite? Even for those who have such access, the questions are: who controls the Internet, who decides what to be shown and what not to be shown, for whose profits, at whose expense and according to whose moral values and standards? Besides, while it is true that we have instant access to people and events through the Internet, we have to be conscious of the illusion that this produces: the hard reality is that the physical, cultural and social distances stubbornly refuse to go. With the Internet, we exist only in a *virtual world*, not a world of reality. Globalization thus creates a false sense of space, and when the chips are down, we still have to face the real world.

I see the present day phenomenon of globalization as a product of modernity (see Giddens 1990, 60; Harvey 1990, 299; Robertson 1992, 142–45; Albrow 1996, 98)—a second phase of it, one may say, with post-modernity as an intervening phase—based specifically on modernity's monolithic conception of culture as synonymous with civilization, and the process of attaining it as evolutionary leading up to the apex, that is, Western culture. Modernity saw culture as something at the center that those at the periphery were to be made to attain. For many reasons including ease of governance, supply of cheap technical labor, commercial interest, etc., concerted effort was made to replace the culture of the periphery with that of the center. The Western school system in the colonies provided the major space for this cultural displacement battle. A product of the Enlightenment and the industrial revolution, modernity is characterized by excessive self-confidence in human rationality, the notion of unlimited human progress that led to the enthronement of human reason and denigration of divine authority in human affairs, and unrestricted human freedom that threw away the voice of human authority and tradition. With the industrial revolution were evolved new ways of production that replaced human labor with machines, a new lifestyle that was more comfortable as opposed to the traditional, new facilities and opportunities that were never there before.

Economically, modernity was structured on the center-periphery configuration whereby the periphery (the colonies) produced raw materials imported cheaply to feed the industries at the center, and the finished products were exported to the periphery in a commercial venture that fueled the economy of the center to the detriment of the periphery. For example, until 1960, when OPEC was formed, the price of petroleum produced in the Third World was determined by the buyers in the West, while the prices of refined petroleum products exported back to the Third World were determined also by the West. Even after the formation of OPEC, the price of petroleum remained at $3.00 per barrel until 1973, the year of the "oil coup," when OPEC unilaterally raised it to $5.11 per barrel. The same situation went for cacao and chocolate, coffee beans and processed coffee, etc. This is a phenomenon that many Third World governments deplored in the 1970s. According to them, rather than economic aid from the West, they wanted equitable trade relations. A postmodern atmosphere in the 1980s created space for a measure of control for these countries over their products. Thus, for example, Nigeria was able to place embargo on the sale of its crude oil to certain countries over the issue of apartheid in South Africa in the 1980s. Today, in the second phase of modernity, however, (that is, globalization), the effectiveness of this control has been neutralized through such international economic apparatuses as the IMF, the World Bank, and the World Trade Organization (WTO). The result has been increased impoverishment of the Third World. This has however not gone without resistance, albeit unsuccessful. In May 1998, a human chain of 50,000 people surrounded the leaders of the G-7 nations as they met in Birmingham, England, to urge them to reduce the debts of the developing countries. The Seattle protest in November of 1999 on the occasion of the WTO meeting also attests to the resistance that these economic measures have generated today.

Politically, modernity was predicated on the basis of a nation-state that would govern the area within its boundaries. Colonies became extensions of the nation-state that exercised responsibility over them. Newly independent nations thus constituted new modernities, and this meant the emergence of multiple modernities. Modern democratic theories gave citizens rights within their *polis* and, in theory at least, sovereignty over their rights and citizenship. But in its globalization phase, the space of both the nation-state and the power of its citizens are potentially undermined through the presence of transnational corporations, a global information and media economy, supranational political and financial institutions, and the rapid penetration of national and regional boundaries by-products, services, and images from a Western globalizing culture (see Cvetkovich and Kellner 1997, 12).

Within the academy modernity produced undifferentiated academic practices that were used in Africa and the Third World based on the Western pattern. With the advent of the post-modern atmosphere, there developed a diversity of methods in academic practices giving space for the development of Third World methodologies. There is, however, today an emerging discernible trend which, in the spirit of globalization, seeks to de-emphasize these diversities and to diminish their cutting edge (see for example Schreiter 1998, 54–60),[3] or seeks to integrate them into the dominant strain. Needless to say that this has also evoked resistance from theologies at the periphery that seek to articulate their identities.

Towards Holistic Globalization and a True Global Village

The experience of globalization in the first sense referred to above—the compression of time and space, the proximity of peoples of diverse cultures through migration, the sense of the world becoming a single place—has inspired the common and popular idea today that our world has become or is becoming a global village. What is often implied by this phrase is that isolationism in whatever form is to be eschewed, and that people must think and act in full awareness of being in constant interaction with other people. While it is true and acceptable that the power of modern means of communication has made it possible to disseminate information through incredible time and space never seen before and that any attitude of isolationism must therefore be eschewed, this alone does not constitute a global village situation. The point I want to make here and which I explore in the rest of the paper is that it is only globalization practiced in a certain manner that leads to a true global village situation, and that the present trend of globalization is not heading in that direction. Currently, the global village concept is only an ideal to be aspired after and made to happen by reversing the current trend in the globalization process.

Having been reared in an African village as a youth, and as an adult still having strong ties to the village, I am often left wondering as to what conception of village we have when we talk of our world today as a global village. It sometimes seems to me that those who vote for this concept passionately as having arrived, may never have lived in a village in their lives. For, what is a village? By sociologists' accounts, what distinguishes a village from a town or city is the presence of a primary *face-to-face* and *reciprocal* relationship in which everybody respects everybody else and knows everybody else by *name, by face, and by location*, and the *concern* of one person is the concern of all. A true global village situation therefore would call for the idea of *radical universality*. This is a universality that arises not from hegemony and harmonization but from a cultural multiplicity that is the contribution of every one concerned. It involves holistic globalization, a globalization from below in which all sectors of the globe participate. It is globalization without oppression, a democratization of power. This can only occur when there is a dialectical interactive process in all aspects of human life involving all sectors of the globe; when there is encouragement of difference rather than homogenization; when there is recognition and respect for the Other; when the distinctive historical and moral claims of other cultures are accepted in their uniqueness and are treated with seriousness, and not as if they were inconsequential. In a situation where the weak economies of the Third World that need protection and strengthening are integrated into the strong economies of the West without regard for the former's needs, one cannot expect to find a true global village situation, for in such a situation, integration means subjugation. In an academic situation, where the game is played by the rules set by one sector of the community without due consideration for diversity, we cannot expect to have a true global village situation. Again, integration results in subjugation.

Currently, what we commonly describe as global village is

only a *unidirectional* globalization. It is the extension of Western cultural practices to other parts of the globe with all the good and evil effects that entails. This cannot lead to or constitute a true global village situation. There is no doubt that this unidirectional globalization has come to stay thanks to modern multimedia resources. But it is important that we be conscious of what it is, and of the distortions that it creates. Above all, it is important to realize that it is within our power (we are not helpless before it) to reverse the process into an interactive and reciprocal one, and thus make it a force of liberation rather than the force of oppression that it currently is.

African Readings in a True Global Village Situation

Let me focus on reading practices within a global village situation. Within the academy in the West, Third World biblical scholarship is regarded largely as outside the mainstream of biblical scholarship. One looks in vain in the traditional Western style journals for occasional acknowledgment of what is happening in the Third World. Analyses of exegetical methodologies by most Western authors do not include Third World methodologies. Academic productions in the Third World (journals, books, conferences, etc.) hardly have a place in Western academic agenda. Knut Holter has given some precise omissions of this nature which he rightly sees as marginalization (Holter 2000, 35). It is my belief that as long as Third World biblical scholarship is consigned to the margin of biblical scholarship and therefore ignored or treated as of no consequence, we shall be still far from living out the global village concept. We will only arrive there when the different voices of biblical interpretation in the globe are acknowledged, heard (not out of curiosity but with full seriousness and respect), and accorded a place side by side with each other; when Third World biblical scholarship features alongside First World scholarship in academic institutions in North America and Europe, just as they do in Africa; and when Third World journals and books are given a place in the libraries of Western academic institutions. Clearly this can only begin to happen when scholars in the West are able to challenge some of the assumptions of the discipline of conventional biblical scholarship. Elisabeth Schüssler Fiorenza who has blazed the trail in initiating such a challenge has argued for "decentering biblical scholarship," for "the ethics of historical reading," and "the ethics of accountability" in biblical scholarship (1988, 3–16). Among other things this would mean "that the voices from the margins of the discipline who raise the issue of power, access and legitimation can participate on equal terms in fashioning a multi-voiced center that is perpetually decentering itself" (2000, 30). "Reading the Bible in the global village," she argues, "requires that one carefully analyzes what stands in the way" of such decentering (2000, 31). In the same way, Daniel Patte (1995) has called for ethically accountable and responsible practice of biblical scholarship that would not be oppressive. To do all this requires courage and a deep sense of self-criticism.

In fairness, I must say that there are signs that Third World biblical scholarship is beginning to be acknowledged within the mainstream. I shall mention just a few cases that I am familiar with. In 1988, John Riches of the University of Glasgow, Scotland and myself from Nigeria were set on an initiative for a cooperative research on the interpretation of the Bible in Africa and in Scotland, a project that turned out to be very instructive and beneficial for both parties. In 1990, the SBL set up the session on "The Bible in Africa, Asia, and Latin America" as a way of articulating the voices from the Third World and establishing dialogue with the First World. In some academic institutions in the USA and Europe there is outreach to Third World experience of biblical interpretation. In addition, I know many Western Scholars who, in various ways, address this issue in their publications like Daniel Patte (*Ethics of Biblical Interpretation*), Willy Schotroff and Wolfgang Stegemann (editors of *God of the Lowly: Socio-Historical Interpretation of the Bible*), Norman Gottwald and Richard Horsley (editors of *The Bible and Liberation: Political and Social Hermeneutics*), and Knut Holter (publisher and editor of *Newsletter on African Old Testament*

Scholarship, now *Bulletin for Old Testament Studies in Africa,* and author of *Tropical Africa and the Old Testament: A Select and Annotated Bibliography,* and *Yahweh in Africa: Essays on Africa and the Old Testament*). I know that in May 2000, the University of Bern, Switzerland announced the award of the Hans-Sigrist Prize to a Latin American (Elsa Tamez) and the doctoral degree *honoraris causa* to an Asian (Seiichi Yagi), and to an African (Justin Ukpong) in recognition of their contributions as Third World biblical scholars to biblical scholarship. I believe there are many other cases to be cited indicating some form of recognition of Third World scholarship within Western academy. However, in my opinion, these are only isolated instances—not enough to constitute the arrival of a "global-village" world of biblical scholarship. These are to be seen as seeds of change that are being sown, and it is the hope of many that an association like the SBL would nurture and promote the growth of such seeds into fruition.

Conclusion

Africa occupies an important position in the history of Christian biblical exegesis. It is in Africa, precisely in the Alexandrian school of biblical interpretation in the third century C.E. that a systematic approach to biblical interpretation in Christianity was first developed. Even with the gradual demise of this approach at the onset of modern biblical criticism, some elements of it, particularly its concentration on the biblical text, still form part of aspects of modern scholarship. However, modern critical biblical scholarship that started in the seventeenth century is young in the continent having reached there only about the middle of the twentieth century. In spite of this late start, modern Africa has made a modest contribution to biblical scholarship and seems poised to establish its voice in the discipline as the third Christian millennium dawns (see Draper 1996, 2).

A lot of serious, substantial, conscientious and sustained work has been taking place in Africa since the last quarter of the twentieth century that does not seem to have exercised mainstream scholarship at least as would have been desired, apparently because such work has been done outside the mainstream scholarly consensus. John Mbiti of Kenya drew the attention of Western theologians to a similar situation in theology in 1976 when he wrote (1976, 16–17):

> We have eaten theology with you (Western theologians); we have drunk theology with you; we have dreamed theology with you. We know you theologically. The question is, do you know us theologically? Would you like to know us theologically?

Nearly twenty years later, in 1995, Grant LeMarquand, himself a Westerner, made an observation that indicates that the situation had not much changed with regard to biblical studies (LeMarquand 1995, 39):

> After teaching New Testament in an African seminary for some years the compiler of this bibliography returned to the West in order to do further studies. I soon became aware that many biblical scholars in the West are almost completely unaware that there even is such a thing as African biblical studies.

More recently Knut Holter has made essentially the same observation (2000, 27). Africans have gone to the West, mastered Western methods of biblical interpretation, but the same can hardly be said about Westerners of African methods of interpretation of the Bible. The thinking in the West seems to be that there can be only one way to biblical interpretation, that is, the Western way in its different forms, and that precludes getting to know other ways. What people do not know always looks strange and weird. The first step to appreciating African biblical scholarship is to know it.

Today African contributions to biblical scholarship can and should no longer be ignored, for continuing to do so would only deprive the discipline of much needed energy and vision to progress. We need to move into a new paradigm contour of biblical scholarship as we enter the Third Millennium—a contour which, among other things, would place Third World biblical scholarship alongside that of the West as a valid and legitimate means of biblical enquiry.

Chapter 2

Villagizing, Globalizing, and Biblical Studies

Musa W. Dube

> Globalization is being touted as the panacea for all economic problems.... But will the world's poor, of whom Africa has a large percentage, benefit from globalization?—Musimbi K. E Kanyoro[1]

> Currently what we commonly describe as a global village is only a unidirectional *globalization*. It is the extension of Western cultural practices to other parts of the globe with all the good and evil effects that entails. This cannot lead to or constitute a true global village situation.—Justin Ukpong[2]

Driving around Cape Town: The Society of Biblical Literature Goes to South Africa!

The 2000 SBL International Meeting gathered in Cape Town, at the Cape Sun Intercontinental Hotel. It was a glorious tower, located in the magnificent business area and only a few kilometers away from the famed Water Front. I flew from Botswana to the Cape Town Airport and then drove straight to the St. Georges Inn, across the street from the Cape Sun. The grounds were paved and perfect. Although I was fully booked into the SBL program, appearing four times, I did not regret that I had no time to tour Cape Town. This was because I had been invited by the Stellenbosch Faculty of Theology to speak about African biblical hermeneutics and my work in 1998. My hosts were very kind. They put me up in their own house. I slept in a huge bed between creamy white satin sheets and I had a shower to myself. They took me out touring to the old winery and showed me the vines that were heavy with grapes. The mountains were glorious and everything was perfect.

My Indian friend Zubeida Jaffer, who works as a parliamentary editor for Independent Newspapers in Cape Town, came to pick me up from Stellenbosch. She said, "I will show you Cape Town." On the way, she told me a story about a young black boy who, in the 1960s, drew a black Jesus and was harassed by the apartheid police. The boy went into exile and now, in the "apartheid-free" South Africa, he is back and the picture hangs in the museum. We drove down from Stellenbosch along the blue seashores of Cape Town. Then she took me to the "Colored only" residential places, then to the "Indian only" residential places and, lastly, she took me to "Black only" residential places, Khayelitsha. And there I cried, for I was no longer a scholar who could speak and be heard in the academic halls of the high and mighty Stellenbosch. I was no longer breathing the fresh air of the green vines, drinking the best wine and sleeping between the best bedroom linen. I was no longer a Motswana, from across the border. I was no longer a tourist. I was black and I occupied the worst place in the geography of apartheid.

For me, this was not post-apartheid history. It was the present and real. I found the wounds of apartheid open and bleeding and they were written on my body. We took off and I spent the night with my friend in the Indian residential place. The following morning she took me to the airport to catch my plane. Just before I disappeared into the departure lounge Zubeida pulled an article from her handbag and gave it to me. I was quite unsuspecting when I began to read the article on my journey. It described her survival as a journalist in the apartheid days—what it meant to investigate and report the injustices of the system, how she had been imprisoned, beaten up and tortured. I arrived in Botswana knowing better about Cape Town.

The drive from Stellenbosch to Khayelitsha was instructive. I realized that without it I could have left Cape Town with the perspective of Stellenbosch, having been completely insulated from the open wounds of apartheid—wounds that are written upon the lands and souls of South African people. The 2000 SBL International Meeting too had gathered in the impeccable hotel to deliberate its scholarly papers. One might as well have been a million miles away from Khayelitsha. Indeed, one could have been anywhere in the first world, but we were in Cape Town in South Africa, the place where racial oppression was practiced and institutionalized since the earliest settlement of Jan Van Reensbeck in 1652. Matthew Collins, one of the SBL organizers of the meeting, informed me that Cape Sun Intercontinental Hotel was chosen as a compromise because, with the race conflicts of South Africa, they could not easily settle for meeting in one of the universities without being seen to take sides. The question is, when the meeting finally took place in the Cape Sun Intercontinental Hotel, who really won and what did SBL and its work lose, besides money? What did we lose?

It was midday, the last day of the SBL 2000 International Meeting, the last night before my departure. I badly needed to go to the Robben Island, the place where Nelson Mandela and other political prisoners were closed up for more than two decades. I dashed into a courtesy bus to catch the last boat to the Island. On the way, I met Vincent Wimbush, with Linda and Lauren, his family, going to the same place. Upon arrival we were told, the tickets were sold out. Desperation must have shown on our faces, for a child of a former Robben Island prisoner, who told us that he had been on this boat many times to go and check on his father, said, "You will get a place. Just wait and do not give up." We waited and we managed to board the boat.

We took a bus drive round the Island and the tour guide, told the story of Robben Island. First we stopped by Robert Sobukwe prison, where he was isolated from all other political prisoners until he broke down. Sobukwe had championed resistance against pass laws. We drove to the quarry, where Mandela and other political prisoners were put to long and senseless hours of hard work under inhuman conditions. We drove to the seashore and watched the huge crystal blue waves rise and fall. We stopped, picked seashells, stones, dipped our hands in the water and breathed the fresh air of the sea. Time ticked. The bus driver and the tour guide had trouble getting us back to the bus. Here was freedom. We drove on and heard about how once Robben Island had also been a place of outcasts, where lepers were confined. We saw the church buildings of those missions that had dedicated themselves to ministering to the lepers. Finally, we drove to the capital prison itself and arrived after the normal tourist hours. There we found a furious tourist guide, who jolted us out of our tourist mood into reality by informing us that he could not take us around, for he had had a long day and for him, this was not tourism, it was real and it was painful. He was a former political prisoner of the place.

And so we had to tour on our own, with the help of our bus tourist guide. We saw the rooms where the political prisoners were kept. We saw their blankets and their toilet buckets. We saw their pictures that included Blacks, Indians, Coloreds, and Jews. Here I did not cry, for the tour guide had repeatedly impressed upon us that Robben Island is a place that represented the triumph of human spirit against all oppression! What I heard her say was, "Don't cry for Mandela and all those who endured the senseless apartheid system. Rather, celebrate their commitment to justice." I heard her saying, "cry for yourself, for the battles that you must wedge against all forms of oppression!" This drive around Cape Town was uppermost in my mind as I reflected on and prepared this response to Justin Ukpong's opening address to the 2000 SBL International Meeting.

The Challenge

Justin Ukpong's opening address challenged the guild to read the Bible in the global village, from the perspective of African readings. My response to his challenge begins by underlining the South African setting of Cape Town, by bringing those dusty shabby homes and roads of Khayelitsha, the lowest of the low places, to the perfectly paved grounds and tiled walls of Cape Sun Intercontinental, to the SBL 2000 International Meeting. It is quite possible that some participants may have undergone sanitized tours that took them through safe and clean routes to homes and farms. Others may have had a chance to walk through the spaces, paths, pains, and scars of apartheid history. Some may have felt the life wounds of this geography and relived it for a moment of their life. Others may have refused to think about this history or to let it touch their very beings. But can the SBL come to South Africa, only six years after the end of the apartheid era, and leave without letting its practice be reconstituted by such a place, such a history, such a call to rededication to the struggle for justice?

My response to Ukpong's essay is, therefore, a call to SBL scholars to respond to the context of their meeting. It is an attempt to drive SBL scholars, who may be tempted to end their work in the glitz of the Cape Sun Intercontinental Hotel, around Cape Town. It is an attempt to bring SBL scholars and their work to be challenged by the other spaces such as Khayelitsha and Robben Island. It seeks to put their biblical hermeneutics within the history of drawing a picture of a black Jesus, where the reigning picture was a white Jesus. It seeks to challenge biblical scholars to become like the black artists, the Zubeidas, the Robert Sobukwes, the Nelson Mandelas, and all those political prisoners, who, while human and vulnerable, took it upon themselves to challenge an oppressive system and to become architects of justice. It is an attempt to hear the voice of a protesting tourist guide at the capital prison jolt us by shouting, "this is not just tourism, it is real and it hurts." It is an attempt to bring us to hear the voice of the bus tourist guide as she bids us not to cry for the political prisoners that endured the most inhuman conditions, but to "think of the battles that we must wedge against all forms of oppression." This challenge calls for our response!

Turning to the contents of Justin Ukpong's opening address, he has challenged the guild in relation to globalization, inculturation, and biblical interpretation. I found Ukpong to be almost reducing "Africa" to something that is unified; that lacks diversity and casting biblical studies as if the discipline has not been undergoing significant changes since the sixties. But I do not wish to focus on these matters. Rather, my response to Ukpong's essay will be more of an elaboration of his points than a criticism.

Globalization Is the Grandson of Colonization

Ukpong's essay traces globalization[3] from colonial movements, links it with structural adjustments regimes of IMF and the age of information super highway of computers. His reviews describe globalization as a "new" world map—where time is no more; space is no more; national boundaries are no more. The world has shrunk to what has been termed the global village. The globe is warming up! His reviews highlight that several scholars see a continuation of yesterday's colonial structures in the acclaimed global era. Ukpong also highlights that many benefits are associated with globalization. Indeed, one author, who sought to underline the remarkable benefits of globalization said, "according to the regional pattern of future gains from globalization *even Africa will gain from globalization* over the next fifteen years"[4] (emphasis mine). Thank you very much. The issue, however, is not so much that one cannot outline and tabulate the benefits of globalization persuasively. For example, I cannot deny that I am writing this essay on my Dell computer, sending e-mails to my friends all over the world, attaching articles to and receiving them from colleagues, reading CNN and BBC news, etc. Neither can I deny that my son comes here to surf the net for jokes, music, games and sports. The issue, however, is that I cannot send e-mails to my mother in the village, I cannot read my home village news from the Internet, I do not read any news posted in my indigenous language. The Dell computer itself is not from the local industry and one cannot ignore how the above listed services have now replaced a number of human resources, leading to retrenchment, unemployment and poverty. There is also the issue of cultural imperialism, where our children can surf the net and play games, listen to music and read jokes that have very little or nothing to do with their context or with other human beings. The real issue about globalization, therefore, is not that it will not benefit many but that it leaves billions out of control in their contexts, economically worse off, dehumanized and that it does not improve the quality of human interactions. The question is pointedly tabled by Kanyoro who asks, "*will the world's poor... benefit from globalization?*"

If we agree with Ukpong's assertion that globalization is a continuation of colonization, then this we must ask about the past and present in our quest to do biblical studies in the global village. We must ask about what we understand by "the global village" and the role we want to play in this "new map" of the world. We must also ask about the power positions that we wish to occupy and advance. It has been underlined, several times, by different scholars that current biblical studies have been engaged in and enabled by colonial projects.[5] It has also been highlighted that current methods of biblical studies are colonizing and that Third World scholars are not taking it lying down.[6]

In the light of Ukpong's descriptions of globalization and the well documented colonial ideology within biblical studies, what does SBL wish to achieve by embarking on a project of *Reading the Bible in the Global Village*? The back cover of the first volume in this series spells out a response, but not a particular position, when it says: "The world of biblical scholarship has not been immune to such changes. Increasingly biblical scholars everywhere are aware of the fact that they are reading the Bible in the global village." What position does SBL and its members wish to assume in the given unequal, oppressive, and exploitative international relations of our "global village"? I certainly do not believe that SBL and its members are among those who sing the praises of globalization, in the light of what Ukpong's paper tell us. For my part, I will assume the "best intentions," namely, that SBL's call to read the Bible in the "global village" seeks to highlight diversity on the globe and the need to read as decolonizing subjects, who do not wish to suppress differences. I assume that SBL and its members want to use many reading methods and to promote human rights, cultural diversity, justice, and liberation in their work. If this is a correct interpretation, the problem is: Does the framework of "global village" in itself help SBL and its members to achieve their goals, or does it inadvertently counteract and subvert their good intentions?

Ukpong's definition of globalization problematizes this framework. He holds that "in a situation where the weak economies of the Third World that need protection and strengthening are integrated into the strong economies of the West without regard for the former's needs, one cannot expect to find a true global situation, for in such a situation, *integration means subjugation*"[7] (emphasis mine). To agree with this definition requires that biblical scholars should assume a certain position towards the "global village" international framework in their work. I would therefore propose that in their reading practices, biblical scholars must constantly ask themselves:

1. Who is globalizing in our biblical reading?
2. Who is being globalized?
3. Who owns the village that we are globalizing?
4. What are the inhabitants of the village saying about being globalized?
5. What if I were to read from and with those in the village?
6. Which global morals can assist a biblical reader to counteract the beastly side of globalization?
7. How can we occupy a position of vigilance and resistance against globalization?
8. What about the village ethics? Can we read from the position of the village for better results than the globe, or should we be combining both?
9. Are we are rejecting, revolutionizing, reforming, or collaborating with globalization?

Ukpong insists that "it is within our power (we are not helpless) to reverse the process into an interactive and reciprocal one, and thus make it a force of liberation rather than of oppression that it currently is."[8] We are challenged, therefore, to think and apply a thousand other alternatives than to surrender to globalization. Since Ukpong's address focused on the inculturation biblical hermeneutics it seems proper to examine its position in relation to the process of globalization/colonization of the present and the past. Does inculturation resist globalization? How can it position itself strategically in this era?

Inculturation as Decolonizing Biblical Hermeneutics

According to Ukpong, inculturation "is a contextual hermeneutic methodology that seeks to make any community of ordinary people and their socio-cultural context the *subject* of interpretation of the Bible. . . . It involves a commitment to the world of the ordinary people and their historical experience, and interaction between ordinary readers and ordinary ways of reading the Bible on the one hand, and academic readers and academic ways of reading on the other."[9] Ukpong's definition notably renders inculturation hermeneutics in the recent South African language of "reading with ordinary readers."[10] This in itself is not objectionable. However, a number of issues are problematic. First, inculturation is much older than this recent South African language of "reading with ordinary readers" and Upkong does not explain how we get to this direct link. Second, inculturation has been associated primarily with upper Sub-Sarahan Africa rather than with South Africa, which is often linked to black theology/ biblical hermeneutics and a sizeable white biblical hermeneutics. Third, while inculturation is about reading both African cultures and the Bible, "reading with ordinary readers" focuses on the Bible. Fourth, Ukpong does not say who defines ordinary readers as such: would they regard themselves as "ordinary readers?"[11] Lastly, he does not address the reservations that have been sounded by some black South African scholars about the approach of "reading with ordinary readers." The latter hold that in the South African context, "reading with ordinary readers" is a position that avoids engaging black theology and race issues of nation.[12] For example, Tinyiko S. Maluleke holds that:

> 1. The phrase "ordinary readers" does not communicate useful, key, or decisive information about the subject it qualifies. Anybody can be and even look ordinary depending on what we are talking about or doing.
> 2. While "ordinary" and "trained" are power-relations categories, the tentative, evasive, and innocuous nature of the terms tend to obscure, trivialize, or palliate the economic, race, and gender (especially as it relates to Black women) basis of the power discrepancy concerned.
> 3. An unmasking of the essential basis of power discrepancy between the so-called "ordinary" and "trained" people in South Africa will lead us back to race, gender, and class as allocators of privilege, wealth and opportunity. This begs the question of why categories that highlight race, gender and class issues ... are deliberately avoided in favor of the obscure phrase, "ordinary people."
> 4. In and of itself, the recognition of a "trained" as opposed to an "ordinary" class of people is quite innocuous if not superfluous. The real question is *how, which,* and *why* people are trained while others are "ordinaried."
> 5. It is not good enough for a hermeneutic of liberation simply to posit and accept the existence of "trained" and "ordinary" readers as a starting point, as if these positions were ordained from above.
> 6. Furthermore, the formulation "ordinary" versus "trained," when used as a hermeneutical starting point, is probably based on an (uncritical) acceptance of the ideologies, choices, and commitments inherent in the "training" of the so-called trained.[13]

Outside Ukpong's definition, inculturation is historically associated with political liberation movements of African countries. Like most resistance movements, it operated at different levels and underwent various stages. It can thus be subdivided into inculturation from above and from below. These can be further subdivided into "collaborating resistance," "radical resistance," "reformative," "liberal," and "romantic." I will use the categories of *below* and *above*, from which some of the above perspectives will be gleaned.

Inculturation from Above

This hermeneutical practice was advocated by ordained academic scholars who wanted to underline the validity of their Christian and African identity. Inculturation followed or even started during colonial times. It sought to resist the colonial reading/interpretations that began by dismissing all aspects of African Religions (ARs) as pagan, exotic, savage, ungodly, childish and dangerous. The proponents of inculturation sought to resist this colonizing missionary approach by adopting different strategies of reading towards the Bible and African Religions/cultures. Their goals were largely geared at showing that there is nothing ungodly about African cultures, that it is by no means the opposite of biblical religions and that ARs are worth preserving. Scholars thus embarked on inculturation reading strategies which:

1. compared the two religions and showed the great similarities;[14]
2. argued that ARs constituted an important ground for planting the Christian gospel;[15]
3. studied the language similarities between Africa and the Hebrew cultures;
4. put significant energy into the study of how Christ may be seen amongst African cultures;[16]
5. insisted on interpreting the biblical text through the African contexts and cultures rather than the ancient biblical settings;[17] and
6. interrogated the ideological base that makes Christianity intolerant towards other religions.[18]

Inculturation was thus an act of resistance, seeking decolonization and liberation. A certain degree of this inculturation resistance, however, operated within the colonial framework by maintaining the priority of Christianity and reducing ARs to *evangelical preparatio* function, whereby the latter were seen as a preparation for Christianity,[19] but not as a complete set of traditions in their own right. Inculturation was thus geared at serving the Christian mission, by seeking for effective methods of evangelizing without dispensing with African cultures. In the process, inculturation hermeneutics took various strategies and underwent a number of stages and was given different names such as accommodation, acculturation, adoption, Africanization, indigenization, inculturation and, sometimes, contextualization.[20]

Some radical voices, however, departed from this "collaborative resistance" by insisting on the complete integrity of ARs.[21] Some argued that in fact, ARs are far superior to the biblical gospel[22] (Setiloane 1976) while others argued that all religions must be treated equally and held to be worthy of study and preservation. This position was best articulated by Canaan Banana who called for a "rewriting of the Bible" that embraces the "rich plurality of human experience."[23]

Inculturation from Below

Inculturation from below, as it has been articulated by the African Independent Churches (AICs), is much older than inculturation from above, since it is traceable to the beginning of the AICs in 1706.[24] Inculturation from below was/is characterized by:

1. an open resistance to colonial government, which was often expressed through the involvement of the AICs in national liberation movements;

2. a refusal to remain in missionary churches, where leadership and interpretation was the sole prerogative of white people;

3. a refusal to dismiss African cultures as pagan and a systematic use of both cultures interchangeably;

4. an articulation of black theology that critiqued white images of Christ and held that Christ and his disciples were black;

5. a clear condemnation of the economic and political subjugation of black people and their kingdoms;

6. leadership that accommodates both women and men; and
7. church institutions that are African founded, owned and financed.

Inculturation from below adopted a radical and nonapologetic hybridity as a stance of resistance and continues to hold this stance. It was more revolutionarily involved, for it sought economic, political and cultural liberation. Scholars who follow inculturation from below regard their scholarly work as an attempt to "read from the community;" to articulate a hermeneutical approach that arises from, for and with the community.[25] They attempt to situate their biblical studies within the framework of resistance and hybridity. According to Tinyiko Maluleke, "much work remains to be done in terms of understanding and articulating precisely how these churches and their members interact with the Bible."[26]

Both these strands of inculturation interact at many points and continue to underline the fact that biblical texts in African contexts interact with other canons, especially those of the ARs. Inculturation is to be expected to continue and to take various forms as long as ARs and biblical text are authoritative texts in the lives of African people. In the context of globalization, inculturation's relevance remains and is even more challenged. The question is: is inculturation strongly positioned to resist globalization? Does it offer an alternative to globalization? How can it reposition itself to resist globalization? The position of inculturation, which is hardly known or studied in Western halls of biblical studies, however, offers SBL scholars a challenge. The challenge underlines the need (1) to do biblical interpretation that does not succumb to colonization and the various forms of international injustice, and (2) consistently to seek ways of reading that accommodates diversity and international justice.

Gender Matters: Inculturation and Globalization

The above categorization of inculturation into upper and lower classes, collaborating and decolonizing, in some ways marks the gender divide that characterizes the approach. Inculturation from above was the realm of ordained church leaders, who were largely, though not exclusively male. The call for a gender inclusive inculturation hermeneutics was sounded by many women, amongst them Mercy A. Oduyoye, Teresa Okure, Musimbi R.E. Kanyoro, Nyambura Njoroge, Isabel Phiri, Teresa Hinga, Bennedatte, and Mbuy Mbeya. Women entered the debate and challenged the exclusively male inculturation hermeneutics[27] by calling for:

1. engendered inculturation hermeneutics;[28]
2. a gender inclusive Christology;[29]
3. a critical reading both of the ARs and of the biblical narrative;[30]
4. a scrutiny of biblical translations and how they have given male gender to God, even where indigenous names and concepts of God were gender neutral and how this affects women in the society;[31] and
5. biblical methods and theories that are drawn from and informed by African culture that highlights the presence of women and empowers them in their search for liberation.[32]

In my own work, I have situated my biblical reading within the paradigm of "inculturation from below" by making attempts to read from the AICs and to articulate the hermeneutical practices of women in the AICs.[33] I have underlined that

> as a woman, I know that most canons marginalize women and represent for the most part the culture of the elites. As an African, I come from a tradition not of textual canons but rather of oral canons—the notion of canon is closely tied to the identity of different cultures. Since imperialism depends upon the suppression of other canons and hence diversity itself, one way of counteracting such oppression is for biblical criticism to become multicultural.[34]

I have repeatedly argued that current feminist biblical practice is working within a colonizing framework because of its lack of attention to religious diversity or acknowledgment of how the

Bible has functioned as a tool of suppressing other cultures.[35] Thus I have called attention to the fact that "we are here as women in biblical religion together with our Other canons, written and unwritten and they demand to be heard and read in their own right."[36]

The work of African women has been credited with sharpening the political edge of biblical and theological hermeneutics.[37] According to Tinyiko S. Maluleke, "closely related are South African Black Theology and African women's theology. In these two theologies the notion of the 'poor' is broken down to mean 'women,' 'African women,' 'Blacks,' and the 'Black working class' so that there is a deliberate emphasis on gender, race and class issues." Maluleke holds that "African women are arguably the one section ... which is engaging in the most passionate, the most vibrant and the most prophetic and challenging in the past decade and a half—at least in Anglophone Africa."[38] Continuing this line of thought, Maluleke holds that

> Whereas Black and African Theologies have for the past half-century argued for the validity of African Christianities and the legitimacy of African culture, African Feminist/Womanist theology is charting a new way. This theology is mounting a critique of both African culture and African Christianity in ways that previous African theologies have not been able to. From these theologies, we may learn how to be truly African yet critical of aspects of African culture.[39]

Ukpong's essay, however, ignores these voices—both women and black theology. He touches on them in passing, if at all. This posture situates Ukpong's approach within the category of "inculturation from above," one that reflects the position of male academic church leaders. Ukpong's stance towards black and women issues also seems to validate the concerns of critics of "reading with ordinary people," who hold that the approach disavows commitment to issues of race, class, and gender. It is important, however, for inculturation hermeneutics to assess if globalization has a gender face:

1. What is the impact of globalization on the lives of women and men?
2. Does globalization empower women and men equally?[40]
3. How can feminist/womanist inculturation hermeneutics maintain an oppositional stance that enhances the lives of women in their struggle for liberation in the era of globalization?

Race Matters: Inculturation and Globalization

Turning to race matters, my introduction to this essay, "Driving around Cape Town," sought to underline the South African context as a situation that calls SBL to a practice that is committed to the struggle against racial discrimination and strives towards economic, political and cultural justice. My analysis sought to underline the role of women and men in challenging the system, by highlighting the contributions of the little black boy who drew a picture of a black Jesus, Zubeida, Sobukwe, our bus tourist guide, Mandela, and other prisoners.

Although Ukpong's essay pays significant attention to First-Third World power relations, he does not pay sufficient attention to black biblical hermeneutics, if at all. Holding that "inculturation hermeneutics" encompasses "a variety of issues—justice issues of gender, race, social, economic, political, religious oppression as well as issues of indigenous cultural identity,"[41] Ukpong subjects black biblical hermeneutics to inculturation, despite the fact that the two are often categorized separately. This mixing in itself is not objectionable. What is problematic, however, is that it hardly gives Ukpong's essay any evident commitment to black biblical hermeneutics that it deserves, given the South African context of the 2000 SBL International Meeting. Further, Upkong does not highlight the present role of black biblical hermeneutics in the post-apartheid era, nor does he sketch for us what he sees as the role and place of black biblical hermeneutics in the age of globalization.

This inadequate attention to race matters, in an SBL International Meeting that is gathered in South Africa (indeed in Africa) for the first time, is regrettable for a number of reasons. First, for the fact that only less than ten years ago the whole world was involved, in different degrees, in dismantling institutionalized racism of South Africa. Second, because six years after such a victory, we need to ask: Is apartheid dead and buried, or it is still alive? Third, we need to ask: Does the international community still have a role to play? Fourth, the United Nations will convene a meeting that focuses on race, which shall meet in South Africa. Lastly, because we need to know if globalization is color-blind or not. With globalization, travel around the globe will be intensified as people search for greener pastures. We must, therefore, ask whether black people, and other people of color, will be welcomed and given opportunities as they travel, or will they be subjected to racial discrimination, while they welcome and open doors to white people from the Western world in their countries. Inculturation hermeneutics that seeks to have an oppositional and liberative role in the age of globalization needs to sharpen its stance toward race issues. The issues of race, in other words, are by no means insignificant in the post-apartheid and globalization era.

For my part, I would like to highlight the racial issue in relation to biblical and religious studies in general. I remember when it was first announced that International SBL would congregate in South Africa six (seven?) years ago. I was still in graduate school and I expected that the conference would take place two to three years before I graduated. Well, it took place two years after I graduated and here I am performing the significant role of responding to its opening address. I remember discussing with Itumeleng Mosala that SBL is coming to South Africa and his response was, "*Ke a gana*. I refuse. SBL is not coming to South Africa. Why South Africa and why now? They are following their white brothers. If they really want to come to Africa, let them go to Botswana, Zimbabwe, or anywhere. There are meeting places in all these countries." It has been indeed a long journey to the 2000 SBL International Meeting on account of race matters. But ever since, I have had a good reason to reflect on Mosala's words, given the number of international religious conferences that have held their meetings in South Africa in the past three years. One can list here SNTS (Pretoria, July-August 1999), the Parliament of World Religions (Cape Town, December 1999), the SBL International Meeting (Cape Town, July 2000), and the International Association for the History of Religions (Durban, August 2000).

South Africa has indeed become a hive of international religious conferences. But what the South Africans have noted is that the one international religious event that Europe would not allow them to have, which they really wanted, is that of football (soccer) World Cup! Why are all these conferences congregating in South Africa? Is it because they have been seriously engaged in the struggle against apartheid and now they want to celebrate the post-apartheid era? Is it because they want to come and empower the victims of apartheid in the study of religion? Who invites them? Why are they not meeting in Zimbabwe, Botswana, Namibia, or any other country in Africa? Who benefits from these conferences? The answers to these questions will be revealing.

Second, I find it very problematic that Justin Ukpong and I, who are black scholars from outside South Africa, were given the privilege of doing the ritual of opening a biblical studies conference held in Cape Town.[42] Where are the black South African biblical scholars? If the answer is we do not have anyone, it does not at all evade or avoid the race issue. That is, why should South Africa, a land that is known for its theological vibrancy, have very few or no black biblical scholars? What are the structures and the content of biblical studies that hinders the grooming of black biblical scholars in South Africa?[43] I happen to know of some qualified and competent black biblical scholars in South Africa, such as Dr. Mmadipoane Masenya and Dr. McGlory Speckman, and I do not understand why they were not invited to participate in the opening session.

Indeed, the racial issue is vibrant in these conferences. One case in point was when I attended SNTS in Pretoria. We were met at the airport by a catering company. The driver had the names of all international participants and delivered each participant to their hotel. I was delivered to the reception, where I found Teresa Okure (from Nigeria) and Eric Anum (Ghana) also under the same fate. We sat there for hours with our bags until Daniel Patte staged a protest, telling the company that if they do not know the name of what is happening, it is called "racism." What was more dramatic for me, however, were the pictures on the walls of the divinity school. Everywhere there were white pictures, such that I just knew that I am treading on a "white-only" space of apartheid, a place where the walls of history refuse to reflect my color as a black person. For once, I could agree with Matthew Collins that, *perhaps*, a meeting in Cape Sun Intercontinental Hotel was a compromise!

On a broader level, the lack of biblical scholars, or their recognition in South Africa is an issue that should challenge SBL to look again at its membership and its color. It is important that the guild should ask:

1. What color is SBL, and why?
2. What routes does SBL travel in the global era, and why?
3. What spaces does SBL occupy: black, white, brown, yellow, or rainbow?

As we begin consciously to do biblical studies in the "global era" we know that some are globalizing and others are being globalized. Some, we presume, are standing in a space of resistance that seeks to counteract globalization and to sprinkle some village spirit on the globe. The alleys of globalization are not race, class, and gender neutral. SBL members should scrutinize the structures, conferences venues, theories, methods, and contents of their programs, as well as the various institutions that have allowed, and continue to allow, biblical studies to be a predominantly white discipline, while Christianity is notably growing among black people, especially in Africa more than on any other continent.[44] The question to ask is: Does the Society of Biblical Literature and its members, in their various institutions of work, intend to take on the rainbow colors of our world or to continue "whitening" the global village in biblical studies?

Villagizing: Do You Know Us Theologically, Do You Even Want to Know Us?

Ukpong's address has problematized the one-way traffic in the global village. Goods, intellectual and material, flow from former colonial centers to Two-Thirds World, but not in a reciprocal style. Two-Thirds World masses find themselves the market place, the consumers, who cannot, however, take their own goods to the West. The biblical studies guild largely occupies and operates within this international economic set-up. Thus biblical books, contents, theories, methods are sold to and bought by Two-Thirds World scholars. Western biblical scholars, on the other hand, remain ignorant of Two-Thirds World biblical and theological hermeneutics and books. If they read them, it is something they rarely teach, practice or apply.[45] For us, on the other hand, we have had to learn every biblical method that was proposed in the West and we have had to apply it regardless of how strange we felt about it. Ukpong raises this problematic relationship by using John Mbiti's 1976 query: "We know you [western scholars] theologically. The question is, do you know us theologically? *Would you like to know us theologically?*"[46] (emphasis mine).

Almost three decades since Mbiti posed this question, it remains relevant. Here we are, five or so decades after inculturation began with the struggle for independence in the 1950s and almost after all African countries have attained some independence, and now Upkong is talking about inculturation hermeneutics to the SBL guild for the first time! I must confess that I felt that Upkong had not sufficiently spelt out the nuances of inculturation; I felt that he had not quoted many of the scholars who have significantly propounded this approach. I thus felt the urge to tabulate the various faces and stages of inculturation to educate the SBL guild (God forbid it)! Why? Shouldn't the SBL guild have traveled with inculturation hermeneutics, just as its members have agonized over historical criticisms, narrative methods, feminist methods, etc.? Having been educated in the West, and having attended SBL meetings frequently for almost a decade, I know that such methods as inculturation biblical hermeneutics have not occupied the attention of an average biblical scholar very much, if at all. In short, I was globalized, but did not find the songs of my village in the academic halls of my training villagizing the globe. This indeed is a hot question for the biblical guild: Does the guild wish to continue to operate within the alleys of the globalization, which, as Ukpong's paper tells us, is colonizing, or does it which to decolonize, by allowing itself to be villagized?

Although I grew up in a village, I do not wish to idealize the village over the globe. In the village, where I grew up the political set-up and leadership were certainly in the hands of men and age was an important factor in our relationships. As a child, I belonged to every parent in the village. All the elders watched my behavior and were free to discipline me anytime they caught me misbehaving. Hilary Rodham Clinton's book *It Takes a Village* recently popularized this village thinking in the United States. It denotes, most of all, the community spirit that pervades the village. As Ukpong notes, in a village there is a *"face-to-face and reciprocal* relationship in which everybody respects everybody else and knows everybody *by name, by face, and by location*, and the *concern* of one person is the concern of all."[47]

Economically, every family had its own land, produced their own crops, and kept their own livestock. If one did not have a field or a home and wished to have it, all they needed was to ask from the village leader *(Kgosi)* and his counselors. One who had no livestock for plowing could use a *mafisa* system to acquire cattle—whereby people were given a number of cattle by some richer farmer to look after and use, while every year they get one cow for themselves. Over a period of five years such individuals will have acquired enough cows of their own for plowing and milk. Underlying this seemingly ideal picture, there were children, women, and servants who were part of the society, who cannot be said to have been enjoying equal rights as men and elders. Village ethics, more often than not, despised some groups of people such as different ethnic groups, left-handed people, homosexuals, and, in some cultures, twins. Besides, the community spirit has its own negative side when too much closeness brings jealous talk and witchcraft accusations. Certainly, the "village model" is not uniform, for there will be as many villages as there are cultures and they will be characterized by their own limitations and strengths. The problems tabulated above also characterize metropolitan cities of various sizes, making it difficult to view the globe and the village as two opposites. In both the globe and the village there is no perfection. Villages, therefore, cannot and do not represent perfection in and of themselves. Villagizing the globe must, therefore, be theorized and pursued in so far as:

1. We cannot ignore that it has many valuable things to offer.
2. It represents those who are on the receiving end of globalization, whose voices must be heard.
3. It makes attempts to add a human or ethical face to the world that is dominated by competition, domination and indifference.[48]
4. It represents the spirit of the 'Earth,' the spirit of being in touch with and in reverence of life in all its forms.

The suppression of the village spirit in the global village became immediately apparent to me when I realized that while I could use the words "globalizing" and "globalization," I did not have the equivalent words of "villagizing" and "villagization." I have coined them here, to highlight the fact that part of counteracting globalization includes creating a multi-directional traffic. The village has something to offer in terms of community care, an economic system that strives to empower all its members and reverence for life. Globalization has something to offer in terms of human rights culture that has been cultivated in the United Nations forums. The latter offer us the ethics of human rights, women's rights, children's rights, cultural rights, environmental rights and international peace. These are admirable facets of our globalization, although their impact has not reached their potential due to lack of application, and although some may object to the very fact that the UN is still located in the West, in New York. Biblical scholars in their various institutions, need to draw more directly from these UN texts *to warm up* the earth village in the right way. If the SBL and its various members selectively draw the best from the globe and village—if they occupy the "earth village" from an angle of resistance against those globalizing forces that increasingly make the world an economically, politically, culturally, and socially repressive place for many billions of people—we can contribute to making the earth our village.

Chapter 3

Unpacking the Package That Is the Bible in African Biblical Scholarship

Gerald O. West

Ruminating on the Meeting

The occasion of the first visit of the Society of Biblical Literature (SBL) to the African continent is cause for some reflection on the relationship between biblical studies in the West/North/First World and biblical studies in Africa. Even a cursory review of the SBL International Meeting in Cape Town, South Africa, in July 2000, indicates adaptions that had to be made in order for the Meeting to be at least partially African. Preliminary consultations between SBL and its members in South Africa (and elsewhere) who wanted this Meeting to engage with its African context brought about some shifts in SBL's normal operating procedure for the International Meeting. The scope of the Meeting was broadened, in recognition of less fixed boundaries in Africa between biblical studies and other theological disciplines. Membership requirements were relaxed, in an attempt to open participation to the vast majority of African scholars, who are not members of SBL. Differential registration costs were established so that African scholars could afford to attend, and some funds were also provided to cover travel and accommodation costs for African participants who had been invited by an African committee. This committee had been established at SBL's request to plan a series of sections that would give the proceedings a distinctively African agenda, and was itself clear acknowledgment that there were specifically African matters that needed to be dealt with. All these signs point to important differences in biblical studies in its Anglo-American and African manifestations. That African scholars turned up (if they received their funding and visas), participated, and were well received and understood by their colleagues from across the oceans signals that though there are differences, there are also some common scholarly concerns among us.

The essays from and reflections on this Meeting found in this volume elaborate, whether implicitly or explicitly, on these similarities and differences. My essay makes a contribution here as well, but not as an end in itself. Rather, my essay seeks to use the occasion of this Meeting at the southern tip of Africa as an impulse to look more closely at African biblical scholarship.

African Biblical Scholarship

Having used the term 'African biblical scholarship,' I must hasten to my first reflection. I must make haste because I want to go on to acknowledge that I am chastened by my colleague Tinyiko Maluleke's critique of my use of terms like this (see Maluleke 2000, 94–95; West 1997). Maluleke is right,

> there cannot and should not be such a thing as "African Biblical Scholarship" if this is envisaged in terms akin to that produced by western-type training. Both African Christians and African Christian theologians have not been able to relate in any exclusive way to the Bible—as a singular collection of texts—in the way that both the historical critical and latter day sociological hermeneutics have done. Except for a small minority, very few Black and African Biblical scholars have been able to do discipline-specific textual biblical studies (94–95).

Maluleke goes on to suggest that like ordinary African Christians, African biblical scholars relate to the Bible as "part of a larger package of resources and legacies which include stories, preaching and language mannerisms, songs, choruses, ecclesiologies, theodicies, catechism manuals and a range of rituals and rites" (95). We must not be misled, says Maluleke, by the overt presence of the Bible among African Christians; while it is "one of the few 'tangible' things" in African Christianity, "The Bible," insists Maluleke, "has been appropriated and continues to be appropriated as part of a larger package of resources" (95). And Africa biblical scholars cannot escape this reality; indeed they are examples of this reality (95):

> Most, if not all African 'biblical' scholars operate as philosophers, missiologists and quasi-systematic theologians (e.g. Dickson, Mbiti and Fashole-Luke). Indeed, it seems that the more Mbiti insisted on the centrality of the Bible in African Theology, the more of a philosopher, missiologist and systematic theologian he became.

So I use the term 'African biblical scholarship' cautiously and carefully, accepting much of what Maluleke has to say on this matter. Elsewhere I have chartered some of the contours of 'African biblical scholarship' (West 2000) and together with Musa Dube provided a glimpse of 'African biblical scholars' at work (West and Dube 2000). In this essay, then, in addition to problematizing these terms, I employ the terms as a means of teasing out and understanding more clearly the forms of engagement between African scholars and the Bible. More specifically, Maluleke's insistence on 'African biblical scholarship' as something quite different from "that produced by western-type training" requires probing. What, I ask in this essay, are some of the distinctive features of 'African biblical scholarship'?

Post-Missionary/Postcolonial

'African biblical scholarship' is indelibly marked by the missionary/colonial encounter.[1] This is obvious; the Bible came to us in Africa as part of a missionary/colonial package.[2] Leaving aside the long history of the Bible in northern Africa, and quite where Africa begins and ends is itself a problem for 'African biblical scholarship'(West 2000, 49), for the vast majority of Africans in West, East, Central and Southern Africa the Bible arrived with nineteenth century European missionary/colonial expansionism (see Sundkler and Steed 2000). Though little attention is given to the Bible in and of itself, the dialectics of the encounters between indigenous Africans and missionaries, explorers and colonial functionaries have been ably chartered (see especially Comaroff and Comaroff 1991; Comaroff and Comaroff 1997). Typically, the Bible is subsumed and assumed under terms like 'Christianity,' 'the message,' 'the Word,' etc. (Landau 1995). Clearly, the Bible is part of the missionary/colonial package in that it is integral to most if not all forms of Christianity, particularly the Protestant forms that were propagated in these parts of Africa. While there may be good reasons for treating the Bible separately, at least heuristically, and I will say more of this later, this has not happened, except when we look at the work of 'African biblical scholars.'

In one of the fullest accounts of African biblical scholarship, without inverted commas, Justin Ukpong analyses important elements of the history and hermeneutics of African biblical scholarship after colonialism. Though he does not refer to African biblical scholarship between the 1930s and the present as post-colonial/missionary, his insightful analysis takes as its starting point the colonial/missionary legacy. In a wonderfully ironic twist, African biblical scholarship turns the tools it has been trained with by western biblical scholarship against the damage (being) done by western missionary and colonial forces.

Ukpong carefully delineates what he means by African biblical scholarship, making it clear that his focus is mainly academic biblical interpretation south of the Sahara (Ukpong 2000, 4). To "some extent a child of... modern methods of western biblical scholarship," African biblical scholarship appropriates but redirects the tools of the trade of post-Enlightenment biblical scholarship, the particular characteristic of this appropriation being "the concern to create an encounter between the biblical text and the Africa context" (Ukpong 2000, 4). Armed with the full array of historical-critical methods, as well as some of the more recent literary and sociological methods, African biblical scholarship responds to "the widespread condemnation of African religion and culture by the Christian missionaries of the nineteenth and twentieth centuries" (Ukpong 2000, 5). The initial phase of this response, the period from the 1930s to the 1970s, tended to be "reactive and apologetic, focused on legitimizing African religion and culture" (Ukpong 2000, 5). Using a comparative approach, which "took the form of showing continuities and discontinuities between the religious culture of Africa and the Bible, particularly the Old Testament," African biblical scholars "sought to legitimize African religion and culture," rejecting the missionary message that African religion and culture were "demonic and immoral" (Ukpong 2000, 5).

In a second, overlapping phase, covering the period from the 1970s to the 1990s, African biblical scholarship became less reactive and more proactive (Ukpong 2000, 7), though the energizing impulse of this phase remains the legacy of colonial and missionary damage. So, during this period there is an attempt to recognize and recover "the presence of Africa and African peoples in the Bible as well as examine their contribution in biblical history," but there is also a conscious drive to correct "negative images about Africa and African peoples embedded in certain traditional readings of some biblical texts" (Ukpong 2000, 7–8). In addition to this focus on "Africa-in-the-Bible studies," the second phase is characterized by a much stronger sense of African religion and culture as the subject of biblical interpretation: "African culture and religion have been seen to be not just a preparation for the gospel, as in the comparative method, but *indispensable resources in the interpretation of the gospel message* and in the development of African Christianity" (Ukpong 2000, 11). Africa is no longer the object of the Bible and Christianity of others (western missionary others), but the subject which makes African objects of the Bible and Christianity.

The third phase of Ukpong's schema, the 1990s to the present, develops an element of the second phase as its primary thrust. The two emerging methodologies of phase two, those of liberation and inculturation, "are carried forward with new orientations" (Ukpong 2000, 15). Missionary and colonial forms still haunt African biblical scholarship, but they no longer dominate its consciousness. Africans are their own primary dialogue partners. From the inculturation trajectory the sense of the African context as the subject of interpretation becomes stronger and stronger, gradually assuming the primary position with respect to the dialogue between the original meaning of the text and its meaning for the African context. From the liberation trajectory, ordinary indigenous Africans emerge from the shadows of their academically trained comrades to take a more prominent place in process of biblical interpretation than previously accorded them. In phase three, then, the African context is seen as both "providing the critical resources for biblical interpretation and the subject of interpretation" (Ukpong 2000, 15).

This final sentence implies more than Ukpong goes on to develop, but that is to be expected in a survey article. In the next section I will go on to read these implications as part of my unpacking of the 'African biblical scholarship' (with a return of the inverted commas) package.

Constituted by Ordinary Indigenous 'Readers' of the Bible

Ukpong's analysis explicitly focuses on academic interpretation of the Bible, deliberately excluding "popular uses of the Bible" (Ukpong 2000, 4). But because ordinary indigenous African 'readers,' whether literate or not, are constitutive of 'African biblical scholarship,' their presence asserts itself in almost any discussion of African biblical scholarship (with or without inverted commas). Ukpong's contribution in the article extensively cited above is his focus on academic African biblical interpretation, but it is mark of our African reality and of Ukpong's engagement with this reality that he cannot bracket ordinary African 'readers' entirely. And this is precisely because *they are a part of academic African biblical interpretation!*

In the words of Teresa Okure, another Nigerian biblical scholar, African biblical scholarship "is inclusive of scholars and nonscholars, the rich and the poor" (Okure 1993, 77). This is not merely a nostalgic or romantic yearning for a lost naivete, as it is in western literary biblical scholarship where the scholarly reader imagines his or her scholarly self in this role. Nor are ordinary Africans merely informants for the enterprise of western scholarship (Smith-Christopher 1995). Okure is making a more telling claim, namely, that ordinary indigenous African 'readers' of the Bible—most of whom are black, poor and marginalized—are constitutive of African biblical scholarship.

Having said this, we still have some way to go in properly characterizing what this means. It is a part of our reality, but it is not a part of our African reality that we have done much reflection about. Ukpong's discussion, in his characterization of the third phase of African biblical scholarship (Ukpong 2000, 15–16), of the contextual Bible study work of the Institute for the Study of the Bible (ISB) in South Africa highlights the engagement and exchange between socially engaged (mainly black organic)[3] biblical scholars and theologians and the importance of "the approach, the perspectives and concerns of the ordinary African readers of the Bible" (Ukpong 2000, 15). As I have argued elsewhere (West 2000), ordinary African 'readers' of the Bible are constitutive of African biblical scholarship in a number of respects. First, as already indicated, because African biblical scholarship concentrates on the correspondence between African experience and the Bible, it locates itself "within the social, political, and ecclesiastical context of Africa" (Holter 1998, 245), a context filled with ordinary African believers in and 'readers' of the Bible. Put more crudely, the directions African biblical scholarship takes and the questions it admits to the scholarly task are shaped more by the life issues—such as AIDS, malaria, unemployment, hunger, etc.—of local African communities than they are by the interpretative interests (Fowl 1990) of the scholarly community. Biblical scholarship belongs in the church and the community, not only in the academy, and, anyway, the community intrudes into the academy, demanding a presence and access to its resources.

Second, certain impulses in biblical scholarship that have

made their way into African biblical interpretation—such as strands of postmodernism, reader-response criticism, post-colonial criticism, liberation and inculturation hermeneutics—have been appropriated precisely because they provide both impetus and theoretical support for the inclusion of ordinary, real, 'readers' (West 1999). Often on the defensive against or intimidated by the scholarly enterprise of the western world, African biblical scholars have reveled in the unraveling of the masters' mystical and exclusive academic empire, unprivileging the dominant discourses and thereby admitting, at last, the contributions of ordinary Africans to the task of critical discourse. The reality of my first point, in other words, is given theoretical coherence by the second, which in turn—in true praxilogical process—leads to fresh understandings of our reality. These discourses have enabled us to see that ordinary indigenous African 'readers' of the Bible constitute our academic work more thoroughly than we had thought. This leads into a third reflection on the constitution of African biblical scholarship by ordinary indigenous Africans.

Third, most African biblical scholars recognize that there remain elements of ordinary readings in their own 'scholarly' reading processes (Patte 1995). This is not an attempt to recover an earlier naivete, but a recognition that we remain, in some senses, ordinary readers, not always giving precedence to the systematic and structure interpretative processes we have learned in our biblical training. We are regularly retrained by African realities, by Africa as the subject of our interpretations. And this reality, Africa as subject, is most profoundly found in the struggles for survival, liberation and life of ordinary Africans with whom African biblical scholars are inextricably bound. We find, for example, that our African contexts begin to take precedence over the original context of the text, even in the work of those with the most historical-critical orientation among us.[4]

Fourth, Per Frostin has argued that one of the defining features of liberation theologies is that their primary dialogue partners are the poor and marginalized (Frostin 1988, 10). This is true for all forms of African theology, not only those strands that may be considered 'liberation' theologies. The theology of African women, South African Black theology, African theology, Reconstruction theology, etc.(see Maluleke 1997) would all admit to ordinary Africans being their primary dialogue partners. Where this impacts on African biblical scholarship is that African biblical scholars are always a part of the African theological project; besides white Afrikaner South African biblical scholarship (and, perhaps, some sectors of African Bible translation scholarship), there is really no separate space for African biblical scholarship, even if some yearn for such space. The driving concerns of African theologies encompass and draw in African biblical scholarship and make it a part of that project. Maluleke's comments about the role of, for example, John Mbiti above are a reminder of the manner in which biblically trained African intellectuals are inexorably conscripted into the agendas of African theologies. In this sense, then, ordinary African Christians, via their participation in African theologies, come to play an important part in African biblical scholarship.

Indigenous Interpretative Resources

This fourth comment leads me into further reflections on the distinctive characteristics of African biblical scholarship, raising as it does for me the question of the contribution of pre-critical interpretative tools to academic biblical scholarship. This is an important, but elusive, characteristic, because most African biblical scholars are not very overt about it. Ordinary African 'readers' of the Bible partially constitute African biblical scholarship in the ways reflected on above, but does this include their ways of dealing with *text*? Their questions and experiences clearly do make a significant contribution, but what about their interpretative strategies with respect to text, the scholar's domain of training and expertise? Ukpong says little on this, emphasizing instead the lived reality they bring to the work of the western trained African biblical scholar.

In my own work I have stressed that we ought to allow the interpretative interests and strategies of ordinary African 'readers' to constitute African biblical scholarship. I am using the phrase 'interpretative interests' here in the way that it is used by Stephen Fowl (Fowl 1990). Briefly, Fowl suggests that instead of talking about the 'meaning' of a text, we explicate 'meaning' in terms of interpretative interests; interpretative interests being those dimensions of text that particular biblical scholars privilege as the location of 'meaning,' whether this be in the text itself (literary, structuralist, etc.), behind the text (historical-critical, socio-historical, etc.) or in-front-of-the-text (symbolic, metaphorical, etc.; see West 1995, 131–73). What, then, are the interpretative interests of ordinary African 'readers' of the Bible, and what role do they play in African biblical scholarship?

The section above goes some way to answering these questions, but only some way. There is no precision as to the interpretative interests of ordinary African 'readers' of the Bible. My own work in this area attempts to go further, but succeeds only in sketching the domain of interpretative interests in rather broad strokes (West 1999, 79–107). I play with and explore a range of metaphors in an attempt to grasp some of the dimensions of ordinary Africans' engagement with the biblical text, arguing that ordinary African 'readers' of the Bible 're-member' a 'dis-membered' Bible, by means of "guerilla exegesis" (Hendricks 1995), by reading with the nose (de Oliveria 1995), by a process of "engraf(ph)ting" (Fulkerson 1994, 152), by "a looseness, even a playfulness" towards text (Wimbush 1991, 88–89), and, now I would add, by "conjuring" with text (Smith 1994). All of this is wonderfully suggestive and provides a host of impulses for digging deeper and becoming more precise. And, as I have said, African biblical scholarship is not averse to these textual resources of ordinary African 'readers' of the Bible, particularly on the countless occasions when African biblical scholars and ordinary African 'readers' of the Bible read together in the churches and communities.

But, I want to ask, what place do such interpretative interests and strategies have in the other locations of African biblical scholarship, the biblical studies classroom of the seminary and university? Because our seminaries and universities are strongly shaped by the encyclopedic model of European (and more recently, North American) tertiary institutions, biblical studies still occupies a place on its own. Now is not the place to debate this, but as long as this situation persists now is the time to ask of the place of the interpretative interests of ordinary African 'readers' of the Bible in our pedagogy. For, it is in these places, outside of the churches and communities, that an important proportion of the next generations of pastors, priests, activists, and scholars will emerge, and their predominant experience, as Ukpong's analysis indicates (see also LeMarquand 2000b) and as Knut Holter would concur from the perspective of African Old Testament scholarship (Holter 2000a; Holter 2000b), is that our classrooms tend to bracket (at best) the textual interpretative 'reading' resources of ordinary Africans.

A large part of placing these reading resources in parenthesis is that we do not know how to characterize them. We have no trouble at all in documenting and displaying the varied interpretative interests and methods of western biblical scholarship; our libraries are full of such secondary accounts of biblical studies methods (even if in many of our libraries the books are rather outdated) and we ourselves are fairly familiar with these methods, having been trained in them, whether in African institutions or elsewhere away from the continent. We, then, perpetuate the cycle, training the next generation to do as we have done. Fortunately, such is the powerful presence of our African realities, even in the corridors of the academy, that once we leave our tertiary retreats we cannot but help being retrained by ordinary African 'readers' of the Bible and their lived experience. But is this lurch in terms of reading practice from outside to inside to outside the academy necessary or desirable?

A negative answer is offered further support by the contention in the work of Vincent Wimbush that early African American (African slaves in America) encounters with the Bible have functioned "as phenomenological, socio-political and cultural foundation" for subsequent periods (Wimbush 1993, 131). If Wimbush is right in asserting that the array of interpretative strategies forged in the earliest encounters of African Americans with the Bible are foundational, in the sense that all other African American readings are in some sense built upon and judged by them, then such analysis has tremendous hermeneutical significance for our current context. What Wimbush's work suggests, and its contribution lies in its heuristic capacity rather than in its detail, is that ordinary African American readers of the Bible embody a long history of biblical hermeneutical strategies that can be traced back to the formative encounters with the Bibles they encounter in the hands of their masters and mistresses, and which they began to appropriate, both by watching how white's used this book and by forging their own interpretative resources so that they could wrest control of this potentially powerful book from them (Wimbush 1991; Wimbush 1993). Further, his work emphasizes the layered nature of ordinary African American biblical interpretation, reminding us that whatever we might do in the academy is just one more layer. Not only do ordinary African American readers of the Bible not come to seminary and university empty handed—without interpretative strategies—but what they do bring has been foundationally shaped by the very earliest encounters of their ancestors with the Bible.

I am persuaded by Wimbush's work, and given some remarkable resonances with our African contexts, believe that his work is worth harnessing for our own research. Implicit in Wimbush's analysis is that we cannot take up the task of identifying and documenting, which I would argue we should be doing, the reading resources of ordinary African 'readers' of the Bible unless we introduce an historical dimension to our hermeneutical concerns. This is the focus of the remainder of my essay.

Conceptualizing a Task That Lies Ahead

In tackling this task, we do well, of course, to remember the concerns of Maluleke with which we began this discussion. And to this I would add another cautionary comment by Maluleke. We African biblical scholars, all of us, assume that the

Bible is central to the lived faith of ordinary African Christians. In fact, it is commonly assumed, even argued, by black and African biblical scholars and theologians that the Bible is a significant resource for African Christians (see Mbiti 1977; Tutu 1983, 124–29). Maluleke himself acknowledges this, pointing to the many ways in which the Bible is a resource in Africa: as the most widely translated book it makes a contribution to the construction of indigenous grammars and texts, it is a basic textbook in primary and higher education, literacy has been closely tied to Bible reading and memorization, it is the

> most accessible basic vernacular literature text, a storybook, a compilation of novels and short stories, a book of prose and poetry, a book of spiritual devotion (i.e. the 'Word of God') as well as a 'science' book that 'explains the origins of all creatures. In some parts of Africa, the dead are buried with the Bible on their chests, and the Bible is buried into the concrete foundations on which new houses are to be built. In many African Independent Churches it is the physical contact between the sick and the Bible that is believed to hasten healing (Maluleke 2000, 91–92).

Clearly African Christians relate to the Bible in various ways, and this is Maluleke's point, that we recognize the diverse ways in which ordinary Africans actually engage with the Bible. In fact, Maluleke goes further, insisting that we probe beneath the apparent place of the Bible in the lives of ordinary indigenous Africans. Leaning on the work of those Black theologians who have gone before him, particularly Itumeleng Mosala and Takatso Mofokeng, Maluleke asks us to reexamine the relationship between black Africans and the Bible.

Mofokeng argues that the Bible is important to black South Africans because besides the Bible there is no

> easily accessible ideological silo or storeroom is being offered to the social classes of our people that are desperately in need of liberation. African traditional religions are too far behind most blacks while Marxism, is to my mind, far ahead of many blacks, especially adult people. In the absence of a better

storeroom of ideological and spiritual food, the Christian religion and the Bible will continue for an undeterminable period of time to be the haven of the Black masses par excellence (Mofokeng 1988, 40).

In other words, ideologically contested though it is, there are good strategic and pragmatic reasons for continuing to use the Bible, so long as it remains the most readily available resource for social transformation. "Preoccupation with Christian doctrines and ideas [and the Bible] was, for black theology therefore, not primarily on account of faith or orthodoxy considerations, but on account of Christianity's apparent appeal to the black masses" (Maluleke 1998, 134). But, Maluleke continues, "What needs to be re-examined now, however, is the extent to which the alleged popularity of Christianity [and the Bible] assumed in South African black theology is indeed an accurate assessment of the religious state of black people" (Maluleke 1998, 134).

However, Maluleke doubts whether "pragmatic and moral arguments can be constructed in a manner that will speak to masses without having to deal with the Bible in the process of such constructions" (Maluleke 1996, 14). The Bible remains in the 1990s, and probably into the millennium, "a 'haven of the Black masses'" (14). And as long as it is a resource, it must be confronted, "precisely at a hermeneutical level" (14). Quite what Maluleke means by this is not clear, but he does offer some clues, which emerge in his dialogue with the biblical hermeneutics of African Theology (Maluleke 1997, 14–16).

He agrees with Mercy Amba Oduyoye, who speaks with many African women,[5] when she says that the problem with the Bible in Africa is that "throughout Africa, the Bible has been and continues to be absolutized: it is one of the oracles that we consult for instant solutions and responses" (Oduyoye 1995, 174, cited in Maluleke 1997, 15). However, continues Maluleke, while many African biblical scholars and theologians are locked into a biblical hermeneutics that makes "exaggerated connections between the Bible and African heritage," "on the whole, and in practice, [ordinary] African Christians are far more innovative and subversive in their appropriation of the Bible than they appear" (Maluleke 1997, 14–15). While they "may mouth the Bible-is-equal-to-the-Word-of-God formula, they are actually creatively pragmatic and selective in their use of the Bible so that the Bible may enhance rather than frustrate their life struggles" (Maluleke 1996, 13). The task before Black Theology, then, is "not only to develop creative Biblical hermeneutic methods, but also to observe and analyze the manner in which African Christians 'read' and view the Bible" (15).

Indeed, and this is where I return to my attempt at characterizing African biblical scholarship, an important task confronting us in such a characterization is "to observe and analyze the manner in which African Christians 'read' and view the Bible." Ordinary black South Africans have adopted a variety of strategies in dealing with an ambiguous Bible, including rejecting it (Mofokeng 1988, 40) and strategically appropriating it as a site of struggle (Mofokeng 1988, 41; Mosala 1986, 184). But, as I have argued (West 1999, 88–89), neither Mofokeng nor Mosala provide the kind of detail required for our project. As I mentioned earlier, my own attempts to reflect on and conjure concepts that elucidate the way in which ordinary black South Africans 'read' the Bible are not detailed enough (West 1999, 89–107). And we have all been concentrating on the *present*, as indeed we should have, given the daily realities of our struggle against apartheid and the lack of leisurely space to do anything different. With the space that liberation has afforded, we must now, I would suggest, not only deepen our analysis of current stances towards the Bible in our context, but we must also follow Wimbush's gaze to the past, to our Bible interpreting African ancestors. We cannot do justice to our task, I would argue, unless we also observe and analyze the manner in which African 'Christians'[6] *have 'read'* and *have viewed* the Bible.

Historical accounts of the early encounters between missionaries and indigenous Africans are plentiful and rich in detail and analysis. But they are pretty thin when it comes to documenting the reception and early interpretation of the Bible. There is much talk of "the Word" (Landau 1995), but on closer examination this tends to stand for the missionaries message in general and not the Bible in particular. That the Bible is seldom treated separately from the arrival and reception of Christianity is not surprising, particularly as it can be argued that the Bible is analytically (in the philosophical sense) bound up with Christianity (Barr 1980, 52). I do not want to dispute the interconnectedness of the Bible and Christianity, but I do not want to conflate them either. We assume too much too quickly if we do not pause to analyze the nature of their interconnectedness more carefully.

We should not assume, for example, that the reception of Christianity and the reception of the Bible are about receiving the same thing; Wimbush's interpretative history of the Bible among African Americans provides compelling reasons for analyzing the reception of the Bible as distinct from but related to the reception of Christianity. While there are many significant differences between African American and indigenous African transactions with the Bible, there are also many striking similarities which make Wimbush's analysis heuristically valuable.

African slaves' initial encounter with the Bible is characterized, according to Wimbush, by a combination of rejection, suspicion, and awe of "Book Religion." During this period the story of European colonization and conquest of "the New World" as told by Wimbush is remarkably similar to the story that indigenous South Africans tell about the coming of European colonization to Southern Africa.

> They conquered native peoples and declared that European customs, languages, and traditions were the law. The Europeans' embrace of the Bible helped to lend this process legitimacy. Since many of them through their reading of and reference to the Bible had already defined themselves as dissenters from the dominant social, political, and religious traditions in their native countries, they found it a rather natural resource in the context of the New World. The Bible func-

tioned as a cultural image-reflector, as a road map to nation-building. It provided the Europeans justification to think of themselves as a "biblical nation," as God's people called to conquer and convert the New World to God's way as they interpreted it (Wimbush 1991:84).

While the Bible did play a role in the missionizing of African slaves, in the earliest encounters its role was not primary and so its impact was indirect. "It was often imbedded within catechetical materials or within elaborate doctrinal statements and formal preaching styles" (Wimbush 1993, 130). When African slaves did encounter the Bible itself, this was done from the perspective of cultures steeped in oral tradition, so the notion of religion and religious power circumscribed by a book was "at first frightful and absurd, thereafter, ... awesome and fascinating" (Wimbush 1993, 131). As illiterate peoples with rich, well-established, and elaborate oral traditions the majority of the first African slaves were suspicious of and usually rejected "Book Religion." However, as Wimbush notes, "It did not take them long to associate the Book of 'Book religion' with power." So early in their encounter with "the Book," before they began to appropriate the Bible in an empowering and affirmative manner, their "capacity and willingness to engage 'the Book' were significant, for they demonstrated the ability of African slaves to adapt themselves to different understandings of reality," and in so doing to survive (Wimbush 1991, 85).

During what Wimbush classifies as the second period of encounter with the Bible, African slaves began to appropriate and own the Bible. With the growth of the non-establishment, evangelical, camp meeting revivalist movements, Africans "began to encounter the Bible on a large and popular scale." As significant numbers of Africans converted to Christianity, even establishing their own churches and denominational groups, they began to embrace the Bible.

What did not go unnoticed among the Africans was the fact that the white world they experienced tended to explain its power and authority by appeal to the Bible. So they embraced the Bible, transforming it from the book of the religion of whites—whether aristocratic slavers or lower class exhorters—into a source of (psychic-spiritual) power, a source of inspiration for learning and affirmation, and into a language world of strong hopes and veiled but stinging critique of slave-holding Christian culture (Wimbush 1993, 131).

The point Wimbush is making here is that African slaves, like their missionized, colonized, and conquered cousins in Africa, adopted and adapted the hermeneutic moves of the European 'masters.' African slaves would have noted the diversity of readings the Bible could inspire, including cultural, political, and denominational (religious) readings. They would also have observed the selective way in which the missionaries and preachers read the Bible; they read certain parts and ignored others. The various forms in which readings of the Bible could be articulated were appropriated and amplified: "in song, prayers, sermons, testimonies, and addresses" (Wimbush 1991, 86). If the missionaries and masters could interpret the Book under the guidance of the Spirit, then so could they.

And interpret they did. They were attracted primarily to the narratives of the Hebrew Bible dealing with the adventures of the Hebrews in bondage and escaping from bondage, to the oracles of the eighth-century prophets and their denunciations of social injustice and visions of social justice, and to the New Testament texts concerning the compassion, passion, and resurrection of Jesus. With these and other texts, the African American Christians laid the foundations for what can be seen as an emerging 'canon.' In their spirituals and in their sermons and testimonies African Americans interpreted the Bible in the light of their experiences. Faith became identification with the heroes and heroines of the Hebrew Bible and with the long-suffering but ultimately victorious Jesus. As the people of God in the Hebrew Bible were once delivered from enslavement, so, the Africans sang and shouted, would they be delivered. As Jesus suffered unjustly but was raised from the dead to new life, so, they sang, would they be 'raised' from their 'social death' to new life. So went the songs, sermons, and testimonies (Wimbush 1991, 86–87).

These various forms—spirituals, sermons, and testimonies—embody the hermeneutical processes whereby African slaves appropriated the Bible as their own property. They "reflect a hermeneutic characterized by a looseness, even playfulness, vis-à-vis the biblical texts themselves;" a looseness and playfulness towards the text which included the following strategies: interpretation "was not controlled by the literal words of the texts, but by social experience"; texts were heard and retold more than read; texts "were engaged as stories that seized and freed the imagination"; biblical texts were usually interpreted collectively; biblical stories "functioned sometimes as allegory, as parable, or as veiled social criticism" in a situation where survival demanded disguised forms of resisting discourse; certain texts in the canon were read and others ignored (Wimbush 1991, 88–89).

In addition to offering a preliminary description of these formative hermeneutical processes, Wimbush also wants to argue that the array of interpretative strategies forged in this period of African American encounter with the Bible are foundational: all other readings would in some sense be built upon and judged by them. The beginning of the African American encounter with the Bible has functioned, according to Wimbush, "as phenomenological, socio-political and cultural foundation" for subsequent periods (Wimbush 1993, 131). The Bible, understood as "the white folk's book," "was accepted but not interpreted in the way that white Christians and the dominant culture in general interpreted it" (Wimbush 1991, 89).

In the absence of a careful analysis and history of the early encounters of indigenous South Africans with the Bible, the first two phases of Wimbush's interpretative history are suggestive, especially in two respects. His characterization of the hermeneutics of encounter as "a looseness, even playfulness" towards the biblical text and his claim that such a hermeneutics is foundational for and constitutive of the hermeneutics of subsequent phases in the ongoing appropriation of the Bible are particularly insightful and significant, and resonate with my own preliminary research and reflections on the Southern African context, and find echoes in the work of some South African Black theologians (West 1999, 86–107). But before we allow such resonances to return us to the place of the Bible in the present, I want to suggest that we allow the impetus of Wimbush's work to push us back into the past, to the earliest encounters between indigenous South Africans and the Bible in order to see if we can detect in more detail the orientation of ordinary African's to the Bible and signs of the interpretative strategies they forged in those early encounters. I turn now to one such encounter in order to explore, briefly, if such a move has anything to offer us in our task.

Unpacking the Package: The Tlhaping Engage with the Bible

Following the death of Dr. van der Kemp, "that valuable man who [pioneered and] superintended the African missions" on behalf of the London Missionary Society (Campbell 1815, v),

> the Directors thought it expedient to request one of their own body, the Rev. John Campbell, to visit the country, personally to inspect the different settlements, and to establish such regulations, in concurrence with Mr. Read and the other missionaries [already in Southern Africa], as might be most conducive to the attainment of the great end proposed—the conversion of the heathen, keeping in view at the same time the promotion of their civilization (Campbell 1815, vi).

The complex and protracted processes that constitute missionary notions and practices of conversion and civilization in Southern Africa have been carefully analyzed by many others, but with particular insight by Jean and John Comaroff in their historical anthropology of mission (Comaroff 1985; Comaroff and Comaroff 1991; Comaroff and Comaroff 1997). Their thorough and theoretically astute work on missionary (and colonial) activity among the Southern Tswana provides a detailed backdrop to my own contribution, an attempt to probe the place of the Bible in the transactions that take place between indigenous Africans and the missionaries. While their work does take note of the Bible in the "long conversation," a recurring metaphor of the Comaroff's, between the Nonconformists and the Southern Tswana, I want to prize the Bible from the Christian missionary package if I can. I may not be able to, but the attempt is important to me as a socially engaged biblical scholar who is trying to understand the role of the Bible in the struggles of indigenous South Africans for survival, liberation, and life.[7] I do not want to too easily assume that the Bible appeared to Africans as it did to the missionaries who b[r]ought it.[8]

Another way in which I have managed the available material for the purposes of this essay is to limit my analysis to one of the very earliest accounts of a Southern Tswana encounter with the Bible that I can find. Unfortunately, this requires that I am largely dependent on missionary narrative constructions of such encounters, but socially engaged biblical scholars (and anthropologists (see Comaroff and Comaroff 1991, xi, 171, 189)) have become adept at "reading against the grain," particularly in contexts like South Africa where, Mosala reminds us, "the appropriation of works and events is always a contradictory process embodying in some form a 'struggle'" (Mosala 1989, 32).

And so I come, with John Campbell, who was, as the Comaroff's say, an astute observer (Comaroff and Comaroff 1991, 178), to see what his narrative of such an encounter might have to offer to the scrutinizing gaze of the Tlhaping, the southernmost group of Southern Tswana ("Bechuana") peoples. For their gaze was no less penetrating and discriminating than that of the missionaries who marched into their lives. And gaze they did; and listen, touch and taste: "the very first exchanges were visual, aural, and tactile, a trade of perceptions" (Comaroff and Comaroff 1991:181).

John Campbell, a director of the London Missionary Society, had been commissioned and sent to the Cape in 1812 in order "to survey the progress and prospects of mission work in the interior" (Comaroff and Comaroff 1991, 178). Campbell made his way from mission post to mission post in the Colony, and when he came to Klaarwater, which was then some distance north of the boundary of the Cape Colony, though the boundary was to follow him some years later (in 1825) almost as far as Klaarwater, he heard that Chief Mothibi of the Tlhaping people a hundred miles further to the north had expressed some interest in receiving missionaries (Comaroff and Comaroff 1991, 178). With barely a pause in Klaarwater, spending no more than a week there, Campbell and his party set off for Dithakong ("Lattakoo"), then the capital of Chief Mothibi, on 15 June 1813.

Though not the first whites or missionaries to make this trek (see below), I pick up their trail and tale as they arrive on the outskirts of Dithakong in the afternoon of 24 June 1813. Having crested a hill, "Lattakoo came all at once into view, lying in a valley between hills, stretching about three or four miles from E. to W." (Campbell 1815, 180). But as they descended the hill towards "the African city," they were "rather surprised that no person was to be seen in any direction, except two or three boys," and the absence of an overt presence continued even as the wagons wound their way between the houses, save for a lone man who "made signs" for them to follow him. The stillness continued, "as if the town had been forsaken of its inhabitants," until they came "opposite to the King's house," at which point they "were conducted" into the Chief's circular court (*kgotla*), "a square,[9] formed by bushes and branches of trees laid one above another, in which," for this space was not forsaken, "several hundreds of people assembled together, and a number of tall men with spears, draw[n] up in military order on the north side of the square." And then the silence was broken! "In a few minutes the square was filled with men, women, and children, who poured in from all quarters, to the number of a thousand or more. The noise from so many tongues, bawling with all their might, was rather confounding, after being so long accustomed to the stillness of the wilderness" (Campbell 1815, 180).

Signed upon and conducted into a dense symbolic space (Comaroff 1985, 54–60; Landau 1995, xvii, 20–25) not of their choosing or understanding, Campbell and company become the objects of Tswana scrutiny. With a feeling of being "completely in their power," Campbell confesses in a letter written some days later, "They narrowly inspected us, made remarks upon us, and without ceremony touched us. . . ."[10] The Tlhaping "see," "feasting their eyes," they "examine," and they "touch."[11] Having been momentarily "separated," and having "lost sight of each in the crowd," the missionaries soon gathered themselves, though they "could hardly find out each other," and devised "a scheme, which after a while answered our purpose; we drew up the waggons in the form of a square, and placed our tent in the centre" (Campbell 1815, 180). Being led into a round "square" not of their own making, they construct a square which they (only partially) control.[12] From this site of some control they plot and execute "the real object" of their visit, which they explain in the following terms to the nine local leaders, representing Chief Mothibi in his absence from the city, who gather in their tent "a little after sun-set" (Campbell 1815, 181).

> Through three interpreters, viz. in the Dutch, Coranna, and Bootchuana languages, I informed them that I had come from a remote country, beyond the sun, where the true God, who made all things was know—that the people of that country had long ago sent some of their brethren to Klaar Water, and other parts of Africa, to tell them many things which they did not know, in order to do them good, and make them better and happier— . . . [that] I had come to Lattakoo to inquire if they were willing to receive teachers—that if they were willing, then teachers should be sent to live among them (Campbell 1815, 182).

The leadership reply that they cannot/may not give an answer until Mothibi returned, after which there is an informal, it would appear, exchange of gifts: tobacco and milk (Campbell 1815, 182). A number of observations, interactions, and transactions are recorded over the next few days as Campbell (impatiently) waits for the arrival of Mothibi. But in the evening of the 27th, when the uncle of the Chief, "Munaneets," comes to their tent with an interpreter, there was "much interesting conversation," during which the Bible is explicitly designated in discourse. Two days earlier, on the first morning after their arrival (25 June) Campbell and his party hold worship in their kitchen, a house in "the square, used by them for some public purpose" but assigned to the missionaries as their kitchen, which is attended by "some of the people" (Campbell 1815, 181). It is hard to imagine the Bible not being present and not being used as either an unopened sacred object or an opened text. Similarly, during worship in the afternoon of the 27th, at which "About forty of the men sat round us very quietly during the whole time" (Campbell 1815, 191), the Bible too must have been present. But the first explicit reference to the Bible in this narrative, where it is separated out from the normal practice and patterns of the missionaries, is in the discussion with the Chief's uncle.

In their constant quest for information and opportunities to provide information, scrutinizing as they are scrutinized, the missionaries "enquired of him their reason for practising circumcision" (Campbell 1815, 191). It is not clear what prompts this question, but quite possibly what appear to be a series of ritual activities each day involving women, perhaps the initiation of young women (Campbell 1815, 185–186, 188, 191, 194–195; Comaroff 1985, 114–118), may, by association, have generated a question to do with male initiation (see Comaroff 1985, 85–115). The Chief's uncle replies that "it came to them from father to son." Sensing, no doubt, an opportunity "to instruct," the missionaries persevere, asking "Do you not know why your fathers did it?" To which the Chief's uncle and his companions answer, "No." Immediately the missionaries respond, Campbell reports, saying: "We told them that our book informed us how it began in the world, and gave them the names of Abraham, Ishmael, and Isaac, as the first persons who were circumcised" (Campbell 1815, 191–92). The illocutionary intent of this information is clearly to establish an earlier, and therefore superior, claim of origin. Origins were becoming increasingly important to the emerging modernity of missionary England, and so the Bible was seen as particularly potent, containing as it did 'the Origin' of all origins.[13] However, what impressed the Chief's uncle and his colleagues was not this claim to an all-encompassing origin, but the naming of the missionaries ancestors, Abraham, Ishmael, and Isaac, which is why "This appeared to them very interesting information, and they all tried to repeat the names we had mentioned, over and over again, looking to us for correction, if they pronounced any of them wrong. Munaneets, and the others who joined the company, appeared anxious to have them fixed on their memories" (Campbell 1815, 192). The book—the Bible—appeared, from the perspective of the Tlhaping, to contain the names of the missionary ancestors, and perhaps, if they picked up the intent of the missionaries proclamation, the ancestors of their ancestors. This was, indeed, interesting, and potentially powerful, information. The missionary attempt to subsume the Tlhaping's oral account of circumcision under their textual, biblical account may have marked the Bible, in the eyes of the Tlhaping, as a site worth watching, and perhaps even occupying; or it may have demonstrated the dangers of this strange object of power.

Impressed, but probably also a little perplexed by this response, the missionaries persist, asking next "if they knew any thing of the origin of mankind, or when they came." The people reply, "saying they came from some country beyond them, pointing to the N. which is the direction in which Judea lies.[14] That two men came out of the water; the one rich, having plenty of cattle, the other poor, having only dogs. One lived by oxen, the other by hunting. One of them fell, and the mark of his foot is on a rock to this day." With no apparent attempt probe this origin story in more detail, but with a clear indication of its (and their circumcision story's) inadequacy, the missionaries immediately "endeavoured to explain to them how knowledge, conveyed by means of books, was more certain than that conveyed by memory from father to son" (Campbell 1815, 192). The Chief's uncle, "Munaneets," is quick to realize the source of this "knowledge," knowing long before Michel Foucault theorized it, the articulations of power and knowledge on each other;[15] for he asks "if they should be taught to understand books." The use of the modal "should" perhaps conveys, as it often does in English, a sense of asking permission; Campbell's reconstruction and representation of this dialogue (via three other languages!) may accurately capture a concern on the part of the Chief's uncle that, given the evident power of the book(s), so openly exhibited by the missionaries, they may not be granted access to the book(s).[16] That the missionaries and the Chief's representatives have in mind 'the book,' in particular, is clear from missionaries' answer: "We answered they would; and when the person we should send (provided Mateebe consented), had learned their language, he would change the Bible from our language into theirs" (Campbell 1815, 192).

One of the local participants was clearly worried about outside instruction, and may also have been worried about the Bible as a new (outside) site and source of power/knowledge, though this is less clear, for during the conversation, Campbell reports, "an old man who is averse to our sending teachers, asked how we made candles, pointing to that which was on our table. He also said," Campbell continues, "he did not need instruction from any one, for the dice which hung from his neck informed him of every thing which happened at a distance; and added, if they were to attend to instructions, they would have no time to hunt or to do any thing" (Campbell 1815, 193). This fascinating exchange, re-presenting as it is a complex exchange, seems to suggest a profound grasp by this "old man"—possibly an *ngaka* (an indigenous doctor/diviner/healer), given that he is wearing a "dice," one of the elements among the bones, shells, and other materials making up the *ditaola* used in divining[17]—of the dangerousness of non-indigenous instruction. The context of the discussion, and the centrality of the Bible in the discussion, if not also centrally positioned in the meeting space, makes it likely that he assumes that the missionaries book(s) are their equivalent of his "dice." My conjecture finds some support from Robert Moffat's account of an incident in which he says, "My books puzzled them," he wrote. "They asked if they were my 'Bola,' prognosticating dice" (see Comaroff and Comaroff 1997, 345; Moffat 1842, 384). Whether his aversion to "instruction" is an aversion to both the source and the interpreter of the source is not clear, but is a question that sits at the center of my analysis. We must not assume that this "old man" shares the assumption of the missionaries that the book and its instruction are one and the same thing. His concern that "if they were to attend to instructions, they would have no time to hunt or to do anything," may reflect rumors of the time schedules and modes of production of established mission station church and school routines to the south, in which case the focus of his aversion is the instruction regime rather than the source of power/knowledge itself, the book.

But I may be imagining a fissure where there is none, for this insightful "old man" may be making a simpler point; by pointing to the candles, and asking how missionaries made them, he may be demonstrating an important difference between knowledge that he and his people would find useful—how to make candles—and knowledge that is potentially damaging and dangerous—instruction about what happens "at a distance," such as circumcision, ancestors, and origins. The book, the source of the latter, but not, it would seem from his analysis, of the former, is as much a problem as the instruction.

Some days later (30 June), with the city still awaiting the arrival of Chief Mothibi, and with many significant interactions transacted each day, including the constant gathering and giving of information, the Bible is again foregrounded. Campbell's major preoccupation during this time is seeking permission to "instruct the people." The local leadership consistently insists that he wait for Mothibi's return, and when Campbell and his men indicate an interest in using the time until Mothibi's return "to visit a large village about a day and a half's journey higher up the country," they receive a visit, that evening—after a busy day full of formative transactions, including Campbell's showing "a person his own face in the looking glass," another missionary brought object saturated with symbolic significance (Comaroff and Comaroff 1997, 170–97)—from Mmahutu, "the queen," Mothibi's senior wife (see Campbell 1815, 200, 207). She entered their tent and said that she "was averse" to their "going any where till Mateebe came," and that at the very least they should leave part of their wagons and party behind. Using this as a lever, the missionaries claim that they would never have thought of leaving Dithakong "even for a day before Mateebe's return" had they "been permitted to instruct the people; but that having nothing to do," they wished to visit that village and hunt. However, they are persuaded not to leave, and once this matter is settled, the missionaries "endeavoured to convey some information" (Campbell 1815, 199).

What follows is a remarkable exchange, signifying as it does a range of possible appropriations of the Bible:

> We explained to her the nature of a letter, by means of which a person could convey his thoughts to a friend at a distance. Mr. A. shewed her one he had received from his wife, by which he knew every thing that had happened at Klaar Water for two days after he left it. This information highly entertained her, especially when told that A. Kok, who brought it, knew nothing of what it contained, which we explained by telling her the use of sealing wax. The bible being on the table gave occasion to explain the nature and use of a book, particularly of that book—how it informed us of God, who made all things; and of the beginning of all things, which seemed to astonish her, and many a look was directed towards the bible (Campbell 1815, 199).

Returning to a theme already raised, the reliability of text over against oral transmission from father to son (see above), the missionaries draw Mmahutu's attention to the power of the letter as text in at least two respects. First, text can re-present "every thing" that happened in a place in a person's absence. Second, text can be made to hide its message from the bearer and reveal its contents only to the intended receiver. Turning from the letter, to a quite different genre of text (from the perspective of the missionaries), the Bible, but a text nevertheless, the missionaries use the interest generated in their exposition of the letter to return to their preoccupation with the contents of the Bible, particularly the matter of origins.

Mmahutu is astonished, but what she is astonished at may not be what the missionaries imagine. Clearly, from her perspective text has power, with some appearing to have more power than others, hence "many a look" at the Bible. Text can reveal and text can hide; text can be manipulated by the people who transact with it. Clearly too, text contains knowledge/power; its contents, for those who have the power to make it speak, has to do with matters of importance to a community. This becomes clearer in a letter written by Campbell to a friend, Mr. David Langton, some days later (27 July) in which he elaborates on this episode. Immediately following the final sentence in the quotation above, the following is added: "Mr Reads eye caught a verse very suitable to our situation in the page that was lying open, viz. Math. 4:16."[18] If this text was read, and the literary context suggests it would have been, Mmahutu would have heard this: "The people which sat in darkness saw great light; and to them which sat in the region and shadow of death light is sprung up." This then makes some sense of Mmahutu's questions, recorded in the next paragraph of the journal entry: "'Will people who are dead, rise up again?' 'Is God under the earth, or where is he?'" (Campbell 1815, 199). But only some sense, for her questions do not seem to deal directly with the passage read. The passage clearly makes sense to the missionaries, being made to bear the full weight of English missionary images of Africa (see Comaroff and Comaroff 1991, 86–125). However, such allusions are probably absent from Mmahutu's hearing of this sentence from the Bible. Whatever she hears, and it may be the word "death," prompts here to bring her own questions to the text/missionaries, disturbed as she and others have become by talk of people rising from the dead, worrying especially that their slain enemies might arise (Comaroff and Comaroff 1997, 342; Moffat 1842, 403–5). I must pause here, both because space prevents me from pursuing the narrative further for now and to allow time for what has transpired to be reflected upon.

Already we see emerging evidence from this very early encounter of a recognition that the Bible is power/knowledge, that as power/knowledge it can be manipulated by those that control it, that it is beginning to be prized from the hands of the missionaries by indigenous experience and indigenous questions, and, most significantly, that the bearer, like the bearer of the letter, might not know the power/knowledge it contains. This last reflection requires particular pause, as we allow this thought to linger and do its subversive work. May it be that Mmahutu wonders whether the missionaries, bearers of the Bible, understand the true nature of what they have brought among the Tlhaping? What this brief case study does demonstrate, though, is that Wimbush is right to insist that we must go back before we can go forward and that Maluleke is right to make us consider more carefully the package that the Bible in Africa is. It also shows the long road we will have to travel with our African ancestors in order to recover their interpretative strategies that form the bedrock of the biblical hermeneutics of our current students in our classrooms. We have barely begun to unpack one early encounter and already we are confronted with the complexities of the Bible as an object of potential power (for good and ill) in the eyes of indigenous South Africans. Yet to be translated into Tswana, the Bible is not yet text in the sense that we are familiar with in the academy, but already it is being transacted with and the package that is the Bible in Africa is beginning to take shape.

Chapter 4

Redefining Power: Reading the Bible in Africa from the Peripheral and Central Positions

Alpheus Masoga

Introduction

This essay discusses the perspectives of both the central and peripheral positions towards reading the Bible in Africa. The connotation central to this essay refers to "trained readers" (West 1993, Draper 1994, and Botha 1994) from institutions of learning with regards to bible historical critical tools, while peripheral has the opposite meaning. As James Cone rightly observes in *God of the Oppressed*:

> Theologians do not normally reveal the true source of their theological reflections. They often tell us about the books that are similar and not so similar to their perspectives, but seldom do they tell us about the non-intellectual factors that are decisive for the arguments advanced on a particular issue (Cone 1977, vi).

In his work entitled, *Theology with a New Voice? The Case for an Oral Theology in the Southern African Context*, Piet Naude (1996, 25) gives a concise outline of the development of the so-called "Oral Theory" which forms the basis for the defense of "Oral theology." He explains why the development of oral theologies in South Africa endowed with literally thousands of

Oral Christian communities has been delayed so far, by pointing out that,

> Yes, the creation of the category "illiterate" is simultaneously the creation of a vulnerable social group with ever increasing opportunities for discrimination and exploitation. Illiterates have been, in the South African context, not merely those unable to read: it is the category of marginalized people, excluded—for many years by law—from education and access to the world of literacy which controlled their lives through documents (pass laws) they could not even read. The current debates on land redistribution and reconstructing education in a new South Africa have their roots inter alia on the dichotomies created by oral-literate social construction in our history. And theologians who take social analysis seriously, must take this matter seriously precisely to avoid a continuation thereof.

The assumptions underpinning the above *asserverations* and the reality they depict, strongly point to images of knowledge, power, economy and dignity "where centralized hands and systems created by and for imperial, colonial and apartheid powers, then it was these social formations which occupied the center of sociality" with adverse results on the *peripheried* hands (Smith 2000, 5).

It is within the context of this periphery *versus* the center that this essay is presented. Basically, the essay explores the concept and practice of power in reading and interpreting Biblical texts. It goes beyond arguing for a shift, and brings home *vibes* of complete *redefinition* of power itself in the context of Biblical texts. Various readings of the Bible texts from Qwa Qwa, Eastern Free State will be used in the essay.

Biblical Hermeneutics and Power Relations

In constructing critical and contextual readings with ordinary readers,[1] West (1995, 68) concludes that "Biblical Studies and trained readers need 'the other,' particularly those 'others' from the margins, in our readings of the Bible. Our readings may be critical, but they are not truly contextual without the presence of ordinary readers." We, argues West (1995), the trained readers, also need to be ready to hear that we might be in possession of resources which are needed by poor and marginalized communities. Some of our biblical training may be useful and empowering to such communities. Again West (1993, 178–79), having read Mark 10:17-22 with ordinary readers, maintains that the exercise "has been a challenging and creative process. We have created a cumulative reading which is not found in any academic commentary nor among ordinary readers in the church and community. However, the interface between academic biblical studies and ordinary readers has produced a reading which is profoundly challenging in our South African context."

The "creative process," West points out, is guided by the *skills* and *tools* to 'read with.' Rightly, West notes the fact that there is ongoing tension between avoiding the insult of speaking for the oppressed and attempting to respond to their voices by challenging and engaging in social and political endeavors (West 1993, 168; Welch 1985, 44). In the opinion of West the tension cannot be resolved. He advises that "we can continue to work creatively within this tension, and we can come to understand its parameters more clearly. We can only do this, however, when we move beyond 'speaking for' the poor and oppressed, and beyond 'listening to'[2] the poor and oppressed, towards 'speaking to' or 'speaking with' the poor and oppressed." Clearly, power and space are key in the submissions made by West. West attempts to look at *interfaces* and corridors of dialogue between the 'trained' and 'ordinary' readership. The question of power encapsulated in terms of *space* and *position* are silently echoed in West's *agigating* process. Unfortunately, for West, the tension does not constitute a major problem, pointing out that "While there are certainly interesting similarities, we must recognize that something fundamentally different is going on in the modes of reading of ordinary readers. The majority of ordinary readers read the Bible precritically... because they have not been trained in critical modes of reading" (1993, 165). West is comfortable with the jargon he employs regardless of the implications it decoys. This can be further noted when he explains the ideological nature of the Biblical text and the role of the ordinary reader. He notes that "for biblical interpreters who recognize the ideological nature of the biblical text and who yet continue to interpret and appropriate the biblical tradition there are at least two key elements in holding together a hermeneutics of suspicion and a hermeneutics of trust." One of these key elements is "the adoption and advocacy of criticality in reading the Bible"; the other is "the commitment to ordinary people "particularly the poor and oppressed, in the text and in their own contexts"[3] (West 1995; cf. Botha 1994, 292; Scheffler 1991, 296; Draper 1991, 255).

Justin Ukpong (1995), looking at the Bible with African eyes, argues that "African biblical scholars, have, until recently, not been able to salvage the situation. Trained as they have been in the tradition of western biblical scholarship, they read the bible through an interpretive grid developed in the western culture, and then seek to apply the result in their own contexts." Ukpong concluded that, at the end of such a process, "has been a visible gap between this academic reading of the bible and the needs of ordinary African Christians" (1995, 4). Ukpong calls out for a new mode of reading the Bible "that would engage the African social and cultural contexts in the process ... and the development of such hermeneutic like the Black hermeneutic ... and the contextual hermeneutic" (*ibid*). Obviously, as in the case of West, Ukpong relents the absence of the African social and cultural contexts in the interpretation of the biblical texts. This *absolute vacuum* according to Ukpong constitutes a serious problem of overshadowing life-orientations in the bible (Taber 1978, 71; cf. Ukpong 1995, 13). Ostensibly so, Western scholarship draws much attention that the African life orientation occupies a peripheral position. The African trained scholar occupies the central position and continues to echo Western training scholarship and dominates the *space*. Ukpong suggests the inculturation hermeneutic in the context of this problem. As he points out, "A preliminary condition for doing inculturation hermeneutic is awareness of, and commitment to, the inculturation movement which seeks strong interaction of the Christian faith with all aspects of African life and thought" (1995, 10). He goes on to suggest several steps of analysis. First, the identification of the interpreter's specific context. Second, analysis of the context of interpretation, "that is the interpreter's context which is to form the background against which the text is to be read" (1995, 11). Third, analysis of the historical context of the text to gain a "proper focus for discussing the text" (1995, 12). Fourth, analysis of the text in the "light of the already contemporary context." This is considered to be having a *plethora* of components, because of its "critical review of current interpretations. Next is textual analysis employing different tools depending on the nature and motif of the text. Most important however is placing the text in its larger contexts within the canon for the purpose of further clarifying the focus of interpretation" (1995, 12).

Ukpong's plea for consideration of *context* is a valid one. However, one fails to see how this can be implemented and accordingly given the power game which has already been noticed between Western readings versus the African readings of the Bible. The five step analysis proposed by Ukpong does not specify the place of the "peripheral reader," but only concentrates on the "central reader" who in this case can be represented by a Western tutor or the African tutored reader. In this case, the African tutored reader according to the Western approach might develop a sensitive reading attitude to the African social and cultural context, but that would certainly not exonerate him or her from a "doubly privileged" position of both reading the African text and using the Western *tools* and *skills*. It should be noted that the author of this essay does not abhor Western training but merely indicates the implications which are drawn in this whole process. This attempt by the author simply sounds an alarm and transmits *vibes* of concern.

Mosala (1989, 15) makes a strong admission that "Black theology's exegetical starting point expresses itself in the notion that the Bible is the revealed word of God." Therefore, in this regard, the task of the trained black theologian is to *explicate* God's word for those who are oppressed and positioned at the *periphery of all happenings* (1989).[4] What is interesting is the fact that Mosala firmly holds the view that, "Just as the church has always been the church of the bourgeoisie, theology and exegesis have always represented bourgeois theological and exegetical interests. And it is a tragedy that rebel theologies like black theology and liberation theology should uncritically adopt the biblical hermeneutics of bourgeois theological interests (1989, 18–19). Mosala's view brings some relief. We note the thin line which does not only affect the theological paradigms but the church itself, the field or plain where *operato* has to be effected. This in my opinion points to the problem. African, in particular, South African, Biblical Hermeneutics faces a number of challenges. Indeed something is wrong somewhere. The church which is referred to by Mosala is definitely positioned centrally. The church has for centuries enjoyed the privilege of, to borrow from Mosala, bourgeoisie benefits. The *other* church is not explicitly mentioned by Mosala, but is implied in his work (1989, 21). It is this *other* church which kept the movement of resistance going, and rallied support for the course of liberation. It voiced silently the malignancy of oppression, strengthened the course for justice, and silently pushed from the periphery the sustainable comprehensive well-being. This is the church which has always stood alongside the bourgeoisie church with its bourgeoisie theological approaches. The space and power it occupied has never being viewed to be constituting any problem in the hermeneutical endeavors but empathetic references[5] are always made to its existence and fundamental hermeneutical strengths (West 1999; Draper 1991; Lategan 1991).

In this context, one area of struggle is to overcome the gap between the periphery and the center. For sometime the periphery has proactively fed into the center for the center's regeneration but without acknowledgment. It does not come to the level of partnership as many scholars have claimed to have been the case (West 1999). One would desire to have a partnership between center and periphery which ultimately goes beyond the two dichotomies. The following question becomes pertinent in this regard: how can the periphery be brought into the mainstream (center)? In my opinion the question should be posed the other way round: Is it possible for the center to move to the periphery? Or to be more vicious: *The time has come for the periphery to occupy its own space without the interference of the center.* Definitely one should not be seen to be perpetuating a situation of *further* asymmetry. This should not be seen to be the case, but instead attempt to allow peripheral growth and sustenance and, in the course enable the periphery to *converse* with the center on an equal footing. Power, as both concept and practice, cannot be ignored in the whole process. Glossing over it would not resolve the endemic condition. It threatens to both corrode and erode the efforts already reached so far. Grappling and acknowledging its serious implications in the process offers one the opportunity to devise new and innovative strategies in dealing with it.

Toward Conversational Biblical Hermeneutic and Theology

So far, we have noticed how power as both concept and practice plays a central role in the interpretation of the text. Even in this case the Bible occupies a central role in the lives of many African people. As Mosala (1991, 44) points out, "The Bible is there in every aspect of South African life in curious and often contradictory ways." And further, this very same text, which is a terrain of "fierce struggles" (Mosala 1991, 44) has to be within the corridors of conversation. It should be within this terrain that both the powerful and the powerless should converse. The text should offer both the center and periphery the opportunity to grow and broaden their horizons. Mosala (1991, 44) states that "In reading the Bible from the people's perspectives, namely, the perspective of liberation, we must confront the fundamental question of the nature of the Biblical text. Biblical study has to revisit this question in the light of the many formerly suppressed struggles, if it does not help to reinforce again the use of the Bible as an instrument of oppression and exploitation." This assertion by Mosala is timely and relevant. The peripheral readers continue to read silently from their context.[6] The Biblical text should offer both the center and periphery a *space* to converse and converge. No Biblical hermeneutic is hermeneutic until it wrestles with the question of power relations. The idea of forging an interface (West, 1993) between the center and periphery does not at all help or come closer to any solution of the problem we are all facing. As Mosala (1991, 44) rightly notes, "In reading the Bible from the people's perspectives, namely, the perspective of liberation, we must confront the fundamental question of the nature of the Biblical Text. Biblical study has to revisit this question in the light of the many formerly suppressed struggles, if it does not help to reinforce gain the use of the Bible as an instrument of oppression and exploitation." Indeed, from Mosala's assertion it becomes apparent that the conversation between the center and periphery is a prerogative one. Displaced discourses have to occupy their space and converse with centralized discourses. The *jargon* dialogue as indicated elsewhere will not suffice. Conversation hermeneutic and theology should be considered as one of the options in narrowing the gap that exists between the two discourses. This will hopefully handle discursive borderlines and open up a possibility for the *fora* of conversation.

Conversation allows openness, presence, life, honest critique, tapestry. In this process, the opportunity arises for the 'trained' readers to gain deeper insight of the realities of the 'peripheral' discourse. Firstly, the 'peripheral' readership brings popular critique into the center scholarship. Regardless of its *un*-orderliness, it is diverse, and addresses and impacts on countless life issues. The issues raised are *problematizations* which undergird the lives and of the common people and are absent from institutionalized published theologians. Whereas the latter creates or *capitalizes* on systems from which only they themselves or a few others benefit. Secondly, the conversational hermeneutic and theology is of presence. The periphery is all about life and opens one to the reality of face-to-face presence and contact. The voices echoed present one with a mirror of life and presence. There is no place for multiplicity of absences, or its empty promises and elusiveness. This, definitely, offers the central readership the opportunity to be immersed in the conversation of presence and contact: real presence and real contact. Thirdly, honesty guides this nuance of hermeneutic and theology. Indeed, one cannot borrow integrity, but integrity should belong somewhere. The peripheral space (*community*) produces and masters its own theological dispositions. It can sometimes mislead the non-peripheral space member to under-estimate echoes from this theological practice. Fourthly, it is communal and co-operative in essence. It connects the disconnected, and opens up stifled channels of energy. It clears up blocked conversations and *jumps* and deconstructs existing boundaries, ultimately reordering these channels and boundaries linking and connecting them for the purpose of advancing the dignity and integrity of all involved. Lastly, open and honest critique is guaranteed in this proposed process. It is inevitable that the Bible constitutes a tapestry of bravery and outspokeness, on the other hand also honest narration of failure and cowardice. Conversational hermeneutic and theology want to be of the same kind. They seek out the bravery of the significant, oppressed and silenced but also report failure. In this case, theology happens in public and not in terms of conceptualized, ritualized and intellectualized discourses which incarcerated and silenced the *prophetic and life-giving* voice. If listened to closely, and within its given *space*, it is definitely not intimidated by any type of power. African readings of the Bible are close or rather situated within the conversational mode. They have stories about life, for life, against life, in life, and on life. Theology is about life and its conversation. We live and continue to converse about our life. It is in this process that we actualize our humanity. Silence constitutes a serious backdrop in life, but forced silence is more acute and endemic than preferred silence. It is within this background that African readings of the Bible should begin to converse with its *periphery*.

Reading John 5:1-10 from the "Organic Pan"

The following text is an illustration of the involvement of peripheral readers I work with in the Phuthaditjhaba area.[7] These readers come from different Independent and Indigenous Churches around Qwa Qwa. There are roughly 30 women and 40 men in the group. The group meets every two weeks in the month for bible study sessions. One of the texts the group worked on is John 5:1-10, commonly known as the healing in the pool of Bethesda. Readers were allowed to formulate their own discourses or subtexts based on the read-text. The primary aim is to encourage readers to be able to speak for themselves and be able to raise their own questions, both critically and out of interest. At first this became a problem, since readers were not offered an opportunity to reflect and ask questions from their background.

The text was read in turn verse by verse. Participants took turns in reading the passage. Then the leader asked readers to give their impressions of the text. In the following dialogue, (L) indicates comments made by the group leader and (R1), (R2), etc., indicate the comments made by various readers in the group.

◆ ◆ ◆

(L) What is the text all about?

(*Various opinions raised randomly*) It is about healing, the sick man, faith, life, miracles of Jesus Christ.

(L) Let us look more closely at the text. What surprises or interests you about this text?

(R1) The image of water. Water is a powerful image used in the text. Verse three points out that a number of disabled people, the blind, the paralyzed, and the lame waited for the moving waters. We definitely use water to heal people. We pray for it before it is used. This is the common powerful symbol which people like and commonly request

(R2) I agree with you water is important in this text. But why does the Lord come down and stir up the waters?

(R3) He was sent by God himself as… mmmm… some kind of representation. Do you see what I mean?

(R2) Then when we as human beings pray and stir water for healing, we act like angels? This is interesting.

(R4) I pray for many people. Most of the people who come to me emerge from many situations of suffering. There are those who come to me seeking employment, there are the sick, those traumatized by their families, school kids who want to be prayed for to pass their exams. Most kids from schools flood my house when the time for exams is near by. I pray for them and ask them to pray for themselves. Usually people who come do not tell you all that trouble them. I usually prepare *sewasho* [a ritual cleansing bath] and pray for the water then allow the person to bathe and tell God what troubles him or her. Washing alone gives them an opportunity to talk to God and feel relieved.

(L) Yes. You do use your own known symbols and language to interpret the text. You are right on target to relate the stirring of water to *sewasho*. Do these people speak loudly or what happens?

(R5) It depends. Sometimes they speak loudly depending on whether they are used to this business or not. While on the other hand others prefer to speak from their inner self because they are shy to speak out. However, this does not mean that they are completely silent.

(R6) Why is this healing (referring to the read-text) taking place in turns? Verse four reads thus, "The first one into the pool after each such disturbance would be cured of whatever disease he had." Do you see what I mean?

(R2) Yes I do. I think that the text attempts to bring the message home, that healing is a difficult process. It is important for the sick or troubled or any other invalid to have a serious commitment about healing. He or she should not be forced into it, but instead has to commit himself or herself to the whole process. This is the central message of the text. It is often common that all healers ask this of a patient who is brought for healing. In this case to be healed willingly is crucial.

(R7) Is it possible for a person to be sick for 38 years? Come on people. This mystifies me. Were there no other ways of making sure that he gets water? Something is missing in this text.

(R8) This comes back to the point made earlier on. Healing goes together with the *intentionality* of the sick person. Commitment plays a very important part in this regard. Surely this man enjoyed being sick. When Jesus confronts him about his condition, "Do you want to get well?" he replies oddly, "I have no one to help me into the pool when the water is stirred. While I am trying to get in, someone else goes down ahead of me." One should expect him to answer "yes" or "no." This is challenging. What should we when confronted by this kind of situation? There are many people in our township who beg and are sick at the same time. What should be our response?

(R9) Thirty-eight years is a long time. I agree something could have been devised, but it was not. That is why Jesus comes up with a rigorous solution. He does not send the man to the pool, but instead he orders him to pick up his mat and walk. He (the sick man) is capable of picking up the mat and can even walk. Something he could not do for thirty-eight years was done in less than five seconds. What a surprise! This text is fascinating.

(R10) I wish to add my contribution in support of the view already pointed out. This man was able to walk. The following verses introduce the Jews who ask the healed man, "It is a Sabbath. The law forbids you carry your mat," but the cured man replied that "The man who made me well said to me, 'Pick up your mat and walk.'"

(L) I am glad that you are able to notice the difference of interest between the Jews and Jesus. As we indicated in our previous introductory session last week, Jesus was interested in the renewal of the complete person and community. We pointed out that we need to make a distinction between a Jew who came from the inner parts and surrounding Jerusalem-Judea, and those who came from the peripheral areas, who were interested in keeping the law which was the strongest power space. For these Jews, it was important for this man to remain in his condition to ratify and nurture their power space. Clearly from the text we do not see the man occupying any power space. He was at the peripheral end, which supported and validated the perpetual power space of the ruling party in first-century Palestinian Judaism. Probably, these powerful rulers of that time could have shouted, "Damn Jesus, why did he do that?"

(R10) You are right. We have seen some of these things on the big screen, or television. The question remains: what is our role in the alleviation of the poor and oppressed in the township and rural areas in which we find ourselves? What about the Church? Most of our Churches are victims of the business plan language. They are trapped in it and it will be difficult for them to get out of it. They speak the same language which the Jews spoke to the healed man. This is not fair."

(L) Friends, we have now come to the end of our bible study session. Let us meet next week."

A hymn was chanted and a member of the group offered a prayer which was relevant to the bible study theme and deliberations.

◆ ◆ ◆

As already indicated, this essay challenges the view that sees peripheral readers as naïve and pre-critical (Draper 1994; West 1995; Botha, 1991; Lategan 1994). We have to begin to understand the criticality which peripheral readers possess. Who determines their naïve and precritical frame reference? Who owns and controls the *jargon* "critical" and "sobriety"? It is a fact that these expressions and many others are formulated and controlled from some powerful space, that of the center. This presentation does not at all discourage the critical engagement between the center and periphery, but merely challenges *central textual operators* to move and allow peripheral readers to occupy their own space and speak for themselves. One notes that another challenge from the central space occupiers would certainly be problematic of the poor not having the *jargon* which is necessary for lobbying, which is also used by the powerful in chambers of power where their *fate* is discussed. As West (1993, 168) points out, "To discover who ordinary are and how they are reading the Bible" the task is to "honestly analyze the relationship between the trained reader and the ordinary reader in liberation hermeneutic." Whose task is this? Which *language* should be used in analyzing this context? And, who is capable of carrying out this task? This brings me to African organic readings of the Bible. *Organic readers* are formerly produced by the periphery and advanced to the center to learn the ropes in the center, and their sole responsibility is the periphery. They have a task to advance the periphery to become itself and not the *copy cat* of the center. To be sure, we need organic readers to be empowered by the periphery and with the mandate of the periphery. Organic reading does not allow any treason but rather empowers and it is always empowered. There is an ongoing relation between the *organic reader* and the *organic reading context*. Power is shared and power is critically negotiated in this context of organic reading. The process allows creative tension and struggle. Ultimately, the on going *agon* itself offers growth, understanding, creativity, criticality, empowerment, and openness. It is within this context that African Bible readings should be modeled. The key question is: To whom are African Bible scholars accountable, and what is their *locus operandi*? Surely, not to the ivory towers that are considered the citadel of excellence. Honest and critical African Bible reading needs organic readers based within their organic context, or organic pan if you will. An organic pan allows freedom of movement, but it is also closed in order to allow the existence of system, its integrity and space. This will ensure that there is no ongoing negative tension in determining the interface between.

Conclusion

To sum up, critical readers or trained readers (West 1995) have to be produced from the organic pan. It is only within this context that the creative center will emerge, determined and controlled by the organic community as a whole. This is the right time to allow power to shift. Let me drive the point home, however harsh it may seem: Commit academic treason when there is time to do so. Surely, no one wants to create a situation of false rhetorical romanticism about theological involvement with the poor and oppressed. The biblical hermeneutic model I am citing requires organic theologians to converse within the organic context and walk within that context, learn critically to respect from within the organic pan that their *truths* are continually coined anew by the ongoing changes and challenges within the pan. This is necessary for the African Theologies which are analyzed and advanced in the present age to take their own shape and bloom. Total immersion into the organic pan and listening with critical silence would be a positive step in the right direction. As Piet Naude (1996, 29–30) concludes:

> It is clear: our work as second order oral theologians has just begun … if we expand our understanding of oppression, broaden our hermeneutical perspectives and leave our comfortable desks to listen to theology, exciting prospects open. Our advantaged location amidst oral communities in South Africa, a new openness after the apartheid era, growing interest from African and local theologians, set the scene for a creative hearing-theology in the South African context. *The voice of the hitherto marginalized voicings must be heard* (emphasis added).

Chapter 5

The Role of Biblical Politics in Contextual Theologies

Norman K. Gottwald

The exegetical-historical thesis of my essay is this: although the Hebrew Bible preserves exceedingly strong articulations of sociopolitical liberation, the actual implementation of these egalitarian ideals and proposals in Israel's history was limited in the extreme. The social ethical and political corollary of this thesis is that we must analyze the sociopolitical conditions in ancient Israel that contributed to a partial realization of social equality and justice and those sociopolitical conditions that in the main frustrated and aborted social equality and justice. The consequent directive for us at the dawn of the twenty-first century is clearly this: we must critically assess the social and political experience of ancient Israel in order neither to overstate nor to minimize what the Bible may contribute to our contemporary quest for social justice and equality. A naive assessment of liberation in the Bible runs the danger of fortifying a naive assessment of the requirements for liberation in our own situations.

Background

The first wave of liberation theology that emerged from Latin America in the 1960s and 1970s, primarily within Catholic circles, was exuberantly positive about the primacy of liberation in the biblical traditions. Black theology picked up the same positive tone. In both instances, the Exodus motif, supplemented by the prophets, was the controlling hermeneutical category for enlisting the Bible in liberation struggles among Latin American peasants and North American blacks. The Bible was seen to be unequivocally supportive of liberation.

The hermeneutical scene began to change when feminist criticism uncovered the extent to which women were subordinated and marginalized in biblical societies. Feminist hermeneutics introduced a critical principle that distinguished between what was liberative and what was oppressive in the biblical witnesses. The same criticality was introduced into examination of the homophobic strand in the Bible.[1] Yet other voices, such as Robert Warrior speaking for Native Americans in the USA and Canada,[2] and Itumeleng Mosala speaking for blacks in South Africa,[3] have underscored that the biblical texts contain many problematic assumptions and judgments that cannot be accepted without serious challenge and even outright rejection because of their oppressive substance and import.

We are now in a situation where wholesale acceptance or rejection of the sociopolitical perspectives in the Bible, couched as they are in religious rhetoric, is simply no longer tenable. The biblical traditions require thorough critical assessment in their own contexts. Only when so assessed can they be a resource for sociopolitical liberation today. In order to make the precarious transition from biblical text to contemporary situation, I suggest that three hermeneutical steps are necessary.

First Hermeneutical Step

The first step is to determine the varieties of politics advocated and practiced by the communities in which biblical writings were produced. This is an arduous task, complicated by literary and historical issues that have no simple resolution. Let me illustrate with two probes into the interplay between Israelite social and political institutions, on the one hand, and Israelite culture and religion, on the other hand. I will look first at the interplay of these factors under the monarchy and then at their interplay in the restored Judahite community.

The Monarchy

Having recently completed an extensive study of the politics of ancient Israel, I have concluded that statist structures and processes in the kingdoms of Israel and Judah were not substantially different from political structures and processes elsewhere in the small to mid-size ancient Near Eastern polities of Syria and Palestine.[4] This judgment requires nuanced clarification.

Israel and Judah were tributary monarchies based on agrarian economies with majority peasant populations, supplemented by trade and small-scale manufacturing. Political elites staffed their modest bureaucracies, collaborating and competing by turns with powerful landowners and merchants, in order to control the peasant surpluses necessary to support the state apparatus and prosper the non-governmental elites. The Israelite states participated in an interregional web of power politics, entailing diplomacy and frequent warfare. They were legitimated by a religious ideology that privileged the ruling elites as bearers of divine blessing, thereby guaranteeing domestic affluence and security against all threats at home and abroad.

The centralized political institutions of Israel and Judah had an impact on the livelihood, the culture and the religion of the majority of Israelites who sustained a traditional village way of life. This impact was deleterious in economic terms since it was these villagers who bore the brunt of taxation and forced labor imposed by the state coupled with onerous rent and debt extracted by prosperous landowners and merchants. The system of village courts was skewed by bribes and corruption. A culture of cooperation and mutual aid among independent cultivators was weakened by the tributary political economy. The local worship, involving various forms of the cult of Yahweh alongside the worship of other deities and which gave ideological support to communitarian village culture, was confronted by an established state cult that arrogated authority and sacrificial offerings to itself.

This imperious pressure of a centralized political culture impinging on decentralized local culture was typical of all the small states in Syria-Palestine, creating a tense and prickly relationship between the political center and the populace of the hinterland. In addition, these conflicts internal to Syro-Palestinian states, were disrupted and complicated by the imperial policies of Assyria and Neo-Babylonia from the mid-ninth to the early sixth centuries B.C.E. The distinctive feature of this struggle between center and hinterland in Israel and Judah— crosscut by intrusive empires—is that, thanks to the Hebrew Bible, we are more fully informed about these tensions and conflicts in Israel and Judah than in any other ancient Near Eastern state. The diverse biblical traditions, among them prophetic, priestly, and wisdom texts, reflect the many-faceted social and religious practices and values that both came into conflict with the state and were coopted by the state for its own purposes in an attempt to retain its power and authority by a combination of ideological persuasion and physical coercion. All the texts of the Hebrew Bible, directly or indirectly, bear the stamp of this political economic struggle which was at the same time a cultural and religious conflict.

The Hebrew Bible retains considerable evidence of an ongoing conflict between state and sectors of society because its formation occurred after the demise of both Israelite kingdoms. The traditionists of restored Judah who gave final shape to the Hebrew Bible were no longer beholden to the old monarchic regimes concerning which they were free to report many traditions that were highly critical of those regimes alongside other traditions that looked with approval on the accomplishments of Israel's political rulers.

Restored Judah

The community of Judahites reconstituted in Palestine under Persian sponsorship, while not possessing sovereign independence, was definitely subject to political forces. First, there was the overarching imperial rule of Persia which established Judah as an administrative sub-unit of its larger empire. Second, there were the native Judahite authorities either appointed by Persia or subject to Persian oversight. Persia's chief interest was to strengthen Judah as a strategic buffer zone against Egypt and Greece. Judahites were constrained in their self-development by the interests of empire. This probably accounts for the fact that the Hebrew Bible has virtually no criticism of Persia compared with its repeated condemnations of Assyria and Neo-Babylonia.

A reforming Yahwism in restored Judah, propelled by a pronounced monotheistic tendency, rejected cultic and ideological elements that had characterized some strains of Yahweh worship during the monarchy. The criteria used to purge Yahwism of elements deemed to be idolatrous were read back into the earlier history so as to give the impression that preexilic Yahwism was intrinsically monotheistic even as the traditions concede that many Israelites were "idolatrous." The result is a very skewed account of Israel's preexilic religion which fails to acknowledge that a variety of Yahwistic practices and beliefs prevailed prior to the movement toward a standardized monotheistic cult that gathered strength after the restoration.

In the Hebrew Bible, the reports of conditions in restored Judah give the impression that Judah was inhabited solely by immigrants from the Babylonian exile, to the neglect of the local populace that had remained continuously in Palestine. It is also claimed that the northern Samarians were illicit Yahweh worshipers who had no place in the cult of Yahweh focused on the rebuilt Jerusalem temple. We also hear virtually nothing about Judahite communities throughout the ancient Near East, in Egypt, Babylon, Syria and Arabia, who developed their own forms of culture and religion in loose connection with Jerusalem. The religious and political perspective of the Hebrew Bible is overwhelmingly focused on Jerusalem repopulated by former "exiles."

As for the impact of colonial rule on Judah, it is evident that Persian, and later Hellenistic, rule imposed conditions that favored the development of a native Judahite elite at the expense of the majority of Judahite peasants. Taxation and debt continued to weigh heavily on the populace, with the benefits of trade and agricultural development accruing principally to the elite elements of society. The indications of these harsh conditions in restoration Judah are not so extensively reported in the Hebrew Bible as are the deprivations of the monarchic period, but they are disclosed now and then with ample clarity (cf. Nehemiah 5).

This brief sketch of the manifold ways in which politics and religion intersected during the monarchy and the restoration era makes it clear that no single reading of their relationship is attainable. Each period, each sector of state and society, and each text must be examined for its peculiar conjoining of politics and religion. The biblical text must be supplemented by archaeology, ancient Near Eastern social and political history, and comparative social sciences in order to approximate an understanding of the contending social, political and religious programs expressed in the biblical texts or forming a background to the texts.

Second Hermeneutical Step

The second step in appropriating biblical texts for liberatory purposes is to assess the extent to which particular forms of Israelite politics conjoined with religion were progressive and the extent to which they were reactionary. It is my contention that the determination of which texts and traditions were progressive and which were reactionary is a complex and debatable matter. In particular, there is a tendency among ethicists and theologians drawing on the Bible to overstate the liberatory intent and effect of many texts because the biblical religious rhetoric obscures the sociopolitical power struggles. At the same time, there is a tendency to overlook the unintended progressive consequences of certain political developments that were in the main reactionary.

In making these claims, I am employing a highly generalized understanding of politics and religion as "progressive" or "liberatory" when they extend the means of livelihood and preserve the integrity of local culture in the interests of the populace at large. By the same token I understand politics and religion as "reactionary" or "oppressive" when they selectively depress the livelihood of the general populace in favor of a privileged elite and when they undermine local culture and religion by imposing a monochromatic culture and religion promoted by the political center. I am also assuming that the same political and religious programs may have both liberatory and oppressive effects. With such highly generalized criteria, it is obvious that there will be different assessments of biblical texts and sociopolitical programs depending on how the criteria are spelled out and applied in detail in each historical context. I think the complexity of the task can be best illustrated by examining three sets of texts widely viewed as positive instances of sociopolitical liberation.

Covenants and Reforms

The books of Kings and Chronicles report a number of covenants between kings and the people of Judah to adhere to the religion of Yahweh and to institute reforms that have religious and political effects. Biblical interpreters generally take these covenanted reforms at face value as progressive developments that purified the religion and extended social benefits to the populace. Aside from the anachronism in viewing these as full-fledged monotheistic reforms, they are widely assumed to indicate that the rulers of Judah, at least on some occasions, limited their authoritarian behavior by adhering to the social equality and justice posited in the covenant attributed to Moses.

However, when the covenanted reforms of Joash, Hezekiah and Josiah are examined more closely, their benefits to the general populace are problematic. Joash's reform consists of ousting queen Athaliah from the throne on the grounds that she sought to destroy the Yahwistic dynasty of David and replace it with a line of rulers devoted to Baal. It is much more likely that Athaliah was aiming to preserve the Davidic dynasty, that she favored toleration for both Baal and Yahweh worship, and that the motivation for dethroning her was due to rivalry within the Davidic dynasty over how Judah should relate to the northern kingdom and to Tyre.[5] Hezekiah's reforms are pictured as a purification of temple worship, restoration of the proper observance of festivals, and, in particular, concentration of all Yahweh worship in Jerusalem. To the extent that this is not an erroneous foreshadowing of Josiah's reforms, the apparent political motivation was to solidify the king's support in Jerusalem by undermining the lineage system in the countryside, and preparing the city for siege once Hezekiah decided to rebel against Assyria.[6] Josiah's reforms elevated Jerusalem to the sole site of Yahweh worship, strengthened his grip on the fiscal resources of the kingdom, enhanced state authority over family and village autonomy, and laid a base for him to attempt to recover the northern territory of Israel that had been lost after the death of Solomon.[7]

If these reforms possessed social programs, they are not described in Kings and Chronicles.

The Covenant Code of Exodus 21–23 is sometimes linked to Hezekiah's reforms, and the social relief measures of Deuteronomy are widely assumed to have been put into effect by Josiah, which may have provided some debt relief to the rural populace that was brought under the fiscal and cultic domination of Jerusalem. If so, these measure seem not have been deep-going or long-lasting, given the critiques of social injustice and cultic corruption by Jeremiah and Ezekiel.

Royal Psalms

There are a number of royal psalms that laud the prosperity and social justice achieved by Israelite rulers under the aegis of the state deity Yahweh. Granted that they are marked by the exaggeration and hyperbole typical of court poetry. Their laudatory rhetoric is typical of the claims made by monarchs throughout the ancient Near East. The extravagant claims can be checked against the more realistic assessments of royal conduct and policies in the biblical narratives and prophetic texts. Even the royal psalms themselves contain inner contradictions, as in the instance of Psalm 72. On one level, the psalm displays supreme confidence that the king secures justice and peace. On another level, the summons to continual prayer on behalf of the king exhibits unease and anxiety that the monarchy may not be living up to the idealistic claims made for it. Also, noticeable in this and other royal psalms, is the absence of reference to the agrarian labor of Israelite peasants who make prosperity possible, as if the king himself has been responsible for planting, cultivating and harvesting the crops attributed to his faithful rule.[8]

Debt Relief

Nehemiah 5 is of particular interest because it is the one biblical text that anchors debt relief in a particular social situation, in contrast to high uncertainty as to how or when the debt relief laws of Deuteronomy and Leviticus were implemented, if indeed they ever were. The outcry of Judahites who suffer from onerous debt at the hands of fellow Judahites of means, and whose children have been delivered into debt slavery, is met by righteous anger from Nehemiah who compels a cancellation of debt. It is unclear whether this edict is intended to forbid future indebtedness. Complicating the apparent simplicity of this debt cancellation, Nehemiah takes credit for not accepting the food allowance due him as governor of the province, presumably because he has private wealth from which he has been able to feed a sizable number of Judahites at his table, probably understood as members of his provincial staff. Also, the clamorous debtors complain of their inability to pay the royal tax which Nehemiah, in his role as governor, was certainly responsible to collect. Thus, it is imaginable that

Nehemiah aimed to keep social peace in Judah by restraining indebtedness and thereby securing the continued payment of the royal tax to Persia. However, realistically viewed, if debts at interest were absolutely forbidden, it is difficult to understand what recourse the hard-pressed peasants of Judah would have had in the face of crop failure and heavy taxation. It appears that Nehemiah's edict, as well as the other debt relief programs mandated in the Hebrew Bible, failed to provide an alternative for impoverished peasants for whom indebtedness to prosperous patrons, however oppressive, was the one alternative to starvation and early death.[9]

My point is that each of these liberatory declarations and actions in ancient Israel had a "down side." The psalmic rhetoric was excessive and fraught with contradictions. The policy decisions professing reform were clouded with mixed motives and had dubious lasting effects. At the same time, we must recognize that the presence of liberatory rhetoric and reforms that profess liberation indicate the resistance of the majority of Israelite commoners to state policies that depressed their livelihood and affronted the dignity of their local culture. Without this pressure from below, we would not find such reform programs in the Hebrew Bible.[10] The aggrieved depressed Israelite majority never succeeded in taking command of the state apparatus, but they nevertheless left a trail of powerful protest in prophecy and wisdom writings, and managed to require the state to make some limited concessions, even when the concessions were not of a lasting nature.

A final point, seldom acknowledged, is that the state structures of ancient Israel, in spite of all their abuses of the general populace, did inadvertently perform a protective function in the nurture of Israelite culture and religion. The kingdoms of Israel and Judah provided a protective shield for the culture and religion to thrive on their own terms and to develop in the various ways that are expressed in the prophetic, priestly, and wisdom traditions of the Hebrew Bible. I say this because, without a native Israelite form of self-government, Israel's culture and religion would scarcely have had the social and cultural space in which to develop sufficient strength to outlast the collapse of political independence. Had the tribes of Israel fallen immediately under Philistine or Damascene rule, without any period of native Israelite state formation, it is highly doubtful that the Israelite culture and religion could have gone on to develop a distinctive character that allowed it to survive and prosper amid rising and falling political fortunes.[11] Accordingly, it seems to me that we must be aware of the contradictory repressive and protective functions of the state in fostering conditions that simultaneously restricted and allowed for the ongoing autonomous development of local Israelite cultural and religion.

Similarly, a measure of "credit" must be given to the great empires of Assyria, Neo-Babylonia, Persia, Alexander and his successors, for providing both a severe challenge to the survivability of Judahite culture and religion, and, at the same time, a protective political cover for Judahite communities, both in Palestine ant throughout the dispersion, to take root and prosper. This "benefit" of imperial rule was a largely unintended side-effect of the pragmatic decisions of the late empires to govern subject peoples as much as possible by local home rule and cultural/religious toleration. Judahites in Palestine and throughout the ancient Near East, as well as Samarians in the north and perhaps also in dispersion, who had grown used to preserving their values and practices under native rule, were thus able to continue to do so under the aegis of foreign powers.[12]

All in all, the theopolitical testimony of ancient Israel is multivalent, ambiguous, and capable of interpretation and appropriation in a variety of ways. This multivalency of Israelite politics and religion precludes the derivation from the Bible of any single definitive program for social justice and human equality. It invites us to abandon simplistic moralistic judgments and to assess the contending political, cultural and religious forces amid which Judahite religion emerged in a monotheistic form and gave birth to the Hebrew Bible.

Third Hermeneutical Step

The third step is to assess which forms of biblical politics are likely to serve progressive and reactionary ends when they are treated as inspirational or exemplary for contemporary politics. This step entails a thorough analysis of the current situation for which progressive political programs are sought. It also entails ethical and theological judgments as to the proper criteria for shaping a society.

The correct starting point must clearly be the needs of the society in which the ethicist and theologian lives, and this requires decisions about the criteria for evaluating the performance of contemporary political regimes with regard to the actual effects of their policies on their "captive"citizenry. The criteria may flow from any number of sources, such as neo-Marxist or anti-capitalist sociopolitical systems, stressing the entitlement of all laborers to the enjoyment of the surplus they produce,[13] or from ethical systems, such as that of John Rawls,[14] or from theological systems, such as that of Douglas Meeks.[15] Neo-Marxist analyses continue to elaborate the fundamental insight that a ruling elite profits one-sidedly from its appropriation of the labor product of workers, whether through private or governmental channels. Rawls stresses the "original position" from which all members of a society are entitled to a share in deciding how they will be ordered politically and provisioned economically. Meeks stresses a view of God as the economist who in ongoing creation pours out lavish means of subsistence to which all humans have an entitled share. Each of these positions can find points of connection with certain strands of the Bible, but it cannot be denied that the Bible contains decidedly reactionary texts and traditions which run counter to all theories and programs premised on a more equitable sharing of power and wealth. Furthermore, the sharing of goods and the honoring of rights among all members of society was never realized in biblical societies once Israel emerged from its tribal period. Such a fully just society and political economy, rather than being lodged in an idyllic biblical past waiting to be recovered, looms ahead of us as a "utopian" hope worth struggling to attain.

In my judgment it is a forlorn hope to search for incontestible validation in the biblical text for sociopolitical reforms applicable today. Such anxious dependence on the Bible to justify needed political reform today can only be reactionary in its ultimate effects. To be sure, we can draw courage and motivation from the thrust toward liberation stated or implied in the concrete struggles and utopian horizons found in many biblical traditions. In the final analysis, however, we must shoulder responsibility for ethical and political programs and options for which aspects of the Bible provide a significant measure of inspiration and motivation, but which ancient Israelites were never able to implement and which give us no coherent template for present theory and praxis. We are in a new situation and on our own.

Conclusion

I conclude that contextual theologies need to develop their own social and political criteria for a just society that are not dependent on moralistic readings of particular biblical texts. Fundamental principles of the right of all people to justice and dignity can find support in certain strands of biblical faith but they must be independently established and asserted as the necessary condition for human liberation in our time. All biblical texts must be carefully assessed for their admixture of liberation and oppression with respect to the particular needs of present societies. Adequate contextual theology requires critical assessment of the contentious political contexts in which biblical texts were produced. Just as we have reached an end to naive trust in the innocence of claims made by contemporary political authorities, so we have come to the end of naive trust in the innocence of biblical text.

Chapter 6

Towards a Postcolonial Reading of Freedom in Paul

Jeremy Punt

There is reason to believe Paul recognized and taught what some Latin American bishops would later call the preferential option for the poor. "God chose what is foolish in the world to shame the wise" he writes to the Corinthians; "God chose what is weak in the world to shame the strong, God chose what is low and despised in the world, even things that are not, to bring to nothing things that are" (1 Cor 1:27-28) (Elliott 1994, 203).

Introduction: Paul in Postcolonial Africa

The time has come when we must ask whether the politico-theologico-religious upheaval in Latin America is not of greater significance for the proper understanding and use of the Bible than is the Reformation itself (Hanks 1983, 61).

The Pauline epistles,[1] as *the* collection of books in the New Testament that emphasize freedom, have been neglected in contemporary theological discussions of freedom and liberation.[2] "Freedom is outstanding among the theological motifs of the New Testament" and "nowhere in the New Testament is the theological motif of freedom so vividly pronounced as it is in the theology of the apostle Paul" (Jones 1984, 11–12). In fact, Pauline perspectives could play as important a role in issues of social justice today, as they did for a different purpose during the sixteenth-century Reformation, and become the driving force of both events to which Hanks refers. However, the antipathy towards Pauline theology is particularly noticeable where theologians emphasized freedom from various kinds of economic and sociopolitical oppression, ranging from *Apartheid* and racism in South Africa, through entrenched and latent patriarchialism the world over, to the reactions to social ostracizing with the accompanying lack of self-esteem, and feelings of unworthiness as espoused in Liberation Theology, Black Theology, and Feminist Theology, to name a few.[3] The neglect to account for Pauline freedom is probably more than ironic, since deliberate exclusion of the perspectives from his letters is noticeable on many different levels and is due to more than one reason.

Far from being a mere twist of fate, it is a combined hermeneutical and theological turn that effectively displaced Paul's writings from earlier and more recent deliberations on the contribution of the New Testament to the liberation of people. As far as the majority of contemporary theologians are concerned, Paul's letters are positioned and classified in such a way that his theme of liberation, and the way in which it may be employed as a perspective on the kinds of bondage people face today, eludes them (Jones 1984, 17). From his *African*-American context, Jones shows that Paul was not traditionally associated with freedom, but often rather seen as the archetypical supporter of the historical bondage of African Americans, slavery. As far as tacit support of, if not complicity in, slavery is concerned, Paul is part of the problem, not of the solution. Even long after the abolishment of slavery, "black religious thinkers found it difficult to deal with Paul because of the opprobrious odium that had been placed on him by past generations of blacks" (Jones 1984, 17).

It is not particularly difficult to show how Paul's writings are read, ever since Augustine's but more especially since the Lutheran tradition's appropriation thereof, as espousing primarily an individualistic, and spiritual freedom[4] (cf. Bosch 1989, 5; GRIC 1989, 52), eschatological in nature, and the ablatives of which are usually seen to consist in the triad of law, sin (or flesh) and death. This line of interpretation is sometimes conveniently referred to as a prominent aspect of the Lutheran captivity of Paul,[5] and constitutes the central moments of what can be called the traditional approach to Paul. It can be argued that the Pauline writings contain some of the most profound contributions to the issue of freedom, on various levels of human existence, both "spiritual" and "material"—to use this traditional if contested contrast.[6] But to appropriate Paul "for all his worth," his letters need to be liberated from the philosophical-theological bondage in which they have been kept for so long. True to the Pauline tradition, however, the interpretation of his letters has to be freed not only *from* an dominant traditional (read, Lutheran) perspective, but requires the freedom *to* include new perspectives on Paul's notions about freedom.[7]

Within the much larger debate, the goal of this paper is rather modest. As a professional biblical scholar at a historically disadvantaged institution in South Africa, standing with one foot in each of the Black and White worlds created by Apartheid in South Africa, my concern to reinterpret what was traditionally taken to be Paul's view on freedom, could be dismissed for being too ambitious. But the paper itself in a more modest way wants to take another look, beyond a textual study, at the broad contours of the social dimension of freedom in Paul, and in particular how the apocalyptic strand in his letters could be understood to influence the assessment of Pauline views on freedom. From the wide array of options available, postcolonial biblical interpretation is suggested as a valuable hermeneutical framework for rereading Paul on freedom, since it contributes heuristic tools and it provides an appropriate ethics of accountability. More importantly, it seeks to read, understand and employ biblical texts in a decidedly anti-imperialistic way.[8]

This is hardly the place for a comprehensive account of postcolonial biblical interpretation, but suffice it to make the following comments. Biblical interpretation, informed by postcolonial theories, questions the co-opting of biblical texts for colonial, imperial and other hegemonic uses, while searching these documents for "the gaps, absences and ellipses, the silences and closures, and so facilitate the recovery of history or narrative that has been suppressed or distorted" (Said, in Sugirtharajah 1998, 18). In this way, postcolonial reading allows one to search for

> alternative hermeneutics while thus overturning and dismantling colonial perspectives. What postcolonialism does is to enable us to question the totalizing tendencies of European reading practices and interpret the texts on our own terms and read them from our own specific locations (Sugirtharajah 1998, 16).

Rereading Paul along these lines would imply moving beyond decades of constructions of Paul's background and ostensibly proper interpretation, to deconstruct and reconstruct Pauline sentiments, in order to formulate alternative positions according to a postcolonial framework.[9]

On a cautionary note, it should be added that while a postcolonial reading attempts to deconstruct colonial interpretation and to simultaneously forge an alternative approach to texts, it must remain ever alert of the "continuing, even if transformed, power" of colonialism and imperialism, and their strategies and tactics (Segovia 1998, 51 n. 2). Indeed, such vigil could help guard against another, ever present danger which a "postcolonial optic," like all other hermeneutical strategies, needs to avoid, namely to become yet another totalizing discourse (cf. Segovia 1998, 64). In an ironic way, postcolonialism can become imperialist and hegemonic in its very efforts to privilege the nationalistic, the neglected, and the peripheral. Such practices derive from postcolonial comparativist strategies which sometimes neglect the "very real differences between cultures and kinds of imperialist oppressions" (Tiffin 1991, xii).

This essay is not intent on offering a theoretical account of Postcolonialism or to demonstrate the value of Postcolonialism for the interpretation of specific Pauline texts. But within the broad perimeters of postcolonial biblical interpretation, the discussion focuses on Pauline notions of freedom, and freedom in a sociopolitical sense in particular. This is accomplished through a rereading and revaluation of the social dimension of Pauline freedom, and by searching for an alternative reading of the apocalyptic tenor in the Pauline epistles, recognizing its often hidden value for sociopolitical interpretation.

The Social Dimension of Pauline Freedom

> So what we have today is a Paul who is trapped. On the one hand he is misrepresented, perverted, corrupted, and misused by the white church to perpetuate institutional racism. On the other hand black theologians castigate and disparage Paul for his seemingly proslavery position (Jones 1984, 31).

Early Christianity's struggles are traditionally taken to be directed more against the Greek or Hellenistic philosophies and culture than against the politics of the Roman Empire (e.g. Sanneh 1989, 50–67). But the traditional view raises a number of questions, first of which is whether the above distinction between culture and empire is tenable? And to what extent can the Empire or Ruler Cult, so pervasive in Paul's world, be equated with either culture or political power to the exclusion of the other?

Staying with traditional perceptions, Paul's political views seem to represent rather the Roman than the Greek perspective, discouraging insurrection (as in Rom 13)[10] and even political activism (cf. 1 Thes 4:11) as means of achieving freedom (cf. Bosch 1989, 4). Such generalizing comments were challenged in the past already, however, when Betz for example argued that the apostle's political ideas have not been explained to any "satisfactory degree" (1977, 7, cf. 32, 39).

It is possible to trace the failure of the majority of New Testament, and in particular Pauline scholars,[11] to recognize the social concerns in the Pauline writings, to the influence of the traditional approach to Paul on the interpretation of these writings. It was, after all, this understanding which embodied the only "proper" approach to Paul, which demanded not only a very individualistic but also an almost exclusively spiritualistic approach to understanding the Pauline documents, "an abstract soteriological perspective" (Pathrapankal 1995, 1014). As long as the opinion prevails that "the real opponent of Paul is the pious Jew" (Käsemann, quoted in Elliott 1994, 227), it is difficult to re-imagine the Pauline letters within their broader sociohistorical context; and the disparaging comments of Jones above become applicable across a wider area of material and theological or spiritual significance.

Against Paul's Sense of Social Freedom

It is lamentable that the perspectives on freedom in the social and political sense of the word have traditionally been loosely appended to discussions of the theme of "spiritual" freedom in Paul. This approach follows the traditional view that the New Testament authors, as followers of Jesus Christ, were not interested in what is called nowadays "political" or "national" freedom.[12] Often, recognition for the presence of the concern with "civil" freedom is found in Paul's letters and the ensuing Pauline tradition, is whittled away with qualifications such as that if freedom of this kind is present here, "then only briefly and in a way that is very revealing" (Gerhardsson 1987, 10). This suggests that Paul's sense of social freedom can only be allowed in derivative form, if at all.

Two main lines of argumentation stand out in the process to deny Pauline interest in socio-political matters. Firstly, traditionally it is denied that the New Testament as a whole or in its constituent parts provide evidence of socio-political concern since its sole concern is spiritual. It is then claimed that it was not "political freedom" that was at issue between "Jews and Christians" in New Testament times. Rather,

> the issue is between that freedom of service to God which the Jews claimed because they were the physical descendants of Abraham, and the liberty which belonged to Christians who had passed from sin to righteousness, from slavery to free-

dom, because they had been born by God by faith in Jesus (Falusi 1973:117).

However, even amidst all the theological language used above, and even if such a scenario is an accurate construction of the contemporary context, the underlying political issue cannot be hidden. The very notion of an exclusive entitlement to God and his promises as expressed by the Jewish sentiment, and this being under threat from a "Christian" perspective which could erode the nationalistic implications of the former, is very political, to say the least.

But secondly, and more commonly, the New Testament in general and the Pauline letters in particular, were often assumed to have been addressed to communities either oblivious of or simply unconcerned with social tensions and strains. For example, Gerhardsson (1987, 17–18) depicts the Pauline presentation of "civil freedom" in an almost eschatological-escapist way:

> The freedom in Christ lies on a plane where social differences becomes unessential—and national and social differences as well (Gal 3:28, Col 3:11).

The most Gerhardsson is willing to concede is that while Paul's declarations regarding social relationships are to an extent relativizing, "they also mean that the social order is allowed to go on as it is."[13] He concludes by arguing that "it is striking that Paul does not use his view of spiritual freedom in Christ to motivate a struggle for civil freedom" (18). Gerhardsson summarizes his argument on what can be called Paul's ineffective socio-political liberation program, with reference to three types of arguments for the apostle's emasculated approach: eschatological (the end of time is near!), tactical (provoking the authorities might bring more hardship), and common-sense (his readers-listeners were not in positions of power, capable of effecting changes corresponding to his message of freedom). He does, however, encourage twentieth-century Christians to follow a different course of action, given the landmark changes especially in the socio-political status and power of many

Christians which renders the second and third reasons inappropriate.

Gerhardsson, however, confuses cause and effect in his analysis of Pauline thought. It is not so much a matter of social and other differences being inconsequential to Christian freedom, as the opposite: freedom in Christ leads to the abolishment of a series of different social and cultural and political (nationalist) distinctions. Gerhardsson fails to acknowledge that the origin of his claim that instead of urging slaves to obtain their freedom, Paul encourages slaves to become more obedient to their masters, comes from the deutero-Pauline tradition with its avowed attempts at domesticating Pauline radicality: Col 3:22-4:1; Eph 6:5-6; 1 Tim 6:1-2; Tit 2:9-10.[14]

Prominently among concerns regarding the relevance of Pauline thought on matters relating to socio-political freedom, Paul's emphasis on apocalyptic-eschatological matters is often pointed out as a serious debilitating factor. However, as Wilder (1961, 415; cf. Lategan 1991, 91) rightly argues, the eschatological and existential freedom "implies and carries with it an active expression of freedom in the historical public area." Therefore "Paul's *eleutheria* is an eschatological freedom operating *in the world*. The eschatological notion is not one of postponement, but one of grounding" (emphasis added). Paul was neither apolitical nor anti-political, and such positions are only defensible within a narrow and biased post-Enlightenment reading of his letters (Bosch 1989, 15), with his apocalyptic tenor serving not as strategy of postponement, but rather as mechanism to plot local details on the global canvas.

Rereading Paul on Freedom in Society

> The sweep of Paul's thought is much broader than is sometimes thought to be the case, especially in some parts of evangelical Protestantism. There are dimensions that certainly include the personal, but are large enough to be described as embracing the cosmos and its future, the church as a world-wide family, and the network of social relationships in which men and women stand (Martin 1981, 3).

It may be true that liberation theologies, expressing concern with social justice, are generally inclined to find its affinity in the New Testament with the Synoptics, rather than with the Johannine or Pauline writings. However, it is probably also true that the latter were largely determinative of the broader Christian theological tradition (Schreiter 1985, 33). Rather than using such arguments as reason for consigning these sections of the New Testament to irrelevance as far as social justice is concerned, they provide impetus to the effort to reread both these texts and the interpretive traditions governing them. Postcolonial biblical interpretation is capable of providing such a rereading, and reversing the ironic state of affairs that, for example, although biblical scholars overwhelmingly point out the socio-economic slavery of the contemporary situation as the context of Paul's insistence on freedom, very few of these scholars manage to offer an interpretation of Pauline freedom which refer to anything else but "spiritual" freedom.[15]

Although Paul agreed with the Jewish notion that freedom is a gift of grace from God, he never conceived of Christ as *sōtēr* (savior) but as the *sōtēria* (salvation) of God.[16] Whereas the Law was perceived in the various forms of Judaism as a covenantal requirement (covenantal nomism à la Sanders), Paul perceived of it as divisive and potentially restrictive. "With the revelation of Christ man [*sic*] is no longer related to God through the Law but by the faith of Christ." Also, although it is probably correct to argue that God's redemption was no longer seen as a political event (only) which will bring the long sought after freedom to the people of Israel, it is debatable whether "Paul does not speak of freedom in political terms, but of bondage to the Law of sin and death" (Abogunrin 1977, 36).

Following the initiatives of, among others, proponents of the New Perspective on Paul, New Testament scholars have other avenues to explore with regard to the Pauline material. Paul is less and less perceived as devastatingly afflicted with a guilt-ridden conscience, or overcome by the graveness of this predicament and thus concerned with finding a gracious God, but rather as a pastor who had to cope with tensions among

Jewish and Gentile Christians in newly-found congregations on the issue of the "how" of salvation, the formation of the community subsequent to salvation, and the resultant issues around identity. Add to this theology's need to address the rapidly changing world scene since the 1960s, and it becomes clearer how it happened that the social aspect of the Pauline concept of freedom came to the fore. It may be interesting to suggest these as some of the reasons for the newly devoted attention to the other than spiritual aspects of freedom in Paul, but the focus here will be turned more to the nature and contents of that discovery.

It is possible therefore to agree that Liberation Theology took the early twentieth-century criticism of an ideal and overly optimistic humanity further with its attempt to uncover and accentuate the influence of socio-political and economic dimensions of our historicity on our consciousness and understanding. The "introspective conscience of the West" (Stendahl) can be faulted for failing within the theological tradition, and biblical sciences in particular, to relate Paul's notion of "justice" to faith also beyond the individual and personal level.

> When we bring a new set of questions to Paul, we find that the justice of God embodies not only God's gratuitous gift of redemption to the sinner, but great power working in the entire world to regain it under divine sovereignty[17] (Tambasco 1982, 126).

Tambasco therefore concludes that Paul is not only concerned with the individual, and his or her salvation but—not regardless of but exactly *because* the correlate of justice is "faith"—"a walking in trust that God is at work in history through Jesus." The instructions directed at the communities receiving the Pauline letters, the insistence on avoiding matters pertaining to "the flesh,"[18] and Paul's advocacy of peace—embracing "corporate and social well-being and not just individual welfare"—all point toward Paul's concern with social matters of this world (1982, 125–27).

Paul's directives on freedom should clearly be understood in ways going beyond the triad of law, sin and death, so distinctly present in Protestant theological traditions. Tuckett argues that Paul's insistence on freedom concerns his "vehement opposition" to have one set of traditions forced onto other people (1991, 319–20). Paul's freedom is only limited by *agapē*, which shows up his understanding of freedom as a relational concept in the first place, and not as a "private matter" (cf. Tuckett 1991, 321, quoting Friedrich; Vollenweider 1989, 229–32). Freedom for Paul is not "total licence," and although it is always "freedom from" something it also "involves some kind of obligation":

> Freedom for the other is what Christian *agapē* works to establish. But freedom for oneself is limited by Christian *agapē* for others. Similarly, Christian freedom is limited by attachment to Christ (Tuckett 1991, 313; cf. Barrett 1985).

It is with the realization that Paul builds his notion of freedom on the "objective situation of the Christian in the world," which has its basis in the eschatological redemption wrought by Jesus and that which is still to come, that the Lutheran and wider Reformation views on freedom can be criticized. The reformationists founded Christian freedom in faith, "on subjective belief" or "spiritual inwardness," which was precipitated by their insistence on "justification doctrine." However, with Paul's emphasis on the "eschatological and cosmic aspect" of freedom, he is capable of directing the focus of freedom to be as much on cultural matters as on "spiritual issues" (Wilder 1961, 416).

A closer look at political freedom in his letters reveals that for Paul it incorporated both strategic and material connotations. Paul's missionary efforts took place within the perimeters of the early Christian mission, which tied in with the Hellenistic Jewish proselyte movement. The very fact that there is a strong communal dimension to freedom in Paul's usage of the term, implies political connotations. As much as the communal implications of "freedom" threatened the established order and its power structure, and not merely posited a neutral alternative, Paul's freedom is not only a "social" matter but quite pointedly has strong political implications[19] (Colloquy 1977, 36–37).

It is further suggested that Paul's political goals were not accidental but strategic. As a religious missionary, he certainly had political ideas and ambitions as well—what Betz called a "definite plan" or "political strategy" (Colloquy 1977, 47). Paul's strategy as "calculated, strategic, political moves to change the present order," is not in tension with the missionary impetus of the impending eschatological reality, the imminent end and the inclusion of the Gentiles. In the case of Romans, Paul had to secure a foothold in order "to bring the Gentiles in." As such, Paul found himself addressing both political and ideological issues, as often happens in missionary and revolutionary movements[20] (Colloquy 1977, 47).

In his attempts at reorganizing the world as an agent God, Paul "turned the world upside down" (*Oi tēn oikoumene anastatōsantes*, Acts 17:6), a reversal sometimes referred to as the "divine comedy" (Anderson 1977, 15; Colloquy 1977, 47). Betz therefore argues that Paul had a

> well worked-out theory of *how* the community can be free, given the circumstances of this world. He had . . . a theology of freedom, a very elaborate theoretical explanation of how it was possible. *That* convinced people and explains as least part of Christianity's missionary success (Colloquy 1977, 48, emphasis in the original).

In his letters, Paul's use of *eleutheria* was deliberate, a concept people would understand, and which would entice them to accept his message about Christ. But, moreover, *eleutheria* described the content of the message of Christ: freedom for all people who put their faith in Christ.

> So Paul's theology, *essentially relational and concerned with the well-being of persons*, took its starting point in what God had done and was still doing in the lives of his people (Martin 1981, 47; emphasis added).

The world-transforming message which Paul transmitted was securely tied to the unmistakable apocalyptic course he steered. As suggested by Martin in the first paragraph of this section, the range of Paul's address should, if anything, not be limited to spiritual concerns as has happened so often in the past, but rather be read from and through an extended scope of reference and concern.

Paul and Apocalyptic

The systematic focus on apocalyptic[21] elements in Pauline thought dates back to the work of Schweitzer, notably in his attempt to understand the apostle in terms of his Jewish background. Some Pauline scholars, for example Ridderbos (1975), argued that Paul's thought is "structured around the topic of eschatology," but the emphasis on apocalyptic goes beyond that. Most recently, however, it is probably Beker's consistent arguments for an interpretation of Paul in terms of "Jewish apocalypticism," which has highlighted the importance of apocalyptic in Paul's letters. Beker has depicted this in a number of writings, with his 1980 work probably being the clearest and most comprehensive argument of his case (esp. chapter 8).[22] Whether one accepts with Beker that Jewish apocalyptic is characterized by the four elements of vindication, universalism, dualism and imminence, and whether these elements can all be traced in Paul's letters, is a matter for another discussion (cf. Matlock 1996, 247ff.). However, although Paul may not be using much of the typical Jewish apocalyptic language, "he writes from the perspective and agenda found in such literature" (Horsley 1995, 1157).

Already in the eschatological notions of Paul's arguments its implications for his theology emerge. Hafemann (1993, 674, 677) argues for reading Paul within the eschatological context in which Paul sees himself. For example, it is "against this backdrop that the question of the exact locus of the "problem" with the Law as its functioned under the old covenant, as well as its role in the new, must be raised"—the impact of Paul's eschatology on his view of the Law needs to be noticed. But in particular Paul's apocalyptic thought should not be seen as an attempt to side-step this world and its burning issues.

> The sense of the imminence of the coming of the Lord heightens rather than negates the imperatives of ethical action. . . . Paul's gospel proclaims the redemption of all creation; it is not an otherworldly hope to escape from material reality (Hays 1996, 26).

Wright (1992, 280–337; esp. 280–99) argues strongly for apocalyptic as very much a "this-worldly perspective." Indeed, attention to the apocalyptic tenor in Paul's writings requires attention to the social implications of apocalyptic, especially in view of the fact that the apocalyptic train of thought issued a challenge to the existing order and power relations.

But the emphasis on Paul's gospel as apocalyptic in nature has met with some criticism. Beker's emphasis on the apocalyptic strain in Paul has for example been criticized (e.g. Deidun 1986, 238–39), on the grounds that Beker himself admits that it is perhaps not so pervasive or at least not the "coherent core" in Paul's letters.[23] Beker's very definition of apocalyptic has been the topic for debate, and whether the traits as listed by Beker would be "essential to Jewish apocalypses' have been questioned, as well as whether all these elements as identified appear in Paul's letters, in any case.[24] Paul's use of apocalyptic did not rule out the use of other contemporary traditions, and all the borrowed material was at any rate reworked—to a large extent transformed and redefined—by Paul in light of his understanding of Jesus Christ, and his death and resurrection.

Nevertheless, to echo Horsley, apocalyptic is characteristic of Pauline thought, going beyond his use of such terminology and language. The implications of this statement can be explored briefly.

Paul's Apocalyptic Challenge to the Imperial Order

The most significant way in which a postcolonial reading of Paul disrupts the standard essentialist, individualist and depoliticized Augustinian-Lutheran Paul, consists in the rediscovery of the anti-imperial stance and program evident in his letters (Horsley 1998, 167–68).

Sugirtharajah (1998, 17) refers in a recent study to the earlier work of Roy Sano on the value of apocalyptic texts for immigrants and communities in diaspora. Sano's argument is that prophetic writings were often used by "white theologians" as both groups operated within "an established nation-state, and have access to power."

> The apocalyptic literature, on the other hand, is suited to immigrants, because this genre emerged at a time in Israel's history when she had lost her sovereignty. More importantly, the apocalyptic writings envisage a total social and political discontinuity and a reversal of roles rather than piecemeal changes.[25]

Whether all the elements of this contrast are equally valid, the salient point is the emphasis on apocalyptic texts' challenge to the existing societal order and configurations of power.[26]

Similarly, Horsley recently (1995; 1998) argued strongly for the recognition of not only the apocalyptic strand running through the Pauline letters, but also for the challenge posed by such apocalyptic thought to the existing socio-political order. Indeed, many of the key words often seen as mere theological terms in Paul's letters—such as *euangelion, sōtēr, pistis, dikaiosunē,* and *ekklēsia*—carried political overtones. These terms are in stark contrast with, and even challenge and oppose important elements of the imperial religion of the *Pax Romana*.

> In the baptismal formula of Gal 3:28 he proclaims that the principal institutional bases of the political-economic order in classical antiquity, slavery, and patriarchal marriage-fam-

ily ... are transcended and replaced in the new assembly(ies) (Horsley 1995, 1157).

Not only does Paul use the language typical of Jewish apocalypticism, but Paul "writes from both the perspective and agenda found in such literature."

Apocalyptic Revelations

> Apocalypse does not signify catastrophe. As revelation, the apocalypse reveals that the monster is a giant with clay feet whose fall will leave open the future for realizing alternatives (Hinkelammert 1997, 43).

The remaking of society, however, is predicated on the appropriate understanding of society and its mechanisms of power and control as evidenced in apocalyptic ideas. "What we have in the apocalyptic texts is ... an unmasking of reality in which the true character of institutions is revealed" (Rowland 1995, 229)—a sentiment echoed by Hinkelammert's quote, when he adds the element of a new perspective on and options for the arrangement of the future. Apocalyptic texts encounter the "seductive realism" of empire and imperial theology head-on (Elliott 1994, 180), and expose its true character. For Paul this meant of course first and foremost the Roman Empire, who through idealization of the Roman government ironically propagated the idea of the *Pax Romana* or peace brought about by the Romans. This so-called peace which was authoritarian and oppressive and led to the growing misery of the masses, which contributed to political and economic instabilities and gave rise to widespread materialism and opportunism (Betz 1977, 4–5), provided the social environment for the fermentation of the idea of freedom. It was not only at macro-political level where the impact of Roman imperialism was felt, but the Jews with their long and revered tradition relating to sacral law and custom found "a thousand irritants in the day-to-day encounters with the Roman provincial administrators" (Meeks 1986, 31).

The historical context of the Pauline letters is the Roman

Empire-dominated Mediterranean world, wherein the Roman emperors referred to themselves as the "saviors of the world," and not only kings. Whereas the title "king" would refer to "dominion over space and people," the title "savior" spans a wider range of meaning and implies power as well as "an imperial ideology that came to a full-fledged maturity in modern centuries, whereby the violence of imperialism was depicted as a redeeming act for the benefit of the subjugated, the so-called 'duty to the natives'" (Dube 1996b, 37–59, esp. 38).

Apocalyptic literature is important both as a mechanism which enables or at least contributes to endurance amidst oppression, but also as medium of response, for example through resistance. Since apocalyptic literature, as found in the Pauline letters too, is clearly "protest literature"[27] (Oakman 1996, 135–36, referring to Ste. Croix), it is appropriate to see its function as going beyond the revelational aspect. It is in this way that apocalyptic literature, by design and apart from everything else it is and does, also poses a challenge to the existing order, securities and powers.

Towards the Construction of a New Societal Order

The perception of the Pauline letters as otherworldly-inclined, oriented to individuals, concerned with the future and so on, is a result more directly attributable to the legacy of Pauline interpretation than the interpretation of his letters as such. Paul clearly neither subscribed to the radical denunciation of temporal economy as found in Apocalypticism or Gnosticism, nor to the appreciation of "performance- and market-oriented society" as found in Jewish missionary wisdom of the time (Georgi 1992, 144, 214 n.8–9). And so for Paul, eschatology was as much part and parcel of the present world (Georgi 1991, 102) as any of the more obvious spatial and temporal concerns he had to deal with. Similarly, Pauline politics was not characterized by "otherworldliness" (Georgi 1991, 30),[28] or passive complacency or fatalism based on future expectation.

On the contrary, Paul's letters consistently appealed to the communities they addressed to engage life to the fullest extent within the first-century context. Encouraged to avoid sinful practices, Paul exhorted his readers towards "hope-full involvement in the here and now" (Bosch 1989, 7). The apocalyptic tenor in Paul's letters provide the grounding or "transcendent data" (Segundo 1986, 89,134–37) for his urging to embrace the new life in Christ, made available by the resurrection of Christ. In fact, Paul's insistence on becoming a "new creation" (2 Cor 5) refers to the whole created order, not only to the "individual's subjective experience" (Hays 1996, 20).

Paul's apocalyptic framework requires a retooling of the universe by setting up an anti-structure (cf. Elliott 1994, 140–80). This is evident for example when Gal 3:28 indicates that the fundamental structures of the universe as expressed by certain "identifiable pairs" or binary oppositions, have been destroyed or at least, have become obsolete. In fact, Gal 6:15 introduces the concept of a *kainē ktisi*, where the new creation replaces the old world, including of course its structures and hierarchical orders (Martyn 1985, 414). Paul undoubtedly insists on an apocalyptic rupture introduced by Christ, symbolized by the formulas *en Christō* and *en Iēsou*, and leading to a new world-order without the sociological oppositions so characteristic of his world. He, however, introduces a new differentiation, namely between flesh and spirit (Gal 5:16ff.). It has rightly been noted that this distinction is not merely one way of distinguishing between spiritual matters as opposed to practical, concrete issues, or setting up a contrast between believers in Christ and non-believers. The flesh/spirit opposition is not disempowering but initiates the anti-structure, and should be embodied in the prototypical anti-structure, namely the church[29] (cf. Combrink 1986, 224).

Only the First Steps?

Some questions, however, still remain: Is Paul's anti-structure not also disempowering, especially as far as the position and status of women, people of different sexual orientation, those belonging to other religions, and so, are concerned? Did the prototypical anti-structure advocated by Paul harbor the seeds in itself which would transform it into the archetype of hierarchy, imperialism, entrenched power, ideological manipulation of others, and so on in the history of the Christian church? Was Paul's a broad concern with the well-being of others and a world, or with achieving his own goals, socio-politically, culturally and theologically?

Why is Paul not as uncompromising on the distinction between slaves and free persons, and men and women, as he is with respect to Jews and Gentiles (Bosch 1989, 7)? Maybe the answer is not as straight-forward as is often implied in putting forward "practical" arguments: The Roman Empire were in absolute control; first-generation "Christianity" was a very small movement among the greater collection of Judaisms of the time; Paul as Johnny-come-lately found himself in a precarious position among the apostles of Christ. The answer may also go beyond the religious argument: Paul was primarily concerned about justification by faith in Christ as the fundamental conviction of Christian faith, that this consumed all his energy, and made him to focus on the Jew-Gentile issue and relegated other societal concerns to second place (Bosch 1989, 8). Is Paul in the end so constrained in his efforts that all he has to offer is a lessening of the impact of dehumanizing and disempowering situations, to be only a humanizing[30] voice—no more but perhaps even less?

Such concerns also have to be addressed seriously, without simply rehashing simplistic, worn-out debates for example on gender issues, such as those between scholars arguing that Paul was nothing less than the worst kind of male chauvinist and those who hold him as the prototypical advocate of women rights. For a start, at least equal attention is due for Paul's socio-political setting and for the interpreters' own interests and ideologies.[31]

Paul and Freedom in Today's Polity

Especially in a day in which the poorest and most vulnerable of our neighbours, in our nation and around the globe—the hungry, the indigent, those driven from their homes and lands by poverty and war—are systematically deprived of the economic and political means of life by people of privilege acting in the name of "Christianity," Paul's message may be heard today as "theology of and for the world in its pain and longing for justice" (Elliott 1997, 384–85, quoting Wright in the last phrase).

At any rate, the realization and acknowledgment that Paul is concerned about more than individuals and their spiritual salvation at that, allows one to reread Paul in our context, characterized by the Two-Thirds World becoming increasingly marginalized amidst trends such as growing globalization, the majority of the world's population or the powerless being exploited by the powerful, and mismanagement and corruption which not only exist but which are seemingly tolerated. Such trends pose the real danger of consigning the larger part of the inhabitants of the earth to a life of poverty, misery, ignorance and oppression. And as long as people in South Africa and elsewhere in the world set stock by the Bible and especially when in certain religious and denominational traditions the Pauline letters play a key role in understanding their religion, their world and themselves, these letters cannot be consigned to the dustbin of user-unfriendly and politically incorrect biblical material. Postcolonial biblical interpretation would allow one to move towards a reconstruction of the meaning of the Pauline material, identifying and recognizing elements which could contribute to imperialist practices while consciously appropriating this material to foster an anti-imperialist consciousness, attitudes and practices.

However, the difficulty in relating Pauline notions and ideas to contemporary societal practice is often characterized by the vastly different social universes which are in play in today's world and Christian communities in particular. This is well illustrated by the contrast between slavery during the time of the New Testament and later slavery, as in "slave-based economies" found in colonial Brazil, the Carribean and antebellum southern USA:[32] temporary versus permanent, hereditary slavery; plural and opportunist origins versus racial (racist)-based slavery; differentiation between class as distinct from status (D. B. Martin) versus joined low status/class; and so on. Without generalizing or trying to romanticize slavery and its devastating effects on individuals as well as systems, the different faces and context of slavery during biblical times has to be acknowledged, at least. This should be ample caution to avoid an all too simplistic application of biblical injunctions concerning slavery to more recent situations. In short, the different character of slavery in biblical times complicates the important task of incorporating biblical texts in formulating socio-political liberatory and life-enhancing arguments.

Even if some would find the Pauline material to have been ineffective for human freedom during the apostle's time, would it mean that, for others who still find value in these documents, they cannot be rehabilitated? As mentioned earlier, after summarizing his argument on what can be called Paul's ineffective socio-political liberation program—with reference to three arguments or reasons for this emasculated approach: eschatological, tactical, and common-sense—Gerhardsson, however, encourages twentieth-century Christians to follow a different course of action. Given the landmark changes especially in the socio-political status and power of many Christians which renders the second and third reasons inappropriate, the "delayed" *eschaton* should encourage Christians to engage the social reality. "What I mean is that we must draw keener conclusions from—the freedom we have in Christ—than Paul did in his situation" (1987, 21).

Elliott's treatment of Romans 9-11 (1997, 371–89) makes it particularly obvious how much a specific interpretive tradition can influence the reading of specific Pauline documents or parts thereof. Although not the major emphasis of his study, Elliott also manages to point out how the traditional approach to Paul—and to some extent what is known as the new perspective on Paul, as well—undergirded by the Baurian opposition between exclusivist Judaism and universalist Christianity, has contributed to a reading of Romans as a charter of a Pauline "law-free" mission. Taking his cue from Paul's "apocalyptic theology of liberation," which requires of Christians the renunciation of supersessionist claims over-against Judaism, Elliott argues that "for Christians of the First World, it also means relinquishing the ideology of privilege over-against the mass of the world's poor" (Elliott 1997, 385). Therefore, a new understanding of Romans is required:

> The Letter to the Romans is an assault against a false theology of privilege on the part of a triumphant Christian majority that vaunts to have supplanted its progenitors and the dispossessed in its midst (Elliott 1997, 384).[33]

Freedom, Politics, and Identity

> Therefore, given the odds against him and the limitations of his situation, it would have been preposterous for Paul (or any other first generation Christian for that matter) to have attempted to develop a program of liberation for the oppressed of the entire Empire (Bosch 1989, 9).

For all the emphasis on Paul's attempts to delineate a particular identity for the followers of Christ, Engberg-Pedersen is at pains to point out that this identity also places them "in a universal scheme that encompasses the whole world" (1995, 502). It is their connectedness to Christ—being in Christ—which allows him to bridge the temporal distance between the death and resurrection of Christ on the one hand, and the coming triumph of God on the other hand.

To be sure, it is not suggested here either that Paul successfully implemented a new world-order on any scale, small or large, or that his views in any simplistic or idealistic way provide a modern ethic for society at large. Paul's concern was first and foremost ecclesiological, aimed at the new communities of faith in which he found himself and all the others who followed Christ (Bosch 1989, 7–10). Whether the acknowledgment that Paul was not preoccupied with the idea of changing unjust societal structures necessarily excludes the possibility that Paul exhibits a broader, societal concern (as Bosch suggested, above), is doubtful. In any case, Paul's apocalyptic vision extends to our time as well, based on the vision of God's coming triumph, requiring of the followers of Christ to work patiently for justice in the present world characterized by corrupt, evil and degenerate structures and conditions.

It has often been pointed out that freedom in Paul is both liberation in the traditional sense of casting off bondage, as well as empowering and enabling: Freedom *from* and freedom *to*! (e.g. Lategan 1991, 91–92). As much as the followers of Paul were challenged by his letters to renounce and work for the abolishment of all structures—religious, socio-political, and others— which enslave people, they are encouraged to promote practices which will be empowering towards themselves, other people and the world at large (cf. Bosch 1989, 12). As much as the good of development may degenerate into developmentalism, freedom can be misplaced in self-enslavement through the quest for self-gratification and a culture of entitlement. The exploitation of other people and the natural environment is relativized in a therapeutic global culture. The modern world is rife with the attitudes of instant self-gratification, the insistence on prosperity, and the hedonistic pursuit of happiness, all too often at the expense of others. Globalization encourages such endeavors, and the pursuit rather than the end-results of such endeavors become people's purpose in life.

A postcolonial perspective on Paul requires of us to ask about the ethics of our interpretation. Since the gospel and its interpretation should be seen as a matter of compromise—as being unavoidably culturally compromised—it leads to the question, not whether the biblical texts[34] and our readings of it are compromised, but rather on whose behalf and for whose benefit it is compromised? It serves us well to be aware of the developments which took place over time in our thinking, in social attitudes and in socio-political realities in the form of systems and institutions (Ringe 1995, 232–47). This might, for example, help to explain the different attitudes towards women co-workers in Paul's letters when compared with Acts. Today, similarly, we have to account for our readings contextually—*in* and *through* a particular context—requiring more from biblical interpreters than developing and being adept at interpretive strategies, exegetical methods and the like. A keen sociological analysis seems inevitable for the development of a relevant contextual and adequate contemporary hermeneutic.

Conclusion

To conclude, it has been observed that Pauline statements on socio-political, including economic, matters are not only often spiritualized by his interpreters,[35] but also that it is typically argued that Paul is relatively unconcerned with politics, economics and social problems emanating from oppressive positions and actions in this regard. This often happens with reference to Paul's eschatological and/or apocalyptic views or assumptions, which would have been seen to function as relativizing agents diverting attention from the material world and its conditions to spiritual, other-worldly matters.[36] Even if only in a preliminary way, this study has shown that the Pauline letters are not silent on socio-political issues, even if texts such as Rom 13 and 1 Thess 4 are often quoted to assert the political acquiescent or even apolitical nature of Paul's gospel. Earliest Christianity including the Pauline letters, far from resembling "an anarchy of Pietism" (Sanneh 1992, 10), resembled local revitalization which came to face opposition from structures of centralized control and power.

Another crucial element in accessing the Pauline material as dialogue partner on issues of social justice, is the well-known notion of *dikaiosunē*, justification or righteousness. If for no other reason than that of so often being seen as the most central theological perspective in the Pauline letters, righteousness should have its implications for issues of social justice explored. However, space does not allow for including its discussion here, and since it in any case properly follows the foregoing argument, will have to await its treatment in a separate, dedicated study. Suffice it to stress here that human working for justice is an expression of justification (Bosch 1989, 10), and to refer to some initial work in this regard (Tamez 1993).

The question is also how to broaden out and plot Pauline stirrings and suggestions beyond a decidedly Christian frame of reference and platform. Or would such an idea smack too much of empire-building, again with ostensibly the best of purposes in mind? Maybe the investigation into the universal in Paul should receive new impetus, as well as stronger engagement into investigations such as Paul's use of images and symbols shared by other religions then and now, such as the important Abraham-figure.

The true successors of Paul will through their ceaseless and patient efforts to right the wrongs of this world, not fall into positions of bitter cynicism and passive fatalism when their best efforts frequently come to naught (Bosch 1989, 16). It is, after all, in Paul's theological perspective the structures of this world which are illusory (1 Cor 7:31). However, in light of the recent scholarly interest in the social aspects of Paul's theology, it is important to note in the post-Apartheid South African society with its many problems and challenges, and where worldly structures matter very much, the inherent challenge in the following statement:

> The successors of Paul today are the theologian-activists, Christian thinkers-and-doers who call the affluent church to live truly in the service of the crucified, who is present in the persons of the struggling poor, the marginalized and oppressed, the sinned against and erased from history, non-persons (1 Cor 1:28-29) (Cook 1981, 495).

These sentiments are echoed by Murphy-O'Connor (1989, 10) in his insistence that interpreters of Paul cannot eschew the commitment to change "the structures in society which are the instruments of oppression." Are we willing to take up this challenge?

Chapter 7

What If We Are Mistaken about the Bible and Christianity in Africa?

Tinyiko S. Maluleke

Post-Events and Passionate Confusion

The twenty-first century has broken into our midst and we are battling to comprehend what it is and what it will be about. Naturally, the 'new situation' is itself understood differently by different people. The prevailing sense is that there is something definitely 'new' about the epoch in which we are living and there is a search for appropriate linguistic metaphors with which to engage and hopefully understand it. This situation has been characterized variously as post-colonial (cf. Dube 1996, 1998a, 1998b, 2000, Sugirtharajah 1998, Mbembe 1988), post-modern or neo-modern (cf. Comaroff and Comaroff 1991, 1997) 'post-cold war,' 'the dawning of the 21st century,' and 'new millennium' (cf. Wickeri *et al.* 2000*).* Within South Africa, we attempt to cover all of these connotations by speaking of the 'Post-Apartheid' situation, which for us is a rather concrete and local way of describing our experience. But the 'post-Apartheid' situation is not merely local, it is part of and caught up in a larger series of *post-events* in which the entire world is caught up. Yet, even before we make the linkages between post-Apartheid and other post-events—for the majority of South African Apartheid is not *post* (in the sense of being past). The language of post-Apartheid is by and large therefore, that of the elite middle, upper and intellectual classes. In the light of this, the designation 'post-Apartheid' not only manages to capture a tiny dimension of the phenomenon of post-events but it also fails to capture the full and continuing force of Apartheid. But this new registrar of phrases and terms are meant as a description and a summons to action. Post-Apartheid (South) Africa is both a description and a summoning to the creation of such a society. In other parts of Africa the program for the creation of a new society has been named on terms of reconstruction (cf. Mana 1992, 1993, 2000).

The search for descriptive notions with which to capture the 'spirit' of our times is still continuing. One term that is being used more and more is 'globalization.' Like so many of its sister notions its meaning is complex, various, contested and even confusing (cf. Santa Ana 1998, Fortman and Goldewijk 1999, Dimmelen 1998). The passionate confusion behind the term is seen by the increasing number of ecumenical consultations meant to discuss it during the past decade[1] as well as the explosion of various monographs on aspects of the theme. In fact at almost every ecumenical consultation one goes to for at least the past five years the notion of globalization is bound to come out—whether it was on the original menu or not. One must admit that there is a some growing clarity at least vis-à-vis certain aspects of globalization in terms of what our basic orientation towards them might be.[2]

A Time to Question 'The Event'

Unfortunately, much of the discourse in search for new metaphors and new language largely leaves much of Africa out. There are many reasons for this. One of these is the basic *Europeanness* of a pre-event—event—post-event scheme, whether such a scheme takes the language of coloniality, modernity or rationality. In this scheme of the things, 'the event' is Euro-American so that African and *other* events can only be its malcontents. Admittedly, post-events and post-rationalities are supposed to subvert 'the event' and explode into smaller, different and various events. But at least two considerations undermine this alleged process; the hugely disproportionate power between the different events the actors in them as well as the fact that 'the event' being challenged was not a truly shared experience. Africans experienced modernity differently from Europeans—in fact maybe Africans never 'experienced' modernity at all, except as slavery and as colonial subjugation. The same applies to the cold-war. Of course the cold war cloud hung over the entire world for fifty years! The Apartheid regime, like Mobutu's were—each in their own ways—the step-children of this war. Similarly the more than three-decades long conflict in Angola cannot be understood apart from the cold-war. We would however be wrong to suppose that Africa was at the center and under as palpable a grip of the cold-war (military and ideological) paranoia that seized the very psyches of USSR and USA citizens—even though Africa was an important 'tool' and 'field' for such paranoia to play itself out. When therefore Africa was caught in this web of events—for indeed it was—it was not as if Africa had no concerns and agendas of her own. My aim in this essay is to retrace, in very small measure, some of Africa's own agendas in matters religious over and against the Christian 'invasion.' Let me hasten to put a halt to the generalization 'Africa' which I have been employing so far. While we may not agree with everything that they say, both Mudimbe (1988, 1992) and Appiah (1992) have taught us to be careful of *what* and *how* we mean by 'Africa.' The former by highlighting the extent to which Africa is an invention while the latter highlights the extent of difference within Africa.

This essay will confine itself to the realm of religion—more specifically to the area of the relationship between Africans and Christianity, between Africans and the Christian Bible as well as the manner in which this relation has been articulated theologically. The present search for metaphors and paradigms offers us space to re-examine some of the basic assumptions upon which African Theology[3] and African Christianity have been thought to be based. My proposal is simply that—and I have hinted at it a few times before (Maluleke 1998a, 1999)—Africans may not be as Christian as all sorts of statistics allege and they may not be as attached to the Bible as it has been thought so far. It is in this context that I raise the question: "what if we were wrong about the centrality of the Bible and the spread of Christianity on the continent?" What would the implications of such a realization for African Christian Theology, Black Theology and the emerging African Women's Theology? The aim of this essay is to frame and pose this question. In fact my sense is that this essay can only offer the very beginnings of a long and complex argument which needs more than one essay to articulate. In this essay we can only state some of the terms of the argument.

Understanding African Christianity More Profoundly

The time has come for Black and African theologians to confront some of the basic presuppositions on which they have been built. This matter seems to me as one fruitful way in which we can navigate the historic seas in which swim at the moment. Both Black Theology and African Theology have largely been based on the assumption that Christianity and its Bible are popular among a large section of African society and have as such become, for better or for worse, key and influential 'texts' in African life (cf. Maluleke 1998a). The assumption takes different octaves and accents in accordance with the orientation of the various hues and personal emphases in African Theology. During the first decade of conscious and deliberate African Theology there was much less certainty about the existence of something called 'African Christianity.' As a matter of fact, one of the doyens of first generation African Theology—theologian and church leader—Bolaji Idowu (1965)—charged that what he saw in the churches of his native country of Nigeria might have been neither Christian nor African but rather some European form of folk religion. Even one of the advocates of the notion of African Christianity, namely John Mbiti, was not always forthright about its existence and its significance. In the introduction to his *Bible and Theology in African Christianity*, Mbiti (1986:ix) described African Christianity as:

> a form of Christianity which combines certain characteristics similar to those of apostolic Christianity with the realities of African life in the present. It is a fascinating form of Christianity. In some ways it is very fresh and fragile; in others it is dynamic and domineering. In some ways it echoes the experiences of the early church; in others it is creatively forging ahead in response to situations of today. In some ways it leans heavily on the religious and cultural background of African peoples; in others it seeks and finds its legitimation and strength in the Bible. In some ways it is deeply African; in others universal. I personally feel moved by and with this African Christendom. *I wish that I could understand it more profoundly and in doing so understand the mysteries of God at work* (emphasis mine).

In the above quote, there is an attempt to maintain a creative tension between the strength and dynamism of the emergent African Christianity on the one hand, and its fragility on the other. One senses that room is made for ambiguity, incompleteness and even a sense of mystery with respect to African Christianity. It is particularly noted that African Christianity exists in the middle of (at least) two pulling forces—the 'religious and cultural background of African people' on the one hand and the Bible on the other. Nor was Mbiti (in p'Bitek 1986, 70) always happy about specific manifestations of African Christianity so he wrote: "Christianity in Kenya has mushroomed denominationally, and the mushroom has turned into a messy soup." Similarly, Kä Mana (2000, 24) described the African Christian scene in the following manner.

> Du nord au sud, d'est en ouest, l'Afrique se présente comme une immense terre où l'exubérance du religieux appelle les spiritualités de tous bords: le plus respectables comme le plus délirantes, celles des institutions traditionnelles vénérables

comme celles des marchands d'illusions, celles de vrais chercheurs de Dieu comme celles des faux-monnayeurs du sacré, celle du souffle profond de l'Évangile comme celle de dangereux terroristes de l'invisible.

Such then is the level of ambiguity and variety on the African religious scene. We need to rekindle the desire to understand African Christianity, its dynamism and power, its fragility and its culpability even as we seek to call the African church to mission. This we must do before we rush back to 'mission' and 'evangelism'—however subtly we may define these. Therefore while I agree with the observation of Mana (2000, 24) that the African religious scene is one in which the churches are: "confrontée à un contexte aussi agité, ou les confusions spirituelles et les ambiguïtés doctrinales risquent de brouiller les repères essentiels de la foi chrétienne..." I would not join Mana as he, to my mind, rather hastily deduces from these observations that "la pensée théologique africaine est de plus en plus appelée à redéfinir la portée et le sens du christianisme pour l'Afrique actuelle...". I think we need to first take careful note of the spiritual confusions and doctrinal ambiguities: what they are, why they are and what they imply before we determine the extent to which they threaten to eclipse some 'marks of the Christian faith.' My suggestion is that a great task for African theologians lies in the moment just before we redefine 'la portée et le sense du christianisme pour l'Afrique actuelle'—i.e. before we venture into redefining the range and direction of Christianity in contemporary Africa. Not that the task of redefining is less important, but it is task better considered after we have taken intelligent note of the spiritual confusions and doctrinal ambiguities of which Mana speaks. It may just be that the product needing redefinition turns out to be something very different from what we imagined before. In fact, I want to suggest that one I of the things we need to start doing is to tone down on the presumed significance of an allegedly massive African Christianity. But I am preempting one of the arguments to follow.

A Timely Message from Heaven: The End of the Present Times[4]

On 31 December 1999 the whole world took turns celebrating the end of the twentieth century and the beginning of the twenty-first. So there was something even more special about 12 midnight on this day—it was not only the end of the year, but the end of the millennium! The world wide panic about an expected computer crash—the so-called Y2K helped to fan the exciting fear and mystery of the end of a millennium. While Y2K virus specialists spent the nights in government and corporate computer centers monitoring the bug, members of the Ugandan Movement for the Restoration of the Ten Commandments of God (MOVEMENT), like hundreds other millenarian groups all over the world, literally awaited the end of the world! The first of January 2000 was for them a truly disappointing day. The sinful generation on earth continued to live on despite their blatant departure from the heart of the Bible— the ten commandments of God! Had all the preparations of the MOVEMENT gone to waste? It is said that many of them had not only fasted to near death but donated most of their prized possessions to the MOVEMENT in preparation for the rapture. It is also suspected that many were either infected with HIV/AIDS or had been survivors in families touched by this dreaded disease. But perhaps all of this does not matter if rapture is around the corner. That is the point, is it not? What might have mattered was that the 1st of January 2000 came and there was no rapture.

Had the prophesy of the leaders of the MOVEMENT failed? What now? How were the leaders of the MOVEMENT—Joseph Kibwetere, Credonia Mwerinde (an alleged former prostitute) and Dominic Kataribaabo (an expelled Catholic deacon)—the seers of the MOVEMENT—to explain this turn of events? The end was the extended from 31 December to 31 January and later to the end of February. Meanwhile some members of the MOVEMENT had started to disappear without trace. Did Joseph Kibwetere not tell the members often that they would be whisked away one by one—as a certain verse in John 14 says—or does it not? Is this not what the Blessed Mother and her Son Jesus had appeared and said to the seers at different times?

On 17 March 2000, more than 500 members of the MOVEMENT were burnt to death in a church building. This happened at the rural village of Kanungu, about 350km south-west of Kampala in Uganda. A few days later the whole world watched gruesome television footage of charred bodies of children and adults. Their death was apparently part of a religious mass suicide pact. Members of the MOVEMENT seem to have been aware of and prepared for some impending rupture shortly before the burning. It is said that many of them had sold and given away most of what they owned. They then went around to invite all members of the MOVEMENT—even those who had backslided—to come to this the 'special' and 'final' service. Worse still, weeks after the special and final service Ugandan Police proceeded to discover the bodies of hundreds other members of the MOVEMENT buried in shallow graves at the homes of some of the leaders. By the first week of May 2000 when I was in Uganda[5], the country was still reeling from this gruesome event. The police could still not pronounce whether the leadership of the MOVEMENT had fled or died with their flock in the fire. During my stay in Uganda, Fr. Dr. John-Mary Walligo, a human rights commissioner and activist in that country told us that there were several surviving members of this cult who were sorry that they 'missed out' on the occasion of the special and final service!

So What is the Message?

The question should be in the plural: What are the messages? There are many possible messages—even conflicting messages. The first thing to note is that as a 'Christian cult' tragedy Kanungu is not unique. Its stands within a gruesome tradition of mass suicides and massacres among and between some Christian fringe groups—which groups have generated a growing body of scholarship (cf. Moore and McGhee 1989a, 1989b, Levi 1982, Chidester 1988). However, while the interpretative insights garnered in these works are most helpful in further research, they are by no means mechanically transplantable from metropolitan USA to rural Uganda. Nor is Kanungu the only African Christian/Biblical cult tragedy—there was Nongqawuse (Peires 1989) and the Bulhoek massacre before (Mandew 1997)[6].

A careful observation of the African scene—even the religious scene—will reveal a lot of untidy stories. As hinted in the brief reference to Mbiti and Mana above, Christianity in Africa—even African Christianity—is not an unqualified success story. Not only have denominationalism reduced Christian churches into a 'messy mushroom soup' but that soup has not always been nutritious but has often been deadly poisonous (cf. Gifford 1991, 1995, 1998). The hideous Apartheid ideology was born and bred in the Christian church. It was a Christian church that considered it:

> desirable and scriptural that our members from the heathen be received and absorbed into our existing congregations wherever possible; but where this measure, *as a result of the weakness of some*, impedes the furtherance of the cause of Christ among the heathen, the congregation from the heathen, already founded and still to be founded, shall enjoy its Christian privileges in a separate building or institution (in De Gruchy 1979, 8).

The 'weakness' referred to in the quotation is a disguise for the racism of White Christians who felt that they could not partake of the Christian sacraments together with Blacks. From this 'momentous' church decision a series of political ones designed to discriminate, oppress and kill Black people all with theological and Biblical justification followed. On the one hand we had the racist outworking of the Christian faith on the continent, justified theologically, internalized and practiced ecclesiastically, politically as well as economically. On the other, we have had the myriad of African (indigenous and missionary) churches who though 'covertly resistant' (Petersen 1995) are nevertheless caught in the web of internalized 'Apartheid theology' as well as being caught in the tragedy of African existential reality—a reality inherited, imported and self-inflicted. As if the scandal of Christian Apartheid theology was not enough we recently had to deal with the tragedy of Christian Rwanda— an outworking of endemic 'Christian Apartheid theology'? For Mana (2000, 77) the Rwandan genocide is "un cauchemar missiologique":

> Des les première heures du genocide, l'interrogation sur le lien entre l'innommable barbarie des massacres et le fait qu'ils aient été perpétrés par un peuple à 90% officiellement chrétien a surgi dans tous les esprits. Comme si tout le monde sentait que se jouait là le drame qui remettait en cause la mission et l'évangelisation de toute l'Afrique (Mana 2000, 79).

Mana is right in the sentiment that the Rwanda genocide put into question the integrity of the evangelization of all of Africa—it is in this sense that he sees it as a missiological nightmare. But Rwanda puts into question not only the past of African Christianity but its present as well—the present integrity of Christian presence in Africa stands accused in the light of Rwanda 1994 and in the light of Kanungu 2000. Mana (2000, 80) suggests that the explanation for Rwanda 1994 should be traced in three areas: abuse of ethnic hostilities by both local and absentee political authorities; murderous colonial involvement in the cultivation of hostilities between Tutsis and Hutus and an inadequate/superficial form of evangelization. This diagnosis refuses to apportion some direct responsibility either on Rwandan Christians or on Christianity—it was what the colonialists, political authorities and missionaries/evangelizers did that caused the genocide to happen. But what if there are more direct connections between the logic of certain aspects of Christian theology and faith with the logic of genocide? Should this not be explored too?

The totality of these factors produce a rather highly strung and unpredictable Christian presence which can explode into either tragedy or celebration, joy or sadness, triumph or disaster any moment and/or from one moment to the next. We do a great disservice when we gloss over the unpredictability, untidiness and highly-strung nature of Christian presence in Africa and rush on to romanticize it. Given this reality the Kanungu tragedy is not that anomalous. Africa has a thousand Kanungu villages and cities saturated with the unpredictable highly strung 'Christianities' which can and do explode as easily into unprovoked celebration as they can explode into wanton tragedy. This is at least the one message, perhaps not from heaven but definitely from Kanungu. The task now facing African theologians is to give up the pretense of a coherent and largely predictable and controllable Christian presence on the continent. African theologians are not doctrinal police seeking to keep the myriad, wayward and unpredictable African churches on the straight and narrow. African theologians should be more than motivational psychologists motivating African Christians and churches to exploit the new millennium by turning their attentions to the project of reconstruction with the same vigor they displayed in the alleged inculturation and liberation (cf. Mana 1999, 2000, Mugambi 1995). Nor is their task exhausted in lauding and elevating African Christianity to the level of being exemplary, leading and a laboratory for the rest of the Christian world (Bediako 1995). Our task is not merely to describe and 'market' African Christianity but to explain it.

Two Types of Optimism[7]

I charge that we have not only understood African Christianity—whatever it is that we mean by it—rather superficially and hurriedly; we might also have been mistaken in being too optimistic about the potential of the 'new millennium' to produce good for Africa and African Christianity—however qualified such optimism might be. Indeed, ill-considered optimism—sometimes bordering on wishful thinking—is the bane of much current theological projection in Africa. On this score I disagree quite fundamentally with the basic spirit of optimism that permeates the works of some of the leading African theologians of our time. Two kinds of optimism are identifiable: *the first* one is a kind of unspoken but palpable optimism about the new millennium (cf. Mugambi 1995, Mana 1992, 1993, 2000)—which I shall, for purposes of shorthand, call 'millennial optimism'—while *the second* type of optimism is a kind of cryptic optimism about the place of the Bible and Christianity in Africa (cf. Mbiti 1986, Sanneh 1989, Bediako 1995, Tutu 1999)[8]—which I will call 'Christianity optimism.'

Millennial optimism is, at least in part, part and parcel of the passionate confusion noted in the first section above. In South Africa and Uganda millennial optimism is also linked to, and partially if only indirectly inspired by, the notions of *Ubuntu* and 'the African renaissance' propagated by Thabo Mbeki president of South Africa and Yoweri Museveni president of Uganda (cf. Katongole 1998, Mbeki 1998). Belonging to those who propagate Christianity optimism are those theologians (cf. Mofokeng 1988, Mosala 1989, Setiloane 1976) who in fact have recognized somewhat the ambiguous nature of both African Christianity and the Bible as well as some White contextual theologians (cf. West[9] 1991, 1999, Cochrane 1999, Petersen 1995) who propagate a carefully nuanced and complex 'new hegemony of agency' by arguing that contextual, grassroots African Christianity is positively *agentic*.

Looking Back at Optimism

The conviction that African Christianity is big, wide-spread and significant appears to have grown steadily from the late 1960s. The works of the 1940s and 1950s were largely apologetics in defense of African culture as a legitimate and largely coherent whole (which for missionaries and Christians meant that African culture was worthy target for Christian evangelism)— following a trend that was started by Kenyatta's *Facing Mount Kenya* and Temples' *Bantu Philosophy*. Christian missionaries and ethnographers had long managed to create a link between all the 'positive' sentiments towards the 'noble savages' and their evangelistic mission. From their point of view what the discourse of discovery of system, logic and coherence in 'primitive' African life was also discourse about the viability and even necessity of their evangelistic task. Soon it became nearly impossible to think positively of African culture and African people without linking them quite fundamentally with Christian mission. This is precisely the question I am broaching in this essay. *Can African people and their cultures be thought of in positive terms without the Christian or Islamic story being made central?*[10] How has it become *normal* to valorize African reality by means of centralizing either Christianity or Islam— whether we do so by means of protest (e.g. African theologies of liberation in their various expressions) or by means of acquiescence (missionary literature) so that it appears inconceivable to do otherwise? Can we find *other* ways of valorizing African reality?

I am not suggesting the summary jettisoning of Africa's heritage of either Christianity or Islam—for that would be wishful thinking. The Christian script has been written onto Africa in ink that will not wash away easily. African deities and by consequence African identities will no longer be able to speak without 'Christian interference.' But must Christian interference be central? From a slightly different angle Mazrui (1986, 12) was asking very similar questions about the impact of Europe in Africa. He asks for example: "Is the westernization of Africa reversible? Was the European colonial impact upon Africa deep or shallow?" His instincts are that Africa should be able to define herself meaningfully without centralizing the European (and I would add the Islamic) episode. But this has proven to be a hazardous exercise. Already during the late nineteenth and early twentieth centuries some missionary ethnographers and evangelists had already started writing all kinds of *apologia* for African culture and African peoples even if the essential aspects of these were written in extremely patronizing terms (cf. Callaway 1868, Junod 1912, Moffat 1852).[11] It was not until the 1930s with the advent of the philosophy of négritude that Africans began to take up the 'cause' themselves—albeit in different terms. In terms of theology many agree that the appearance of the conference proceedings titled *Les prêtres noirs s'interrogent* which appeared in 1956 and many of whose contributors were clearly influenced by the négritude philosophy was an important landmark.

Christianity Optimism

'Christianity optimism' is at least mostly up-front and often owns up. It takes various accents and shapes. Recent works especially those that propagate what I have termed the new hegemony of agency earlier (West 1999, Cochrane 1999, Petersen 1995) above—offer the most sophisticated and most nuanced optimism about the state, potential and possibilities of Christianity in Africa. Many of those theologians who subscribe to millennial optimism (cf. Mugambi 1995 and Mana 1993, 2000) also subscribe to Christianity optimism. Therefore the distinction between the two types of optimism is mainly pedagogical for in reality there is much overlap. Yet the two types of optimism carry essentially different visions of the church and in Africa.

In the case of millennial optimism, the vision is largely one of a Constatinian-type programmatic church which leads and facilitates the projects of reconstruction rather from above. The ambition of Christianity optimism is to elevate a grass-root African church of the poor whose members are constructing and deconstructing theologies of survival and agency (cf. Haddad 2001)[12] over against the powers that be. Another difference between the two types of optimism is that whereas millennial optimism is inspired mainly by external factors of a grand political scale, a considerable section of those who propagate Christianity optimism proceed on an in-built mistrust of the great factors out there, concentrating rather on the less grand-scale struggles of survival and day-to-day/day-by-day forms of liberation. In this category I would put the works of the three white contextual (or prophetic) theologians Petersen (1995), Cochrane (1999), and West (1999). Each in their own ways tries to link with marginalized African Christians and readers of the Bible. All three suppose not only that the Bible and/or Christianity is good for poor Africans but that poor Africans are equal to the task of 'reading' the Bible and 'doing' theology albeit in unconventional ways. In this way, through creative interaction with the Bible and Christianity, poor Africans are able to negotiate and 'survive' their material destitution.

This line of argument—which I have termed 'the new hegemony of agency'—is enticing, but it could be misleading. Poor Africans have less to gain from being declared the creative, 'surviving oppressed'—of course they are, what choice do they have? The question is: what have the protagonists of this version of Christianity optimism to gain from the discourse? Does it help them sleep better at night, to suppose that marginalized and poor Africans are not that destitute after all?

However there are protagonists of Christianity optimism who straddle between the two types of optimism. One is thinking here of the likes of Bediako (1995) and Sanneh (1989), both of whom combine an optimism about the new epoch in which the South (Africa in particular) is now able to take up Christian leadership with an optimism about Africa Christianity as an authentic and 'original' form of Christianity—a Christianity that owes as much to 'lowly Africans' as it does to the high-powered missionary endeavors.

South African Black theologians—like their counterparts in the USA—cannot be accused of taking an uncritical stance towards white Christianity and its Bible. Theirs has been a devastating critique of racist and exploitative white Christianity and a rejection of a 'white' Jesus. Indeed, over the years, many a South African Black Theology conference has returned again and again to the niggling questions: Is Christianity ally or foe? What does it mean to be Black oppressed and Christian at the same time, seeing that the oppressors are fellow Christians? Do we really need Christianity in order to be or to do? Some have asked this question while looking to African Traditional Religion for help while other ask this question while looking to modern secular ideologies for help. Those like Gabriel

Setiloane who believed that African Traditional Religions were just as good as Christianity, nevertheless stayed within the Christian fold—as ministers of religion. Indeed these issues and questions have been the stuff of which South African Black Theology has been made. However, when all is said and done Black Theology has chosen to "use the Bible to get the land back [and hopefully] get the land back without losing the Bible" (Mosala 1987, 194). This is a telling choice. In what is arguably the best essay that articulates the dilemma of being a Black Christian, Mofokeng (1988, 55) explains the same choice in terms of a last resort:

> In this situation of very limited ideological options, Black theologians who are committed to the struggle for liberation and are organically connected to the struggling Christian people, have chosen to honestly do their best to shape the Bible into a formidable weapon in the hands of the oppressed instead of just leaving it to confuse, frustrate and destroy our people.

From Mofokeng's statement it is clear that the Bible is thought of as something prone to and capable of *confusing, frustrating* and even *destroying*. Nevertheless Black theologians like him and Mosala opt to attempt the difficult (and some would say the impossible) task of 'shaping the Bible into a formidable weapon' so that although it was used to take the land of Black people away, it may now be used to get the land back. In is noteworthy that it was not the pull of the Bible or its contents *per se* that led to this position but it was the situation of limited ideological options which left Black theologians and Black Christians alike with few other options. In this, the starting point for the Christianity optimism of Black theologians differs from the starting point of the white prophetic theologians discussed above—who, otherwise share this optimism with them. For Black theologians subscription to Christianity optimism is a reluctant, last resort affair. Now the crucial question is: What if we now live at a time where and when there are other ideological options open to African Christians? What if Black Theology has been wrong in the assumption that millions of Africans regard the Bible and Christianity as a haven? What if what is actually going on in African Christianity is not 'Christian' in the sense that it is commonly understood? Would Black Theology be brave and consistent enough to consider other platforms for constructing their theological and religious discourse?

Millennial Optimism

It is not easy to identify this type of optimism because it seldom owns up to its optimism. The language used is kerygmatic and even didactic—calling on African theologians, churches and Christians to decisive action in the new millennium. With good reason too. The summons has largely been one of reconstruction rather than celebration or naked optimism. Crediting the AACC—particularly José Chipenda and André Karamaga as the initiators of the project of reconstruction, Mana (1993, 46) explains it thus:

> ... ce concept rend compte des besoins et des attentes de nos peuples et de nos Églises. Il englobe des nécessités et des urgences qui concernent tous les domaines de la vie de notre continent. Après l'échec de nos trente ans d'indépendance, nous avons à reconstruire des économies, des politiques humaines, des sociétes créatrices et des cultures d'initiative historique. *Notre théologie ne peut donc qu'être une théologie de la reconstruction,* avec ce que cela exige de connaisance du terraine, de lucidité dans les choix des moyens, de rationalité dans la conduite des travaux, de profonduer dans la conception des espaces à vivre et d'imagination prospective pour inventer l'Afrique nouvelle (emphasis mine).

The terrain within which Mana pitches his reconstruction tent is the language of crisis brought about by past and present failure. Thirty years of failed independence has left many African societies devastated so that 'our theology can only be a theology of reconstruction'—a theology which allegedly encompasses all the areas of the life of the continent and caters for the hopes and needs of Africans. In his first three chapters,

Mugambi (1995) paints a similar picture. But these are rather tall statements for the thirty years of independence have not just and only been 'failure'. The 'crisis' in which Africa finds herself demands slower and more careful consideration than merely as an introduction to a new paradigm of Christian theology. The real premise—not always clearly and openly articulated—on which the proposal is based is a sense of optimism about the new times in which Africa finds herself. Mana's (1993, 10) view of the times in which we live is a little betrayed when he says:

> Les idéologies qui ont dominé les années des indépendances africaines en se fondant sur les nécessités des luttes anti-coloniales et de l'identité culturelle s'emoussent et s'essouflent. *L'orage des philosophies de l'autheticité cède la place à un ciel plus serein*, où les préoccupations fondamentales sont celles de démocratie, de liberté et de droits de l'homme comme conditions pour la construction d'une Afrique nouvelle, la promotion de son développement économique et l'amélioration de ses structures sociales et culturelles (emphasis mine).

For Mana therefore the new skies are much calmer than those of the days of anti-colonialism and the quest for cultural identity. It is this assumption that betrays the millennial nature of Mana's optimism. Mugambi (1995) sees the new window of opportunity in terms of the end of the cold war—so that because of that, it is no longer necessary to engage in either liberation of inculturation theological projects. However, between the two, it is Mana who tries harder to enflesh what he means by a theology of reconstruction. What both of them seem to share is the largely unspoken optimism about the new millennium. In our opinion such optimism is not only grossly misplaced but the protagonists err in not being up-front about the optimism, its nature and whence it comes. It also strikes one as too easy a buying into progressivist propaganda on the basis of which we the world is getting better and better every millennium which achievements accumulating on top of each other as the years pile on. In a sense therefore the theology of reconstruction—at least as propagated by both Mana and Mugambi—is a theology of millennial optimism. By this we mean that it is fundamentally built on a positive disposition towards the new millennium even if its protagonists are critical of the appalling circumstances in which Africa finds herself. The millennial and global ambitions of Bediako's version of millennial optimism are apparent in the statement with which he closes his book:

> An important dimension of Africa's role as 'laboratory' for the world may, therefore, include the vindication in the modern world of the viability of Christian religious discourse, as not outworn and to be discarded, or about which to be embarrassed, but rather as fully coherent with human experience, and fully meaningful within the history of the world's redemption. (Bediako 1995, 265)

In this scheme of things, African Christianity has global significance—as a laboratory—in the light of the waning of Christianity in other parts of the world. This assertion contains an important challenge to African Christianity and African Christian theologians—for it is an immense responsibility to be situated in the midst of one of the leading laboratories for Christian religious discourse in the world of today! However if Christian religious discourse is not something to be embarrassed about, certain articulations and enactments of African Christianity—such as Rwanda 1994, Apartheid South Africa and more recently Kanungu 2000—are *embarrassing*. The answer is neither to gloss over the embarrassments or to ignore them totally. It is our task to confront African Christian potential in all its glory and all its embarrassing moments. The new millennium must be probed and be probed deep. The answers are complex and multi-faceted but we will be better off attempting these in their complexity rather than building our theological enterprise on some superficial common-sense notion of the new millennium.

To End: A Story That Continues

Around 1700 a young Ghanaian boy of seven or eight was kidnapped or, in his own words, "robbed of my parents" by a Dutch captain of a merchant and a slave trader on the Ghanaian coast line (cf. Kpobi 1993). The captain gifted the boy to his friend, yet another merchant. His second master took him to the Netherlands and gave him a name—a rather long name—for no one could remember the little boy's real name. Fortunately for him, his new owner, for some reason, chose to keep him as an adopted child rather than as a slave as was the common practice at the time. In the Netherlands, he became *Jacobus Elisa Johannes Capitein* and was dully instructed on the Christian faith and became as Dutch as any adopted child could be. Around 1740 Capitein completed five years of theological studies at the University of Leiden. The title of his dissertation which was well-liked at the time was: "Politico-Theological Dissertation Concerning Slavery, As Not contrary to Christian Freedom." In it he joined those who at that time, argued that slavery was compatible with Christianity. To support his arguments he refers to age old 'tactics': reference to the curse of Ham (Gen 9:25) and his descendants; the epistles of Paul especially sections which appeared to accept and favor slavery and the letter to Philemon; distinguishing spiritual slavery (which was unacceptable) from physical slavery (which was acceptable). For obvious reasons, Capitein's views were popular in Holland that his dissertation went into fourth printing. Subsequently he was ordained as minister in the Netherlands Reformed Church and became the first African Protestant minister of religion. He was immediately employed as missionary and pastor by the Amsterdam-based West India Company. His first and only station was Elmina castle—captured by the Dutch from the Portuguese—Cape Coast, Ghana. Here Capitein became pastor and missionary to the Dutch soldiers and officials living there. Notably, he was not sent to minister to the slaves who were frequently stationed there *en route* to Europe or America.

Stung by the low morals of the Dutch merchants, officials, and soldiers resident in the self-contained castle of Elmina, Capitein became a stern moralist and preacher. Thus he invited the disdain and even hatred of the Dutch and a measure of indifference of the locals at Elmina whose young he tried to evangelize through education. But alas, Capitein died suddenly within five years of his ministry at Elmina. It is not clear what the cause of his death was for the military authorities at Elmina omitted to record the cause of his death. All sorts of rumors abound about the cause of his death. There were rumors that his sudden death in 1747 was caused by murder either at the hands of the Dutch soldiers or the Elmina's local African community. The former is more likely since Capitein had more to do with the Dutch at Elmina than with either the slaves or the locals. Another rumor that did the rounds was that whilst at Elmina, Capitein had lapsed in faith due to the disdain and low morals of the Dutch and due to his increased contacts with the locals, so that he went back to heathenism and disappeared into the Ghanaian interior, never to be seen again. What is true is that for a while before his death, Capitein was a depressed man, in great financial troubles and much alienated—so much so that he sent several letters to his employers threatening resignation so that at times his employers resorted to sending him tobacco and alcohol to revive his spirits and keep him in the job. Maybe Capitein died of 'loneliness' and frustration. Maybe he died of the realization that his theology was of no use to the herds of slaves living in the dungeons underneath. It was the hollow and haunting eyes of emasculated slaves bodies, clutching on the iron bars, invoking Capitein's mercy and imploring him to remember his ancestry that killed him. Or was it the absurdity of the words of Psalm 132:13-14 pasted on the door to the chapel in Elmina that drove Capitein insane? How can the Lord have chosen a place like Elmina as his dwelling place?

Let us pause and reflect seriously on the Capitein in *us*—as African Christians. While it is true that up to about the seventh century, African Christianity was not heavily sponsored by either colonialism or slavery, it is true that modern day African Christianity emerged out of the context of slavery and racist colonialism. To be an African Christian has come to be an enigma and a *Capitein*. It is to be converted as slave to the religion of your very masters and thereby to share in the complicity. Like Capitein, many African Christians realize how impotent their theological resources are as they look into the eyes of Africa's modern day slaves. Indeed many of these resources are not meant to serve the slaves but to serve the elite who live in self-contained modern-day fortresses insulated from the noise and the smell of Africa's Elmina and Kanungu villages. This then is the challenge we face: To be honest about the Capitein in us. To have the courage to confront Elmina—ancient and modern. To have the audacity to acknowledge that the Bible might not be as central to African life as we make it out to be. To acknowledge that African Christianity is ambiguous and unpredictable and that our job is first and foremost to understand rather than to correct this situation.

Chapter 8

Response

Vincent L. Wimbush

It is an honor for me to respond to this collection of essays, to have been part of some of the discussions that led to and are reflected in the essays and, most significant for me personally, to be able to interact and collaborate with some of my Black African brothers and sisters. That the essays are associated with a multi-racial gathering, in this case an academic conference, in South Africa—and in Cape Town no less—is poignant enough. That the gathering was facilitated by the Society of Biblical Literature is for me quite incredible. My history of membership and active participation in and challenges to SBL will not allow me to miss the significance of the moment. Although I am not licensed to speak for all those SBL members who are understood to belong to "underrepresented" groups, I cannot refrain from pointing to the collection of essays and the gathering that inspired it as historic. From one SBL member's point of view, it is a measure of restraint to say that whether in Cape Town or New York, whether before or after the fall of (a narrowly defined) apartheid, whether in heightened consciousness of or in total indifference to what apartheid was and meant, SBL, a bastion of traditionalism in the way that nearly all western academic guilds are, has not always been open to the facilitation of conversations of the type that the collection represents. So all the usual and unusual communication problems, frustrations, doubts, suspicions, disagreements that are generally associated with collections of essays and that are in several instances registered in this particular collection of essays notwithstanding, this particular collection is a great moment, an historic moment and project. If only in a minor key, I am pleased and proud to be associated with it.

What is this collection of essays about? What in more specific terms is its importance? It may be most appropriate and helpful first to indicate what the collection *not* about.

The collection is not and cannot be about interpretation of texts. Although some of the essayists discuss some biblical texts and some others seem to argue quite seriously about the appropriate ways to approach the Bible in general, it is clear that this collection is about something other than interpretations of texts—of any sort. The selection of essayists as a group (all with two exceptions are Black Africans); the essayists' topics (none with primary focus upon the interpretation of particular texts); the larger conference setting and its charged significance; and in terms of the usual demographics of conferees for SBL International Meetings the much more African-mixed constitution for the Cape Town meeting—these factors and considerations make it clear that the collection of essays could hardly be primarily about the interpretation of texts. The title *Reading the Bible in the Global Village* does not contradict this argument. What "Reading" as cultural practice may mean and what "the Bible" as object of interpretation may refer to are certainly to be qualified by whatever the "Global Village" may mean. "Reading the Bible" may then point to practices quite different from, perhaps even antithetical to, those practices and understandings and assumptions associated with SBL. More pointedly, it is certainly possible that what Africans—not at all well represented in the ranks of SBL—may understand by the title may be quite different from what most members of SBL mean by it, including what it means to interpret texts.

This collection is also not (primarily) about Africans. Or even about whatever might be claimed to be "African" biblical interpretation. Although most of the original presenters and essayists are (Black) Africans, they do not appear to have been selected with a view to their capacity or agreement to represent or address directly aspects of (Black) African religious sentiment in general or biblical interpretation in particular. Had this been the agenda I suspect a different line up of presenters and essayists would have been conscripted. This is less a comment about either the "African"-ness or the scholarly acumen of the essayists; it is recognition of the need to conceptualize and problematize and organize a program or session about African biblical interpretation on terms that seem here to have been lacking. That some African traditions are described, that some African-specific perspectives, criticisms and sentiments are articulated, and again that African scholars and religious leaders are represented—these facts about the collection are clear. But what is also clear is that there are too many basic and preliminary questions and issues are left unaddressed to justify labeling the collection of essays as African biblical interpretation without much qualification.

Regarding methods and approaches and perspectives, I would argue that although contributors to this collection reflect familiarity with and even expertise in several different (western) modernist and postmodernist discourses and theories of interpretation, the very fact that there is a mix of such with no explicit or implicit privileging of one or combination of such suggests much. Presenters were clearly not chosen in terms of their allegiance to or practice of a particular guild interpretive school of thought or critical method. Although there are in the book some fascinating representations of and discussions about interpretive practices and strategies that are not normally associated with western biblical scholarship, it is nonetheless clear that the line up of presenters and essayists does not reflect any particularly clear agenda regarding the representation of alternate methods and practices. There may be intimations of such, promises of such representation. But this collection of essays seems not to have had as its purpose presentation of any particular critical approach or perspective or practice—western, African, Black African.

So the collection is not text-focused, it is not consistently and explicitly and programmatically and conceptually Africacentered, and it is not reflective of any one critical method or approach or perspective. But enough about what the collection is not. I turn briefly to a consideration of what it *is*, or at least what it promises.

It is the con-fusion of all the above—the rather playful and not tightly wound attention to some texts; the sensitivity to the challenge that the setting in Africa and the idea of "Africa" represent to biblical interpretation; and the genuine openness to different methods and approaches and perspectives—and the resultant de-centering and de-stabilization of the discourse, that marks the collection as historic and fascinating and most important as a harbinger of a radical epistemic challenge. The latter I understand to encompass more than critical method; it has to do more pointedly with what one can know and how one can know it. I think this collection of essays points to a radical challenge for certain scholars about what it is that they claim to know, what it is that they can know, what are or ought to be their practices in relation to that complex abbreviation "Bible."

The essays presented here do not consistently and explicitly address these issues. It is at any rate not the essays themselves that could or should address completely these matters. It is not simply the contents or arguments in the essays that raise these issues. It is the entire *situation* within which the essays appear that needs to be considered or interpreted here. It is the combination of the meeting held in Africa (again, in Cape Town, South Africa, no less), some Black African biblical scholars and religious virtuosi coming into speech and onto the stage of a part of the western academy (SBL), the rather open mix of topics and issues and texts addressed, and the mix of methods and approaches represented—these promised the de-stabilization, the more fundamental questioning, of the agenda and orientation and politics of the discourses about the Bible. In the way that the Black presence has always tended to disturb, even haunt, western discourses and practices, so the more dramatic Black presence at the SBL International Meeting in Cape Town, South African appropriately dramatized and threw into question some of the ongoing practices and orientations of the overwhelmingly white western guild of biblical scholars. It made clear what issues and problematics are not addressed, what practices are absent, what orientations and sentiments are missing. It forced us to take stock of what has been and continues to be unquestioned and taken for granted.

My hope is that this volume will remain a touchstone for the continuation of the questioning and probing that the more dramatic Black presence provokes. Such questioning and probing will likely lead not to a simple opposition between critical and non-critical practices, but to different understandings of what the "critical" might mean. That the meaning of "critical" may through the Black presence be challenged, qualified, and expanded should be considered positive for our common enterprise—interpretation.

Notes

Notes to Chapter 1

1. By trained Bible readers is meant people who have received formal training in the biblical science. What untrained Bible readers do is to unconsciously follow the methods embodied in the Bible readings in which they were brought up.

2. For the difference between critical and uncritical use of the historical method by Africans see Ukpong 1999c, 5.

3. See Robert Schreiter's call for considering "cultural flows" as a new source for rooting Third World contextual theologies (Schreiter 1998, 54–60).

Notes to Chapter 2

1. See Musimbi R. A. Kanyoro, "Reading the Bible From an African Perspective," *The Ecumenical Review* 51/1 (1999): 18–24.

2. Justin S. Ukpong, "Reading the Bible in a Global Village," pp. 34–35 above.

3. See Musa W. Dube, "Fifty Years of Bleeding: A Storytelling Feminist Reading of Mark 5:24-43," *The Ecumenical Review* 51/1 (1999): 16.

4. See Hebert Oberharhansli, "Globalization and Sustainable Prosperity," in *Sustainability and Globalization* (ed. Julio de Santa Ana; Geneva: WCC, 1998), 107.

5. See Miriam Peskowitz, "Tropes of Travel." *Semeia* 75 (1996): 189.

6. See Fernando F. Segovia, "And They Began to Speak in Other Tongues: Competing Modes of Discourse in Contemporary Biblical Criticism," in *Reading From This Place: Social Location and Biblical Interpretation in the United States* (ed. Fernando. F. Segovia, and Mary Ann Tolbert; Minneapolis: Fortress, 1995), 1–32. See also R.S. Sugirtharajah, "Critics, Tools, and the Global Arena," in *Reading*

The Bible in the Global Village: Helsinki (Atlanta: Society of Biblical Literature, 2000), 49–60.

7. Ukpong, p. 34 above.

8. Ukpong, p. 35 above.

9. Ukpong, p. 12 above.

10. Although the process of reading with grassroots readers is traceable to earlier times, (Latin America) the language of "reading with ordinary readers" is particularly associated with Gerald West and his work the Institute for Contextual Theology in Natal. See Gerald West and Musa W. Dube, "Reading With: African Overtures," *Semeia* 73 (1996).

11. See Teresia Hinga, "A Response to 'Reading With': Critical and Ordinary Readings" *Semeia* 73 (1996): 277–84.

12. See Tinyiko S. Maluleke "The Bible among African Christians: A Missiological Perspective," in *To Cast Fire Upon the Earth*, ed. Teresa Okure (Natal: Cluster, 2000), 92–93.

13. Tinyiko S. Maluleke, "The Bible among African Christians," 93–94.

14. See Kwesi Dickson, "Continuity and Discontinuity between the Old Testament and African Life and Thought," in *African Theology en Route: Papers From the Pan-African Conference of Third World Theologians* (ed. Kofi Appiah-Kubi and Sergo Torres; Maryknoll, NY; Orbis, 1979), 95ff. See also his *African Theology* (Maryknoll, NY: Orbis, 1984).

15. See John Mbiti, "The Biblical Basis for Present Trends in African Theology," in Appiah-Kubi and Torres, *African Theology en Route*.

16. For a good summary, see Pricilla Pope-Levison & John R. Levison, "Jesus in Africa," in their *Jesus in Global Contexts* (Louisville: Westminster John Knox, 1989), 89–127.

17. See Teresa Okure, "Feminist Interpretations in Africa," in *Searching the Scriptures, Volume 1: A Feminist Introduction* (ed. Elisabeth Schussler Fiorenza; New York: Crossroad, 1993), 76–85.

18. See Kwesi Dickson, *Uncompleted Mission: Christianity and Exclusivism* (Maryknoll, NY: Orbis, 1991).

19. See Seratwa Ntloedibe-Kuswani, "A Religious Life of an African: A God-given Praeparatio Evanglica?" in *Talitha Cum: Theologies of African Women* (eds. Nyambura J. Njoroge and Musa W. Dube; Natal: Cluster Publications, 2001), 97–120.

20. See Emmanuel Martey, *African Theology: Inculturation and Liberation* (Maryknoll, NY: Orbis, 1993), 67. See also Mercy A. Oduyoye, *Hearing and Knowing: Theological Reflections on Christianity in Africa* (Maryknoll, NY: Orbis, 1993), 69–76.

21. See Bolaji Idowu, *Towards an Indigenous Church* (London: Oxford University Press, 1995), and Gabriel Setiloane "Where Are We in African Theology?" in Appiah-Kubi and Torres, *African Theology en Route*.

22. See Gabriel M. Setiloane, *The Image of God among the Sotho-Tswana* (Rotterdam: Balkema, 1976).

23. See Canaan Banana, "The Case for a New Bible," in *Voices From the Margin: Interpreting the Bible in the Third World* (ed. R. S. Sugirtharajah; 2d edition; Maryknoll, NY: Orbis, 1995), 80.

24. See Inus Daneel, *Quest for Belonging* (Gweru: Mambo, 1987) for the history of AICs.

25. See Musa W. Dube, "Readings of *Semoya*: Botswana Women's Interpretations of Matt 15:21-28," *Semeia* 73 (1996): 111–26. See also Robin M. Peterson, "Time, Resistance and Reconstruction: Rethinking Kairos Theology" (Ph.D. diss., University of Chicago, 1995).

26. See Tinyiko S. Maluleke, "The Bible among African Christians: Missiological Perspective," in *To Cast Fire upon the Earth* (ed. Teresa Okure; Natal: Cluster, 2000), 105.

27. See Nyambura Njoroge, "The Missing Voice: African Women Doing Theology," *Journal of Theology in Southern Africa* 99 (1997): 77–83, for a good summary on the activities of African women theologians.

28. See Musimbi R. A. Kanyoro, "Cultural Hermeneutics: An African Contribution," in *Women's Visions: Theological Reflections, Celebration and Action* (ed. Ofelia Ortega; Geneva: WCC, 1995), 18–28, and "Reading the Bible from an African Perspective," *The Ecumenical Review* 51/1 (1999): 18–24.

29. See Mercy A. Oduyoye and Elisabeth Amoah's, "The Christ for African Women," in *With Passion and Compassion* (ed. Fabela V. and Mercy Oduyoye; Maryknoll: Orbis, 1988).

30. See Dora Mbuwayesango, "Childlessness and Woman-to-Woman Relationship in Genesis and in African Patriarchal Society: Sara and Hagar From a Zimbabwean Woman's Perspective (Gen. 16:1-16; 21:8-21), *Semeia* 78 (1997): 27–36; Mmadipoane

Masenya, "Esther and Northern Sotho Stories: One African–South African Woman's Commentary," in *Other Ways of Reading: African Women and the Bible*, ed. Musa W. Dube (Atlanta: Society of Biblical Literature, 2001); and Mercy A. Oduyoye, *Daughters of Anowa: African Women and Patriarchy* (Maryknoll, NY: Orbis, 1995).

31. See Musimbi Kanyoro, "Translation," in *Dictionary of Feminist need Theologies* (ed. Letty Russell and J. Shannon Clarkson; Louisville: Westminster John Knox, 1996), 303; Gomang Seratwa Ntloedibe-Kuswani, "Translating the Divine: The Case of Modimo in the Setswana Bible," in Dube, *Other Ways of Reading*, 78–100; and Dora R. Mbuwayesango, "How Local Divine Powers Were Suppressed: A Case of Mwari of the Shona," also in Dube, *Other Ways of Reading*, 63–77.

32. Some of these methods and theories are on divination, storytelling and *Bosadi* (Womanhood). See Musa W. Dube, "Divining the Text for International Relations, Matt 15:21-28," in *Transformative Encounters: Jesus and Women Re-viewed* (ed. Ingrid Kitzberger; Leiden: Brill, 2000), 313–28; "Fifty Years of Bleeding," *The Ecumenical Review* 51/1 (1999): 11–17; and Mmadipoane Masenya, "Reading the Bible the *Bosadi* (Womanhood) Way, *Bulletin for Contextual Theology in Southern Africa and Africa* 4 (1997): 15–16.

33. See Musa W. Dube "Readings of *Semoya*," 111–24.

34. See Musa W. Dube, "Go Therefore and Make Disciples of All Nations: Matt 28:19*a*: A Postcolonial Perspective on Biblical Criticism and Pedagogy," in *Teaching the Bible: The Discourse an Politics of Biblical Pedagogy* (ed. Fernando F. Segovia and Mary Ann Tolbert; Maryknoll, NY: Orbis, 1998), 224–46.

35. See Musa W. Dube, "Scripture, Feminism, and Postcolonial Contexts," *Concilium* (1998/4): 50–53.

36. See Musa W. Dube, "Towards a Postcolonial Feminist Interpretation of the Bible," *Semeia 78* (1997): 13.

37. Martey, 82–86.

38. Tinyiko S. Maluleke, "African Theology after Apartheid and after the Cold War—An Emerging Paradigm" (paper presented at the SBL International Meeting, Cape Town, South Africa, July 2000).

39. See Tinyiko S. Maluleke, "Half a Century of African Christian Theologies: Elements of Emerging Agenda for the

Twenty-First Century," *Journal of Theology for Southern Africa* 99 (1997): 22.

40. See Yassine Fall, ed., *Africa: Gender Globalization and Resistance* (New York: AAWord, 1999) for this assessment.

41. Ukpong, p. 13 above.

42. I raised this question in SNTS Hamanskraal post-conference, August 1999, when I noted that the majority of the black participants were from outside South Africa. Only three or so black scholars from South Africa attended. Similarly, the outpouring number of academic religious conferences held in South Africa have repeatedly featured the likes of Jesse Mugambi, Justin Upkong, Teresa Okure, and myself, while the likes of Dr. Masenya Mmadipoane, Prof Tinyiko S. Maluleke, Dr. McGlory Speckman, and Dr. Motlhabi Mokgethi, to mention just a few, are not given the privilege to open conferences that are taking place in their own lands after such a long struggle against apartheid. One cannot argue that scholars from upper Africa are more distinguished in their work than those in South Africa. What is evident is that there is a race issue at play in this conference set up.

43. For the analysis of apartheid and the grooming of a Black South African intellectual, see Tinyiko S. Maluleke, "African Intellectuals, African Culture, and the White Academy in South Africa: Some Implications for Christian Theology in Africa," *Journal of Constructive Theology* 2/1 (1996): 16–21.

44. See Knult Holter, *Yahweh in Africa: Essays on Africa and the Old Testament* (New York: Peter Lang, 2000), 28.

45. Significant change has been brought by those Two-Thirds World scholars who have taken the "voyage into" the Western academic halls and operated in exile. Their work has problematized this set up, almost forcing, with a notable success, Western scholarship to engage Two-Thirds World works. In African studies, one can name here the likes of V. Y. Mudimbe, Ali Mazrui, Appiah Kwame, Ngungi wa Thiongo, Henry Louis Gates, Jr., et al. In biblical Studies, one can name the likes of R. S. Sugirtharajah, Fernando F. Segovia, Kwok Pui Lan, Vincent Wimbush, Randall Bailey, Renita Weems, et al. In other disciplines, the likes of Edward Said and Gayatri C. Spivak have certainly brought Western scholarship to pay attention to Two-Thirds World scholarship.

46. Ukpong, p. 38 above.

47. Ukpong, p. 34 above.

48. See Christopher Lind, *Something is Wrong Somewhere: Globalization, Community and the Moral Economy of Farm Crisis* (Halifax: Fernwood, 1995), 40–42.

I am grateful to my colleagues Dr. Joseph Gaie and Dr. Peter Mwikwisa who read an early form of this essay and gave me their feedback. *Leka moso bagaetsho*!

Notes to Chapter 3

1. In this essay I am not going to explicate the complexities elided by my use of the composite 'missionary/colonial.' Every African locality and almost every commentator has a slightly different experience and interpretation of the complicity between mission and colonialism. My own understanding of this relationship is strongly shaped by the work of the Comaroffs on southern Africa cited below.

2. Obvious as this may be, African biblical scholars have not used the specific designation 'post-colonial' for their work until quite recently (see Dube 2000).

3. Because I, a white male South African biblical scholar, reflect and write about these things, as part of my participation in the work of the ISB, it is often, but mistakenly, assumed that the ISB interface is one of white middle-class biblical scholars like myself reading with black poor and marginalized Bible 'readers.'

4. I would argue that this is can be detected in the work of two of our most adept historical-critical scholars, Justin Ukpong and Jonathan Draper (see their work in LeMarquand 2000a).

5. See for example Dube 1997; Masenya 1997; Mbuwayesango 1997; Sibeko and Haddad 1997.

6. I use inverted commas as a reminder that my problematizing of the place of the Bible in Africans' appropriation of the missionary package may turn out to pose important questions about any unitary understanding of Christianity.

7. My task is a genealogical one, in Michel Foucault's sense, in that it is a "union of erudite knowledge and local memories ['popular knowledge'] which allows us to establish a historical knowledge of struggles and to make use of this knowledge tactically today" (Foucault 1980, 83).

8. My project is similar, but with a twist of perspective, to that proposed by Paul Landau, when he argues that historians of religion have too readily subsumed indigenous practices into religious categories that make sense to European researchers generally and missionary Christianity in particular (Landau 1999).

9. The "square" would have been round (see references cited above); that it is described as "a square" demonstrates both some recognition of the political space into which they had been brought and the desire to re-vision what they found (see Comaroff and Comaroff 1991, 182–183).

10. J. Campbell, Klaarwater, 26 July 1813 [CWM. Africa. South Africa. Incoming correspondence. Box 5–2-D].

11. J. Campbell, Klaarwater, 26 July 1813 [CWM. Africa. South Africa. Incoming correspondence. Box 5–2-D].

12. Campbell never quite copes with the way in which local people, mainly the leadership, just walk into "our tent" (Campbell 1815, 181, 184).

13. The English were, of course, about to have their views on origins thoroughly shaken and stirred by an English explorer and naturalist (Darwin 1963 [1859]); the beginnings of this paradigm shift (in the Kuhnian sense (Kuhn 1970)) can be detected in the missionary message (see below).

14. This is a puzzling reference; could it mean biblical Judea, and if so, might the missionaries have here 'seen' confirmed the origin of all peoples, even these 'sons of Ham,' from this distant land in and of the Bible? That Campbell thought in such categories is evident from a letter to Mr David Langton dated 27 July 1813, in which Campbell apologizes for not having written sooner, saying that he has "written much from this land of Ham." Campbell then goes on to present him with an account of his visit to Dithakong [J. Campbell, Klaar Water, 27 July 1813 [CWM. Africa. South Africa. Incoming correspondence. Box 5–2-D].

15. I use the term power/knowledge deliberately, realizing the hardworking hyphen (in the French *pouvoir-savoir*) and slash (in the English) bear a heavy load of theory. Accepting Foucault's invitation "to see what we can make of" his fragments of analysis (79), my use is intended to allude to this theory, especially to the fragmentary nature of Foucault's theory (79), to the implicit contrast of "idle knowledge" (79) with local forms of knowledge and

criticism, subjugated knowledges (81–82), and their emergence as sites of contestation and struggle over against "the tyranny of globalizing discourses" (83) and their appropriation as genealogies which wage war on the effects of power of dominant discourses (84), whether scientific (Foucault's focus) or other forms of dominating discourse. In particular, my use picks up on Foucault's analysis of the articulation of each on the other, namely, that "the exercise of power itself creates and causes to emerge new objects of knowledge and accumulates new bodies of information," that the "exercise of power perpetually creates knowledge and, conversely, knowledge constantly induces effects of power," and that it "is not possible for power to be exercise without knowledge, it is impossible for knowledge not to engender power" (52) (Foucault 1980).

16. William J. Burchell's earlier stay among the Tlhaping, and his more secretive employment of text generally and the Bible specifically, may have contributed to this question (see Burchell 1824, 391).

17. I am grateful to Mogapi Motsomaesi and Mantso 'Smadz' Matsepe for elucidating and helping me to interpret elements of this encounter.

18. J. Campbell, Klaar Water, 27 July 1813 [CWM. Africa. South Africa. Incoming correspondence. Box 5–2-D].

Notes to Chapter 4

1. West uses the term 'reader' in the phrase 'ordinary reader' to "allude to the shift in hermeneutics towards the reader. He maintains that the use of the term 'reader' is metaphorical to include "the many who are illiterate, but who listen to, discuss, and retell the Bible" and are encouraged to read the text carefully and closely (1993, 168, 171; 1999, 10–11).

2. This presupposes, maintains West (1993, 168), "the speaking voice of a wholly self-knowing subject free from ideology."

3. Draper (1991, 235) maintains that, "Ordinary readers of the Bible in South Africa have remained, by and large, within a pre-critical, naïve frame of reference. The Bible is read with little insight into either its historical context or the influence of the reader's context on the process of interpretation," but, he asserts,

"God is at work among the poor of the oppressed, but the good news that power comes from below, that the system is coming to an end, that the Church belongs to them, that justice and peace are on the horizon" (255).

4. See James Cone, *God of the Oppressed* (1975). In this regard, the Bible is viewed with serious light because it is absolute "nonideological Word of God that can be made ideological only by being applied to the situation of oppression" (Mosala 1989, 16).

5. See West's *Some Parameters of the Hermeneutic Debate in the South African Context* (1992, 10*)*. He refers to the work of the Institute for the Study of the Bible, University of Natal, Pietermaritzburg, the School of Theology which, West points out that, it will continue "to play a significant role in the life of Christians in South Africa, the primary aim of the ISB is to establish an interface between biblical and ordinary readers of the bible in the church and community that will facilitate social transformation."

6. See J. Botha, *How Do We 'Read the Context'* (1994).

7. Adapted from Masoga (2000, 20–25), *Weeping City, Shanty Town Jesus: Introduction to Conversational Theology.*

Notes to Chapter 5

1. Gary D. Comstock, *Gay Theology Without Apology* (Cleveland: Pilgrim Press, 1993).

2. Robert Warrior, "Canaanites, Cowboys, and Indians: Deliverance, Conquest, and Liberation Theology Today," *Christianity and Crisis* 29 (1989): 261–65.

3. Itumeleng J. Mosala, *Biblical Hermeneutics and Black Theology in South Africa* (Grand Rapids: Eerdmans, 1986).

4. Norman K. Gottwald, *The Politics of Ancient Israel* [The Library of Ancient Israel] (Louisville: Westminster John Knox Press, 2001), chap. 4.

5. Gottwald, *Politics*, pp. 77–78, 216, 272 n 50.

6. Baruch Halpern, "Jerusalem and the Lineages in the Seventh Century B.C.E.: Kinship and the Rise of Individual Moral Rights,." in *Law and Ideology in Monarchic Israel*, ed. B. Halpern and D. W. Hobson. (JSOTSup 124; Sheffield: Sheffield Academic Press, 1991), pp. 27, 47–48, 73–79

7. William E. Claburn, "The Fiscal Basis of Josiah's Reform," *JBL*

92 (1973): 11–22; Shigeyuki Nakanose, *Josiah's Passover. Sociology and the Liberating Bible* (Maryknoll: Orbis Books, 1993); Naomi Steinberg, "The Deuteronomic Code and the Politics of State Centralization," in *The Bible and the Politics of Exegesis*, ed. D. Jobling et al. (Cleveland: Pilgrim Press, 1991), 161–70.

8. David Jobling, "Deconstruction and the Political Analysis of Biblical Texts: A Jamesonian Reading of Psalm 72," *Semeia* 59 (1992): 95–127; Walter Houston, "The King's 'Preferential Option for the Poor': Rhetoric, Ideology and Ethics in Psalm 72," *Biblical Interpretation* 7 (1999): 341–67.

9. Norman K. Gottwald, "The Expropriators and the Expropriated in Nehemiah 5," in *Concepts of Class in Ancient Israel*, ed. M. R. Sneed [South Florida Studies in the History of Judaism, 201] (Atlanta: Scholars Press, 1999), pp. 1–19; see also, Gottwald, "The Biblical Jubilee: In Whose Interests?," in *The Jubilee Challenge. Utopia or Possibility?*, ed. H. Ucko (Geneva: WCC, 1997), pp. 33–40, and Itumeleng J. Mosala, "The Politics of Debt and the Liberation of the Scriptures" in *Tracking a Classic: The Tribes of Yahweh Twenty Years On*, ed. Roland Boer (Sheffield: Sheffield Academic Press), 2001.

10. Gottwald, *Politics*, pp. 231–35; James C. Scott, *Weapons of the Weak: Everyday Forms of Peasant Resistance* (New Haven: Yale University Press, 1985; Daniel Miller, Michael Rowlands and Christopher Tilley, eds., *Domination and Resistance* (London: Unwin Hyman, 1989).

11. Gottwald, *Politics*, pp. 216–22, 248.

12. Gottwald, *Politics*, pp. 238–42, 248–49, 258 n 27.

13. Frederick Jameson and Masao Miyoshi, eds., *The Cultures of Globalization* (Durham: Duke University Press, 1998).

14. John Rawls, *A Theory of Justice* (Cambridge: Harvard University Press, 1971).

15. M. Douglas Meeks, *God the Economist: The Doctrine of God and Political Economy* (Minneapolis: Fortress Press, 1989).

Notes to Chapter 6

1. That is, the seven undisputed letters of Paul: Romans, 1 and 2 Corinthians, Galatians, Philippians, 1 Thessalonians and Philemon. The deutero-Paulines provide evidence of later and different considerations than those emphasized here and are

probably related to concerns about ecclesiastical order and power of the institutional kind. Some Pauline scholars, however, challenge this very distinction, cf. Kittredge 1998, 12, 35.

2. As this is a discussion on freedom in its theological and hermeneutical appropriations, and particularly focused on the Pauline writings of the New Testament, no attempt will be made to deal extensively with current thought on freedom or liberty, and liberation, as discussed in the social sciences. Suffice it to mention that since the Enlightenment, theologians have endeavored to formulate acceptable notions of human autonomy, leading to a wide range and variety of different treatments of this idea. For fuller discussions of theological discussions on freedom, cf. e.g. Brown 1981 and Dyson 1985, 56, who deals with the influence of Marx, Freud, and Existentialism on the contemporary discussion on freedom.

3. In formulating biblical perspectives on the liberation of people across the world from oppression, those which could be derived from the Pauline letters are, in fact, effectively absent. Recently, however, and although a decided minority, some biblical scholars have challenged the neglect of Paul on issues of freedom and have subsequently embarked upon a new reading of Paul; e.g. Elliot (1994, 1997); Jones (1984); Lewis (1991); Segundo (1986); and Tamez (1993).

4. This is admittedly only an aspect of Augustine's thinking regarding both the Pauline letters and the idea of freedom. Cf. Dyson (1985, 69–71) for a more balanced, although concise description of Augustine's explanation of freedom according to the distinction between *libertas minor* and *libertas major*. *Libertas minor* is the "ground of the free will or liberty of choice," whereas the other refers to "the liberty of fulfillment." Because "democratic" rights and freedoms imply a freedom *from*, *libertas minor* does not guarantee that a human being will indeed achieve his/er end in life. On the other hand, *libertas major* concerns people's "freedom of being," "the realization of the perfection of their nature in God."

Naturally, although *libertas major* is the freedom sought after in the end—the purpose of human life—*libertas minor* provides the "necessary condition" for that purpose to be realized. Therefore the two "liberties" could not be perceived the one without the other: *libertas minor* as subjective and individual freedom alone means to put oneself "at the mercy of whatever secular forces happens to be dominant at the time"; *libertas major* without actual freedom of choice, "becomes a theological, and then a socio-political, positivism and totalitarianism."

In Luther's appropriation of Augustine, however, *libertas minor* becomes dominant and exclusive, and the ruler can no longer be opposed. Luther's dictum was: "A Christian man [sic] is the most free Lord of all, and subject to none; a Christian man [sic] is the most dutiful servant of all, and subject to everyone."

Pannenberg's argument on freedom of choice and "the full-fledged realization of human freedom" almost equals the Augustinian sentiments above (1981, 293–94).

5. So many developments in various areas of human understanding and knowledge impacted on the interpretation of the Pauline letters since Luther, that it must be stressed that the appropriateness of a term such as "Lutheran legacy" is situated in its reference to the origin of this particular line of interpretation. However, it is interesting to note how Freud's psychology of religion with its emphasis on the "disordered inner self" and subsequent individualism (cf. Dyson 1985, 58–59) provides many striking resemblances with the Lutheran reading of Paul.

The Lutheran framework does not only refer to Luther's interpretation of Paul, but also to the tradition which found its inception in Luther's thought. For example, Pannenberg (1981, 292) argues that particularly on the notion of "justification," Luther's immediate successors (Melanchthon in particular) transformed his "profound insight" about faith and transformed "justification" into "a somewhat wooden, juridical matter, while in Luther's language it has a mystical flavor."

6. It is at least an anachronistic separation and contrast, since in biblical times the religious and the secular were experienced as one, a unity, and not as separate realms of existence (cf. Bosch 1989, 4).

7. Space does not allow the repetition of my argument elsewhere, namely that such a new hermeneutical perspective depends heavily on Paul's own hermeneutics in his engagement with the scriptures of Israel. Indeed, concerns such as those raised by the virtual exclusion of Paul from theological positions on human freedom, requires first of all a new appreciation for Paul's

hermeneutical freedom. The argument, therefore, needs to be extended to a consideration of how Paul's hermeneutics, which itself is an act of freedom, interacts with his notion of freedom in the theological and ethical senses of the word.

8. "Empire is deconstructed and transcended in a process of interpretation 'that is vitally critical, that refuses the short-term blandishments of separatist and triumphalist slogans in favor of the larger, more generous human realities of community *among* cultures, peoples, and societies'" (Draper 1993, 1–3, quoting Said).

9. Postcolonialism should be distinguished from Postmodernism, although they are sometimes presented as two sides of the same coin. Boer (1998, 25) argues that postmodernism is properly seen as both cultural phenomenon and socio-economic development ("late capitalism"), and postmodernism therefore can be understood as "an intense dialectical opposition between globalization and disintegration." Postcolonialism exhibits the same dialectical opposition, but rather than following in the wake of Postmodernism it is actually "constitutive of the postmodern moment in the first place" (26). However, a number of criticisms against the postmodern project have been leveled from the side of postcolonial critics. For example, postmodernists tends to posit another "grand narrative" in the most absolute sense ever, itself; postmodernism is often perceived as being nothing else but (cultural and intellectual) neo-colonialism—a "Euro-American western hegemony"; postmodernism's largely unconcerned attitude to politics limits its effectiveness; postmodernism is often as much a rejection of modernism as a subtle re-inscription thereof (cf. Bosch 1995, 15–25); postmodernism "fetishes" notions of "difference" and "otherness"; postmodernism is "marketed" as "a general movement which addresses global concerns" and is therefore limited in its ability to address local issues; postmodernism's antipathy towards "representation" disallows the much needed postcolonialist post-naive realism; and so on (Tiffin 1997, vii–xv).

10. However, cf. also Elliott (1994, 214–26) who reads Rom 13:1-7 as an exhortation against rivalry, and juxtaposes it with Rom 13:11-14 with its apocalyptic-prophetic emphasis on God's imminent "redisposition of powers."

11. The few exceptions would include Beker (1980, 1982); Dunn (1993); Elliott (1994; 1997); and Georgi (1991a; 1991b; 1992).

12. Cf. Falusi (1973, 125–26), who refers after elaborate discussions on freedom from the law, sin, and death, briefly to "the ethical dimension of freedom." Similarly, Abogunrin (1977, 28–40) elaborates on freedom and emphasizes that Paul's concern in this regard was spiritual, only to contradict himself a few lines from the end of his article, claiming that "Paul was intensely interested in the Empire, its spiritual and social life" (40).

13. A slightly different emphasis, but with the same result, is found in France (1986, 16–17) when he suggests that Paul "envisages a situation where there will continue to be masters and slaves, and gives practical guidance on the proper Christian attitude in those states" and he refers then to Eph 6:5-9 and Col 3:22-4:1. However, Paul's insistence on spiritual freedom "makes men [sic] equal" and therefore Paul "undercuts the value-system of a slave-owning society."

14. Gerhardsson's interpretation of Philem 8-21 and 1 Cor 7:21 as Paul encouraging good slavery attitudes, stands in stark contrast with recent studies finding Paul promoting emancipation. Cf. e.g. Petersen (1985) on Philemon; on 1 Cor 7:21, e.g. Bartch et al. (1983, 509); Dawes (1990, 681–97) from the perspective of a rhetorical analysis; Osiek (1992, 177–78). France (1986, 17) concedes that Paul's advice in 1 Cor 7:21 advocates that slaves accepts emancipation when offered, but that his concern is with "the individual's choice, not with the disruption of the system." It is not clear how he reaches this conclusion!

15. The neglect of the social aspects of Paul's gospel includes also the disregard for the social dimension of "justification." Recently, however, scholars like Dahl, Dunn, Georgi, and Tamez have addressed this deficiency, which arguably boils down to the translation of *dikaiosunē* in all its derivatives, as a forensic term.

16. As far as social criticism is concerned, "the Christian confession that Jesus is Lord includes the proclamation that all powers and principalities are subject to him" (Dahl 1977, 18).

17. Cf. Georgi's study of the Pauline letters from the perspective of "theocracy," claiming that this was Paul's ultimate vision for the world (1991b). Hengel argues that Paul's thought should be understood in terms of pre-70 C.E. Pharisaism with, among other emphases, its strong theocratic-political concern (1991, 51).

18. Tambasco argues that "the flesh" can refer to at least four

matters: sins of sensuality, of heathen religion, of community conflicts, and of intemperance. The third of these could indicate "structural sin" (1982, 126).

19. Betz even argued that Paul "stops just short of being an instigator to disobedience" (Colloquy 1977, 37).

20. "No conviction of Paul is as political (or, if you wish, as secular) as the one about the new unity between Jew and Gentile" (Bosch 1989, 7). Bosch points to the ideological and political implications attached to the Jewish law as instrument of both identity and exclusion; unfortunately, he still interprets "works of the Law" as referring to the increasingly difficult to maintain notion of Jewish works-righteousness.

21. The general debates on "apocalyptic" in its various configurations will not be attended to here. For some brief indications of these debates, cf. Aune 1993, 25–35; Matlock 1996; Stegner 1993, 506–7.

22. Beker is by no means the only scholar to argue for apocalyptic as a key element in Pauline thought. Cf. also Barr 1995, 65–68; Soards 1987, esp. 37ff.; etc. For a review of how the apocalyptic Paul is both veiled and unveiled, cf. Matlock 1996. Even the few authors mentioned here exhibit a wide range of perspectives on apocalyptic.

23. Beker admits that Galatians focuses on the "eschatological present" and does not really exhibit a "futurist, apocalyptic" perspective (1980, 58; cf. Deidun 1986, 238).

24. As a counter argument, it is suggested that Paul's theology is apocalyptic, not because it adheres to the traits as outlined by Beker and others, but in so far as it displays a "perspective of discontinuity" (Keck 1984, 229–41). Discontinuity is a subtler expression of direct challenge leveled at the powers that be.

25. Malina and Rohrbaugh (1998, 7–16) have recently, in their attempt to explain the peculiarities of the language found in the Fourth Gospel as antilanguage put to service of antisociety, referred to John's call for *new values*. In contrast, one finds in Paul (and the Synoptics) an emphasis on *new structures* which are to replace the old ones: e g, "kingdom of God," "church," "body of Christ" and those "in Christ." Malina and Rohrbaugh ascribe this emphasis to Paul's priority for what Halliday calls the "ideational" dimension of language (6). But Paul's call for new structures can be

understood more properly as the result of his apocalyptic frame of mind, rather than his engagement with a certain linguistic dimension, although these two factors need not be mutually exclusive.

26. Cf. e.g. Hengel (1974, 47–53) on the criticism of property in the apocalyptic tradition.

27. Cf. also Meeks (1986, 29–32). It should therefore not be interpreted as "consolation literature" (Elliott 1994, 164).

28. Hengel insists that Pauline thought should be understood in relation to pre-70 C.E. Pharisaism, and here the relevance would be the pharisaic emphasis on political theocracy (1991, 51). For theocracy in Pauline thought, cf. also Georgi (1991b).

29. Where Paul leads by example, and to the dismay of and in opposition to the Jerusalem leaders (cf. Gal 2:11)!

30. It is clear from the New Testament that very often the followers of Christ merely attempted—as Israel did in the Old Testament—to humanize the slave-master relationship without calling the institution and practice of slavery into question (Segundo 1986, 164). This was important since "mistreatment in both Roman and Jewish moral ideology indicated weakness of character on the part of the one in power. Restraint, discipline, and evenness were the ideal" (Osiek 1992, 178). And among the Stoic philosophers "the slowly growing perception of moral equality among "brothers" and "sisters" already pondered . . . was beginning to create cultural complications in a society in which status depended upon birth, class, and the status of one's patron" (Osiek 1992, 178). However, cf. Keener and Usry (1997, 36–38,175–76 n.48): Paul's [sic] insistence in Eph 6:9 on the equality of master and slave implies he viewed slavery as "against nature" and therefore immoral. This was the expressed position of Aristotle, and the Jewish sects of the Essenes and the Therapeutae who used wording similar to that of Paul.

31. Cf. e.g. the argument from admittedly a different context (Mach 1993, 166–79), namely that apocalyptic can easily become elitist ideology of the elect among the elect, through use of certain "scriptural" legitimization. While serving as justification for intergroup boundaries, apocalyptic reasoning can become subservient to intra-group hierarchy.

32. Referring to Carney, Osiek (1992, 178) finds the decline of slavery not in moral objections, but in economic reasons: slavery

was simply inefficient. The reasons for this ineffectiveness were the cost-intensive method of production; an economic system based on power and coercion rather than motivation to achieve maximal profit; requiring a large capital outlay whilst returns were low and slow; no incentive to technologize; reinforcement of class prejudices and disdain of manual labor; an ethos of "conspicuous consumption"; and, the impoverishment of the rural lower free classes—as much as the main reason for the *original* establishment of the institution of slavery, and its maintenance, was economic in nature (Witvliet 1985, esp. 49)! Recognizing the economic driving force behind slavery, as with South African *Apartheid*, does not lessen, but if anything, increases the moral abhorrence for these systems.

33. Meyer (1997, 350) argues: "Such triumphalism among Christians is not only the soil on which a patronizing view of Judaism grows (and worse, where Christendom dominates, a questioning of the Jew's right to existence); it is irreconcilable with Paul's understanding of justification." As for Judaism, cf. Neusner (1989, 30 n.19) for the "isolationist and triumphalist position" found in Orthodox Judaism with regard to the "Judeo-Christian encounter."

34. Cf. Davies (1995, 322) "Inevitably, therefore, these [sc NT] writings reflect a variety of attempted balances between separation from and involvement in the larger social complexes."

35. And the interpretation of Pauline material is not unique in this; cf. e.g. Birch and Rasmussen (1978, 9) on the Gospels.

36. Some reasons offered for Paul's perceived disinterestedness were mentioned above and would typically include the eschatological-apocalyptical theme (however, cf the warning of Nürnberger 1978, 170), the argument that early Christians were structurally prisoners of the system(s) of the time, and claims that Paul's attention were to individual and spiritual matters. Scholars often almost subconsciously propagate Paul's illusory silence on social matters rather than propose a new interpretation of his letters; cf. Sider (1977, 182) "Why have missionaries so often taught Romans but not Amos to new converts in poor lands." On the other hand, cf Elliott's rereadings of Paul, and Romans in particular, showing upon Paul's all but acquiescent socio-political advocacy (1994, 93–230; 1997, 371–89).

Notes to Chapter 7

1. During the past 18 months alone I can think of no less than five such consultations. In May 2000, the mission organization *Missio* initiated a consultation on the jubilee at the Uganda Martyrs University, Nkozi, Uganda. The AACC convened a 'Jubilee 2000 Convocation' in Lome Togo during November 2000. EATWOT Africa and the WCC summoned Africa's young theologians to a discussion of globalization and theology in Africa at Abokobi, outside Accra, Ghana in October 2000. During September 2000, the National Initiative for the Contextualization of Theological Education in South Africa also held a conference in Johannesburg on the theme "Theology and Globalization in South Africa."

2. Writing from the point of view of environmental ethics, Rasmussen (1996) eschews and in the process subverts the notion of globalization by insisting on speaking of 'earth' rather than the rather utilitarian and market orientated notion of 'globe.' 'earth community' rather than 'global community' and 'earth ethics' rather than 'global ethics' (See also Habel 2000). Similarly, the notion of 'intercontextuality' (cf. Wickeri, et al. 2000) invoked alongside 'the role of religion in the new millennium' is yet another one with potential to engage globalization in creative ways—that is insofar it implies a questioning of those aspects and interpretations of globalization that have the ambition of abolishing all contexts so that only one global context remains. Unfortunately Wickeri and his collaborators do not really develop this notion in this work. Another avenue where it seems that we are finding some creative ways of discussing some of the new challenges we face is the avenue of the related discourses about difference (thanks to the inspiration of the Parisian school of philosophy), plurality and more recently reconciliation. Unfortunately many of these discourses are too European and/or North American premised as they are on the premodern-modern-postmodern scheme—a scheme in which Africa does not sit comfortably.

3. By the term 'African Theology' I mean to include both South African Black Theology as well as African Women's Theology. However, whenever the distinctions are important they will be made.

4. This is part of the title of the handbook of the Movement for

the Restoration of the Ten Commandments of God. The full title is: *A Timely Message from Heaven: The End of the Present Times. Delivered Through the Seers with Orders to Inaugurate a Movement for the Restoration of the Ten Commandments of God* (1991). It seems to have bee written by Dominic Kataribaabo, one of the founders of the MOVEMENT.

5. I was at Uganda to read a paper at a Conference summoned by the Germany based Catholic Mission organization called *Missio* in cooperation with the Uganda Martyrs University (1–5 May 2000) on the theme "Jubilee Contextualized in Marginalized Africa Today."

6. The Bulhoek massacre of members of an African Initiated Church called *the Israelites* is a fact a peculiar cult tragedy. White allegedly Christian soldiers of the Apartheid regime mowed down dozens of members of this sect for refusing to vacate a disputed piece of land.

7. Optimism is being used in a specialized sense. By 'optimism' here I mean more than the opposite of pessimism. Indeed the opposite of the optimism of which I speak is not pessimism but honest, structured, observant and intelligent realism. Optimism is the often unspoken and (often unaccounted for) belief that Christianity in Africa is either mainly positive and or has mainly positive potential; and that it is a significant if not key factor in the shape of Africa and in the identities of Africans. Furthermore this optimism proceeds by either being unwilling or unable to look at the unseemly side of Christian presence on the continent in an honest and structured manner. More recently this optimism has linked up with the euphoric optimism riding on the beginning of a new millennium and on notions of the world as a global village in which technological advancement reigns supreme.

8. It is noteworthy that a good deal of African American scholarship also tends to hold what I would see as a mainly positive if not optimistic view of the place and significance both the Bible and Christianity among African Americans (cf. Felder 1991; Hopkins 2000; Wimbush 2000), however my focus is on continental African theologies. My sense is that the same question I am raising for the African context can be raised for the African-American situation, albeit with differing nuances. That task is however, best done by an African America.

9. I acknowledge the academic stimulation, friendship and dialogue with Gerald West—in personal conversation and exchange of notes and article drafts. Many of the nascent ideas have been embedded in several pieces I have already published. Conversations (even disagreement) with West has helped me to attempt developing some of these ideas further.

10. Even Mazrui's enticing charge (1986, 14)that the European impact on Africa was "no more than an episode in millennia of African history" is marred by his apparent Islamic bias in elevating three traditions in what he calls Africa's triple heritage of cultures which are: indigenous traditions, Islamic ways and Western tendencies (115). In his scheme Christianity becomes part of 'Western tendencies' while Islam becomes part of 'Islamic ways' and not part of 'Arabic tendencies.' Is there a hint of optimism about Islam here?

11. Chidester (1996) would argue that much of the *apologia* literature to which I refer would belong to the period after the conquest of Africans by Europeans, i.e. once the conflicts over land, trade, labor, and political autonomy were resolved in favor of Europeans then and only then could Europeans suddenly discover African religious systems and cultures. As such therefore even this apparently favorable literature was a function of the power relations.

12. Haddad (2001) offers a fresh, creative and gripping argument about the survival strategies and agentic potential of poor and marginalized African women whose only resource is usually their faith in God.

References

Abogunrin, Samuel Oyinloye. 1977. The Background of St Paul's Concept of Freedom. *Orita* 11:28–40.

———. 1980. The Modern Search of Historical Jesus in Relation to Christianity in Africa. *Africa Theological Journal* 9/3:18–29.

Albrow, Martin. 1996. *The Modern Age*. Stanford, CA: Stanford University Press.

Anderson, W. S. 1977. Response. Pages 14–15 in *Paul's Concept of Freedom in the Context of Hellenistic Discussions about the Possibilities of Human Freedom*. Protocol of the 26th Colloquy. Edited by Wilhelm H. Wuellner. Berkeley, CA: The Center for Hermeneutical Studies in Hellenistic and Modern Culture.

Anyanwu, K. C. 1981. The African World-view and Theory of Knowledge. In *African Philosophy: an Introduction to the Main Philosophical Trends in Contemporary Africa*. Edited by E. A. Ruch and K. C. Anyanwu. Rome: Catholic Book Agency.

Aune, David E. 1993. Apocalypticism. Pages 25–35 in *Dictionary of Paul and His Letters*. Edited by Gerald F. Hawthorne, Ralph P. Martin, and Daniel G. Reid. Downers Grove, IL: InterVarsity Press.

Baëta, C. G. 1962. *Prophetism in Ghana: A Study of Some "Spiritual" Churches*. London: SCM.

Bailey, Randall C. 1998. The Danger of Ignoring One's Own Cultural Bias in Interpreting the Text. Pages 67–90 in *The Postcolonial Bible, Vol. 1: Bible and Postcolonialism*. Edited by R. S. Surgirtharajah. Sheffield: Sheffield Academic Press.

Barr, David L. 1995. *New Testament Story: An Introduction*. 2nd ed. Belmont, CA: Wadsworth.

Barr, James. 1980. *The Scope and Authority of the Bible*. London: SCM.

Barrett, David B., ed. 1962. *World Christian Encyclopedia: A Comparative Survey of Churches and Religions in the Modern World AD 1900–2000*. Nairobi: Oxford University Press

———. 1968. *Schism and Renewal in Africa: An Analysis of Six Thousand*

REFERENCES

Contemporary Religious Movements. Nairobi: Oxford University Press.

———. 1970. AD 2000: 350 Million Christians in Africa. *International Review of Mission* 59:39–54.

Barrett, C. K. 1985. *Freedom and Obligation: A Study of the Epistle to the Galatians*. Philadelphia: Westminster.

Bartsch, H. W., K. Heiligenthal, H. Grieve, R. Mehl, and A Schwan. 1983. Freiheit. Pages 497–549 in *Theologische Realenzyklopädie*. Edited by G. Krause and G. Müller. Berlin and New York: De Gruyter.

Bediako, Kwame. 1995. *Christianity in Africa: The Renewal of a Non-Western Religion*. Maryknoll, NY: Orbis.

Beker, J. Christiaan. 1980. *Paul, the Apostle: The Triumph of God in Life and Thought*. Edinburgh: T&T Clark.

———. 1982. *Paul's Apocalyptic Gospel: The Coming Triumph of God*. Philadelphia: Fortress.

Betz, Hans Dieter. 1977. Paul's Concept of Freedom in the Context of Hellenistic Discussions about the Possibilities of Human Freedom. Pages 1–13 in *Paul's Concept of Freedom in the Context of Hellenistic Discussions about the Possibilities of Human Freedom*. Protocol of the Twenty-sixth Colloquy. Edited by Wilhelm H. Wuellner. Berkeley, CA: The Center for Hermeneutical Studies in Hellenistic and Modern Culture.

Beyer, Peter. 1994. *Religion and Globalization*. London: Sage.

Birch, Bruce C. and Larry L. Rasmussen. 1978. *The Predicament of the Prosperous*. Philadelphia: Westminster.

Boer, Roland. 1998. Remembering Babylon: Postcolonialism and Australian Biblical Studies. Pages 24–48 in *The Postcolonial Bible, Vol. 1: Bible and Postcolonialism*. Edited by R. S. Sugirtharajah. Sheffield: Sheffield Academic Press.

Boesak, Allan. 1982. *The Finger of God: Sermon on Faith and Responsibility*. Maryknoll, NY: Orbis.

Bosch, David J. 1995. *Believing in the Future. Towards a Missiology of Western Culture*. Christian Mission and Modern Culture. Valley Forge, PA: Trinity Press International.

———. 1989. Paul on Human Hopes. *Journal of Theology in South Africa* 67:3–16.

Botha, J. (1994). How Do We Read the Context? *Neotestamentica*, 28/2:291–307.

Brecher, Jeremy, and Tim Costello. 1994. *Global Village or Global Pillage: Economic Reconstruction from the Bottom Up*. 2d Edition. Cambridge, MA: South End Press.

References

Brown, Delwin. 1981. *To Set At Liberty: Christian Faith and Human Freedom.* Maryknoll: Orbis.

Bujo, Bénezet. 1992. *African Theology in its Social Context.* Maryknoll, NY: Orbis.

Burchell, William J. 1824. *Travels in the Interior of Southern Africa*, Vol. 2. London: Longman, Hurst, Rees, Orme, Brown, and Green.

Callaway, Henry. 1868. *The Religious System of the Amazulu.* Springvale: Springvale Mission Press.

Campbell, John. 1815. *Travels in South Africa: Undertaken at the Request of Missionary Society.* 3d edition. London: Black, Parry, & Co. Reprint, Cape Town: C. Struik, 1974.

Chidester, David. 1988. *Salvation and Suicide. An Interpretation of Jim Jones, the People's Temple, and Jonestown.* Indianapolis: Indiana University Press.

―――. 1996. *Savage Systems: Colonialism and Comparative Religion in Southern Africa.* Cape Town: University of Cape Town Press.

Cochrane, James R. 1999. *Circles of Dignity: Community Wisdom and Theological Reflection.* Minneapolis: Fortress.

Colloquy. 1977. Pages 31-48 in *Paul's Concept of Freedom in the Context of Hellenistic Discussions about the Possibilities of Human Freedom.* Protocol of the Twenty-sixth Colloquy. Edited by Wilhelm H. Wuellner. Berkeley, CA: The Center for Hermeneutical Studies in Hellenistic and Modern Culture.

Comaroff, Jean. 1985. *Body of Power, Spirit of Resistance: The Culture and History of a South African People.* Chicago: University of Chicago Press.

Comaroff, John, and Jean Comaroff. 1986. Christianity and Colonialism in South Africa. *American Ethnologist* 13:1-20.

―――. 1988. Through the Looking-glass: Colonial Encounters of the First Kind. *Journal of Historical Sociology* 1/1:6-13.

―――. 1989. The Colonization of Consciousness in South Africa. *Economy and Society* 12:267-95.

―――. 1991. *Of Revelation and Revolution, Vol. 1: Christianity, Colonialism and Consciousness in South Africa.* Chicago: University of Chicago Press.

―――. 1997. *Of Revelation and Revolution, Vol. 2: The Dialectics of Modernity on a South African Frontier.* Chicago: University of Chicago Press.

Combrink, H. J. B. 1986. Perspektiewe uit die Skrif. Pages 211-34 in *Die Ng Kerk en Apartheid.* Edited by J. Kinghorn. Braamfontein: Macmillan.

Cone, James. 1977. *God of the Oppressed*. New York: Seabury Press.
Cook, R. B.. 1981. Paul the Organizer. *Missiology* 9/4:485–98.
Croatto, José Severino. 1987. *Biblical Hermeneutics: Towards a Theory of Reading as the Production of Meaning*. Maryknoll, NY: Orbis.
Cvetkovich, Ann, and Douglas Kellner. 1997. *Articulating the Global and the Local: Globalization and Cultural Studies*. Boulder, CO, and Oxford: Westview.
Dahl, Nils Alstrup. 1977. *Studies in Paul: Theology for the Early Christian Mission*. Minneapolis: Augsburg.
Dallmayr, Fred. 1998. *Alternative Visions: Paths in the Global Village*. New York: Rowman and Littlefield.
Daneel, M. L. 1971. *Old and New in Southern Shona Independent Churches*. New York: Mouton Publishers.
———. 1987. *Quest for Belonging*. Gweru: Mambo Press.
Darwin, Charles. 1963 [1859]. *The Origin of Species: by Means of Natural Selection of the Preservation of Favoured Races in the Struggle for Life*. New York: Washington Square Press.
Davies, Margaret. 1995. Work and Slavery in the New Testament: Impoverishments of Traditions. Pages 315–47 in *The Bible in Ethics: The Second Sheffield Colloquium*. Edited by John W. Rogerson, Margaret Davies, & M. Daniel Carroll R. JSOT Supplement Series, Vol. 207. Sheffield: Sheffield Academic Press.
Dawes, G. W. 1990. But If You Can Gain Your Freedom (1 Corinthians 7:17-24). *Catholic Biblical Quarterly* 52/4:681–97.
De Oliveria, Rosangela Soares. 1995. Feminist Theology in Brazil. In *Women's Vision: Theological Reflection, Celebration, Action*. Edited by O. Ortega. Geneva: WCC.
De Gruchy, John W. 1979. *The Church Struggle in South Africa*. Cape Town: David Philip.
Deidun, T. 1986. Theological Trends: Some Recent Attempts at Explaining Paul's Theology. *The Way* 26:230–42.
Des Prêters Noires S'interrogent. 1956. Paris: Cerf.
Dickson, Kwesi. 1984. *Theology in Africa*. Maryknoll, NY: Orbis.
Draper, Jonathan A. 1991. For the Kingdom Is Inside of You and It Is Outside You: Contextualization Exegesis in South Africa. Pages 235–58 in *Text and Interpretation: New Approaches in the Criticism of the New Testament*. Edited by P. J. Hartin and J. H. Petzer. Leiden: Brill.
———. 1993. The Bible in African Literature: A "Contrapuntal Perspective." *Bulletin of Contextual Theology* 3/3:1–3.
———. 1996. Great and Little Traditions: Challenges to the Domi-

nant Western Paradigm of Biblical Interpretation. *Bulletin of Contextual Theology* 6/1:1–3.

———. 1994. Jesus and the Renewal of Local Community in Galilee. *Journal of Theology for Southern Africa* 87:29–42.

Drimmelen, Rob Van. 1998. *Faith in Global Economy. A Primer for Christians.* Geneva: WCC.

Dube, Musa W. 1996a. Readings of *Semoya*: Botswana Women's Interpretations of Matthew 15:21-28. *Semeia* 73:111–29.

———. 1996b. Reading for Decolonization (John 4:1-42). *Semeia* 75: 37–59.

———. 1997. Towards a Postcolonial Feminist Interpretation of the Bible. *Semeia* 78:11–26.

———. 1998a. Go Therefore unto the World: A Postcolonial Perspective on Biblical Pedagogy. Pages 224–46 in *Teaching the Bible*. Edited by Mary Ann Tolbert and Fernando Segovia. Maryknoll, NY: Orbis.

———. 1998b. Scripture, Feminism, and Postcolonial Contexts. *Concilium* 4:45–52.

———. 2000. *Postcolonial Feminist Interpretation of the Bible*. St Louis: Chalice.

———, ed. 2001.*Other Ways of Reading: African Women and the Bible*. Atlanta: Society of Biblical Literature, and Geneva: WCC.

Dunn, J. D. G. 1993. *Christian Liberty: A New Testament Perspective*. The Didsbury Lectures. Carlisle: Paternoster.

Dyson, A. O. 1985. Freedom in Christ and Contemporary Concepts of Freedom. *Studia Theologica* 39: 55–72.

Elliott, Neil. 1994. *Liberating Paul. The Justice of God and the Politics of the Apostle*. Maryknoll, NY: Orbis.

———. 1997. Figure and Ground in the Interpretation of Romans 9-11. Pages 371–89 in *The Theological Interpretation of Scripture: Classic and Contemporary Readings*. Edited by Stephen E. Fowl. Oxford: Blackwell.

Engberg-Pedersen, Troels. 1995. Galatians in Romans 5-8 and Paul's Construction of the Identity of Christ Believers. Pages 477–505 in *Texts and Contexts: Biblical Texts in Their Textual and Situational Contexts: Essays in Honor of Lars Hartman*. Edited by Tord Fornberg and David Hellholm. Oslo: Scandinavian University Press.

Falusi, G. 1973. The Christian View of Freedom. *Orita* 7(2):113–28.

Fashole-Luke, Edward W. 1976. The Quest for African Christian Theologies. In *Third World Theologies*. Volume 3 of *Mission Trends*.

Edited by Gerald H. Anderson and Thomas F. Stransky. Grand Rapids: Eerdmans.

Felder, Cain Hope, ed. 1991. *Stoney the Road We Trod: African American Biblical Interpretation*. Minneapolis: Fortress

———. 1994. *Troubling Biblical Waters: Race, Class, and Family*. Maryknoll, NY: Orbis.

Fiorenza, Elisabeth Schüssler. 1988. The Ethics of Biblical Interpretation: Decentering Biblical Scholarship. *Journal of Biblical Literature* 107:3–17.

———. 2000. Defending the Center, Trivializing the Margins. Pages 29–48 in Heikki Räisänen et al., *Reading the Bible in the Global Village: Helsinki*. Atlanta: Society of Biblical Literature.

Fish, Stanley. 1980. *Is There a Text in this Class? The Authority of Interpretive Communities*. Cambridge: Harvard University Press.

Fornberg, Tord, and David Hellholm, eds. 1995. *Texts and Contexts: Biblical Texts in Their Textual and Situational Contexts: Essays in Honor of Lars Hartman*. Oslo: Scandinavian University Press.

Fortman, Bas De Gaay and Berma Klein Goldewijk. 1999. *God and the Goods: Global Economy in a Civilizational Perspective*. Geneva: WCC.

Foucault, Michel. 1980. *Power/Knowledge: Selected Writings and Other Interviews 1972–1977*. Edited by C. Gordon. New York: Pantheon.

Fowl, Stephen E. 1990. The Ethics of Interpretation; Or, What's Left over after the Elimination of Meaning. In *the Bible in Three Dimensions: Essays in Celebration of the Fortieth Anniversary of the Department of Biblical Studies, University of Sheffield*, Edited by D. J. A. Clines, S. E. Fowl and S. E. Porter. Sheffield: JSOT Press.

———, ed. 1997. *The Theological Interpretation of Scripture: Classic and Contemporary Readings*. Oxford: Blackwell.

France, R. T. 1986. Liberation in the New Testament. *Evangelical Quarterly* 58/1:3–23.

Friedman, Jonathan. 1994. *Cultural Identity and Global Process*. London: Sage.

Frostin, Per. 1988. *Liberation Theology in Tanzania and South Africa: A First World Interpretation*. Lund: Lund University Press.

Fulkerson, Mary McClintock. 1994. *Changing the Subject: Women's Discourses and Feminist Theology*. Minneapolis: Fortress.

Georgi, Dieter. 1991a. Auf dem Weg zu Einer Urbanen Theologie. Denkanstösse Zur Funktion Universitär Verfasster Wissenschaft- lichen Theologie. Pages 1–14 in *Einer Metropole. Proceedings of the Symposion: Protestantismus als Integrative Kraft in der Multikul-turellem Gesellschaft?, Frankfurt Am Main, October 31, 1991 to 3 Nov 1991*.

REFERENCES

———. 1991b. *Theocracy in Paul's Praxis and Theology*. Translated by David E. Green. 1987. Minneapolis: Fortress.

———. 1992. *Remembering the Poor: The History of Paul's Collection for Jerusalem*. 1965. Nashville: Abingdon.

Gerhardsson, B. 1987. *Eleutheria* ("Freedom") in the Bible. Pages 3–23 in *Scripture: Meaning and Method. Essays Presented to Anthony Tyrrell Hanson on His Seventieth Birthday*, Edited by B. P. Thompson. Hull: Hull University Press.

Giddens, Anthony. 1990. *The Consequences of Modernity*. Cambridge: Polity Press.

Gifford, Paul. 1991. *The New Crusaders: Christianity and the New Right in Southern Africa*. London: Pluto.

———, ed. 1995. *Christian Churches and the Democratization of Africa*. Leiden: Brill.

———. 1998. *African Christianity: Its Public Role*. Bloomington: Indiana University Press.

Gottwald, Norman K., and Richard A. Horsley, eds. 1993. *The Bible and Liberation: Political and Social Hermeneutics*. Maryknoll, NY: Orbis.

GRIC (Muslim-Christian Research Group). 1989. *The Challenge of the Scriptures. The Bible and the Qur'an*. Faith Meets Faith Series. Translated by Stuart E Brown. Maryknoll: Orbis.

Habel, Norman C., ed. 2000. *Readings from the Perspective of Earth*. Sheffield: Sheffield Academic Press.

Haddad, Beverly Gail. 2001. African Women's Theologies of Survival: Intersecting Faith, Feminisms and Development. Ph.D. Thesis, University of Natal, Pietermaritzburg.

Hafemann, Scott J. 1993. Paul and His Interpreters. Pages 666–79 in *Dictionary of Paul and His Letters*. Gerald F. Hawthorne, Ralph P. Martin, and Daniel G. Reid. Downers Grove, IL: InterVarsity Press.

Hanks, Thomas D. 1983. *God So Loved the Third World: The Biblical Vocabulary of Oppression*. Translated by James C. Dekker. Maryknoll, NY: Orbis.

Hartin, Patrick J. 1992. *Third World Challenges in the Teaching of Biblical Studies: Occasional Papers* 25. Claremont: The Institute for Antiquity and Christianity.

Harvey, David. 1990. *The Condition of Postmodernity*. Oxford: Blackwell.

Hastings, Adrian. 1976. *African Christianity: An Essay in Interpretation*. London: Chapman.

———. 1994. *The Church in Africa, 1450–1950*. Oxford: Clarendon.

Hays, Richard B. 1996. *The Moral Vision of the New Testament: A Contemporary Introduction to New Testament Ethics*. San Francisco: HarperSanFrancisco.

Hendricks, Osayande Obery. 1995. Guerrilla Exegesis: 'Struggle' as a Scholarly Vocation: A Postmodern Approach to African-American Interpretation. *Semeia* 72:73–90.

Hengel, Martin. 1974. *Property and Riches in the Early Church: Aspects of a Social History of Early Christianity*. Translated by John Bowden. London: SCM.

———. 1991. *The Pre-Christian Paul*. Translated by John Bowden. London, SCM and Philadelphia: Trinity Press International.

Hinkelhammert, F. J. 1997. Liberation Theology in the Economic and Social Context of Latin America: Economy and Theology, or the Irrationality of the Rationalized. Pages 25–52 in *Liberation Theologies, Postmodernity, and the Americas*. Edited by David Batstone, et al. London & New York: Routledge.

Holter, Knut. 1996. *Tropical Africa and the Old Testament: A Select and Annotated Bibliography*. Oslo: University of Oslo.

———. 1998. It's Not Only a Question of Money! African Old Testament Scholarship between the Myths and Meanings of the South and the Money and Methods of the North. *Old Testament Essays* 11:240–54.

———. 2000a. Old Testament Scholarship in Sub-Saharan African North of the Limpopo River. In *The Bible in Africa: Transactions, Trajectories, and Trends*. Edited by Gerald. O. West and Musa W. Dube. Leiden: Brill.

———. 2000b. *Yahweh in Africa: Essays on Africa and the Old Testament*. New York: Peter Lang.

Hopkins, Dwight. 2000. *Down, Up, and Over: Slave Religion and Black Theology*. Minneapolis: Fortress.

Horsley, Richard A. 1995. Innovation in Search of Reorientation. New Testament Studies Rediscovering its Subject Matter. *Journal of the American Academy of Religion* 62/4:1127–66.

———. 1998. Submerged Biblical Histories and Imperial Biblical Studies. Pages 152–73 in *The Postcolonial Bible, Vol. 1: Bible and Postcolonialism*. Edited by R. S. Sugirtharajah. Sheffield: Sheffield Academic Press.

Idowu, Bolaji. 1965. *Towards an Indigenous Church*. Oxford: Oxford University Press

Iser, Wolfgang. 1978. *The Act of Reading: A Theory of Aesthetic Response*. Baltimore: John Hopkins University Press.

Isichei, Elizabeth. 1995. *A History of Christianity in Africa.* Grand Rapids: Eerdmans
Jones, Amos, Jr. 1984. *Paul's Message of Freedom: What Does it Mean to the Black Church?* Valley Forge, PA: Judson.
Junod, Henri-Alexander. 1912. *The Life of a South African Tribe.* 2 vols. Lausanne: Bridel.
Kataribaabo, Dominic, Credonia Mwerinde, and Joseph Kibwetere. 1991. *A Timely Message from Heaven: The End of the Present Times. Delivered through the Seers with Orders to Inaugurate a Movement for the Restoration of the Ten Commandments of God.* N.p.
Katongole, Emmanuel. 1998. African Renaissance and the Challenge of Narrative Theology in Africa: Which Story/Whose Renaissance? *Journal of Theology for Southern Africa* 102:29–39.
Keck, Leander E. 1984. Paul and Apocalyptic Theology. *Interpretation* 38/3:229–41.
Kittredge, Cynthia Briggs. 1998. *Community and Authority: The Rhetoric of Obedience in the Pauline Tradition.* Harrisburg, PA: Trinity Press International.
Kpobi, David Nii Anum. 1993. *Mission in Chains: The Life, Theology, and Ministry of the Ex-slave Jacobus Capitein (1717–1747) with a Translation of His Major Publications.* Zoetermeer: Boeckencentrum.
Kuhn, Thomas S. 1970. *The Structure of Scientific Revolutions.* 2d edition. Chicago: University of Chicago Press.
Landau, Paul Stuart. 1995. *The Realm of the Word: Language, Gender, and Christianity in a Southern African Kingdom.* Portsmouth: Heinemann.
———. 1999. "Religion" and Christian Conversion in African History: A New Model. *Journal of Religious History* 23/1:8–30.
Lategan, Bernard C. 1991. New Testament Anthropological Perspectives in a Time of Reconstruction. *Journal of Theology in South Africa* 76:86–94.
———. 1994. Reception: Theory and Practice in Reading Romans 13. Pages 145–69 in *Text and Interpretation: New Approaches in the Criticism of the New Testament.* Edited by P. J. Hartin and J. H. Petzer. Leiden: Brill.
Lemarquand, Grant. 1995. Bibliography of the Bible in Africa. *Journal of Inculturation Theology* 2/1:39–139.
———. 2000a. A Bibliography of the Bible in Africa. In *The Bible in Africa: Transactions, Trajectories, and Trends.* Edited by Gerald O. West and Musa W. Dube. Leiden: Brill.
———. 2000b. New Testament Exegesis in (Modern) Africa. In *The Bi-*

ble in Africa: Transactions, Trajectories, and Trends. Edited by Gerald O. West and Musa W. Dube. Leiden: Brill.

Levi, Ken, ed. 1982. *Violence and Religious Commitment: Implications of Jim Jones's People's Temple Movement.* University Park, PA: Pennsylvania State University Press.

Lewis, L. A. 1991. An African American Appraisal of the Philemon-Paul-Onesimus Triangle. In *Stony the Road We Trod: African American Biblical Interpretation*, ed. Cain Hope Felder, 232–46. Minneapolis: Fortress.

Lienhardt, Geoffrey. 1961. *Divinity and Experience: The Religion of the Dinka.* Oxford: Oxford University Press.

Mach, Michael. 1993. The Social Implications of Scripture-interpretation in Second Temple Judaism. Pages 166–79 in *The Sociology of Sacred Texts.* Edited by J. Davies and I. Wollaston. Sheffield: Sheffield Academic Press.

Maimela, Simon S. 1991. Black Theology and the Quest for a God of Liberation. Pages 41–59 in *Theology at the End of Modernity: Essays in Honor of Gordon Kaufman.* Edited by Sheila Greeve Devaney. Philadelphia: Trinity Press International.

Malina, Bruce J., and Richard L. Rohrbaugh. 1998. *Social-science Commentary on the Gospel of John.* Minneapolis: Fortress.

Maluleke, Tinyiko S. 1996. Black and African Theologies in the New World Order: A Time to Drink from Our Own Wells. *Journal of Theology for Southern Africa* 96:3–19.

———. 1997. Half a Century of African Christian Theologies: Elements of the Emerging Agenda for the Twenty-First Century. *Journal of Theology for Southern Africa* 99:4–23.

———. 1998a. African Traditional Religions in Christian Mission and Christian Scholarship: Re-opening a Debate That Never Started. *Religion and Theology* 5/2:121–37.

———. 1998b. "Christianity in a Distressed Africa. A Time to Own and Own Up." *Missionalia* 26:3 (December 1998), 324–40.

———. 1999a. "Black Theology as Public Discourse." Concept paper, Multi-event 99 Academic Conference, October 1999, Cape Town, South Africa. See <http://www.ricsa.org.za>.

———. 1999b. "Pour Une Foi Avec De Profondes Racines. *Itiniraires* 28:13–15.

———. 2000a. The Bible among African Christians: A Missiological Perspective. Pages 87–112 in *To Cast Fire upon the Earth: Bible and Mission Collaborating in Today's Multicultural Global Context.* Edited by Teresa Okure. Pietermaritzburg: Cluster.

———. 2000b. A Historical Quest for a Black Presence That "Walks." Pages 229–50 in *Orality, Memory & the Past. Listening to the Voices of Black Clergy under Colonialism and Apartheid*. Edited by Philippe Denis. Pietermaritzburg: Cluster.

———. 2000c. The Rediscovery of the Agency of Africans. *Journal of Theology for Southern Africa* 108:19–37.

Mana, Kä. 1992. *Foi Chréttienne, Crise Africaine et Reconstruction de l'Afrique. Sense et Enjeux Des Théologies Africaines Contemporaines*. Nairobi: CETA/AACC.

———. 1993. *Theologie Africaine Pour Temps De Crise. Christianisme et Reconstruction De l'Afrique*. Paris: Karthala.

———. 2000. *La Nouvelle Évangélisation en Afrique*. Paris: Karthala; Yaoundé: Clé.

Mandew, Martin. 1997. War, Memory, Salvation: The Bulhoek Massacre and the Construction of a Contextual Soteriology. Ph.D. Thesis, University of Natal, Pietermaritzburg.

Marber, Peter. 1998. *From Third World to Third Class: The Future of Emerging Markets in the Global Economy*. Reading, MA: Perseus Books.

Martin, Ralph P. 1981. *Reconciliation: A Study of Paul's Theology*. London: Marshall, Morgan & Scott.

Martyn, J. Louis. 1985. Apocalyptic Antinomies in Paul's Letter to the Galatians. *New Testament Studies* 31:410–24.

Masenya, Madipoane. 1997. Proverbs 31:10-31 in a South African Context: A Reading for the Liberation of African (Northern Sotho) Women. *Semeia* 78:55–68.

Masoga, Mogomme Alpheus. 2000. *Weeping City, Shanty Town Jesus: Introduction to Conversational Theology*. Cape Town: Salty Print.

Matlock, R. Barry. 1996. *Unveiling the Apocalyptic Paul: Paul's Interpreters and the Rhetoric of Criticism*. JSNT Supplement Series, Vol. 127. Sheffield: Sheffield Academic Press.

Mbeki, Thabo. 1998. *Africa: The Time Has Come*. Cape Town: Mafube.

Mbembe, Achille. 1988. *L'Afriques Iindociles. Christianisme, Pouvoir et Etat en Société Postcoloniale*. Paris: Karthala.

Mbiti, John S. 1969. *African Religions and Philosophy*. London: Heinemann.

———. 1970. *Concepts of God in Africa*. London: SPCK.

———. 1971. *New Testament Eschatology in an African Background. A Study of the Encounter between New Testament Theology and African Traditional Concepts*. London: Oxford University Press.

———. 1975. *Introduction to African Religion*. Nairobi: Heinemann.

———. 1976. Theological Impotence and the Universality of the Church. In *Mission Trends No. 3: Third World Theologies*. Edited by Gerald H. Anderson and Thomas F. Stransky. New York: Paulist, and Grand Rapids: Eerdmans.

———. 1977. The Biblical Basis for Present Trends in African Theology. Pages 83–94 in *African Theology En Route: Papers from the Pan-African Conference of Third World Theologians, Accra, December 1977*. Edited by Kofi Appiah-Kubi and Sergio Torres. Maryknoll, NY: Orbis.

———. 1986. *Bible and Theology in African Christianity*. Nairobi: Oxford University Press.

Mbuwayesango, Dora Rudo. 1997. Childlessness and Women-to-Women Relationships in Genesis and in African Patriarchal Society: Sarah and Hagar from a Zimbabwean Woman's Perspective (Gen 16:1-16; 21:8-21). *Semeia* 78:27–36.

Meeks, Wayne A. 1986. *The Moral World of the First Christians*. Philadelphia: Westminster.

Metuh, Emefie Ikenga. 1981. *God and Man in African Religion*. London: Geoffrey Chapman.

Meyer, John W. 1980. The World Polity and the Authority of the Nation-State. In *Studies of the Modern World System*. Edited by Albert Bergesen. New York: Academic Press.

Meyer, Paul W. 1997. Romans 10:4 and the 'End' of the Law. Pages 338–55 in *The Theological Interpretation of Scripture: Classic and Contemporary Readings*. Edited by Stephen E. Fowl. Oxford: Blackwell.

Míguez Bonino, José. 1999. Gen 11:1-9—A Latin American Perspective. In *Return to Babel: Global Perspectives on the Bible*. Edited by John R. Levinson and Priscilla Pope-Levinson. Louisville: Westminster John Knox.

Mittleman, James H. 2000. *The Globalization Syndrome: Transformation and Resistance*. Princeton: Princeton University Press.

Moffat, Robert. 1842. *Missionary Labours and Scenes in Southern Africa*. London: John Snow. Reprint 1969, New York: Johnson Reprint Corporation.

Mofokeng, Takatso. 1988. Black Christians, the Bible and Liberation. *Journal of Black Theology in South Africa*. 2/1:34–42.

Moore, Rebecca, and Fielding M. McGhee, III. 1989a. *New Religious Movements, Mass Suicide and the People's Temple. Scholarly Perspectives on a Tragedy*. Lewiston: Edwin Mellen.

———. 1989b. *The Need for a Second Look at Jonestown*. Lewiston: Edwin Mellen.

Mosala, Itumeleng J. 1986. The Use of the Bible in Black Theology. Pages 175–99 in *The Unquestionable Right to Be Free: Essays in Black Theology*. Edited by Itumeleng J. Mosala and Butie Tlhagale. Johannesburg: Skotaville and Maryknoll, NY: Orbis.

———. 1987. *Biblical Hermeneutics and Black Theology in South Africa*. Ph.D. Thesis, University of Cape Town.

———. 1989. *Biblical Hermeneutics and Black Theology in South Africa*. Grand Rapids: Eerdmans.

———. (1991). Land, Class and the Bible in South Africa Today. *Journal of Black Theology in South Africa*, 5/2:40–45.

Motlhabi, Mokgethi G. 1994. Black or African Theology? Toward and Integral African Theology. *Journal of Black Theology in South Africa* 8/2:113–41.

Mudimbe, V. Y. 1988. *The Invention of Africa: Gnosis, Philosophy, and the Order of Knowledge*. Bloomington: Indiana University Press.

———. *The Idea of Africa*. London: James Curry and Bloomington: Indiana University Press.

Mugambi, J. N. K. 1995. *From Liberation to Reconstruction: African Christian Theology after the Cold War*. Nairobi: East African Educational Publishers.

Mukerji, Chandra, and Michael Schudson. 1991. *Rethinking Popular Culture: Contemporary Perspectives in Cultural Studies*. Berkeley and Los Angeles: University of California Press.

Murphy-O'Connor, Jerome. 1989. *Becoming Human Together: The Pastoral Anthropology of St. Paul*. Good News Studies, Vol 2. Wilmington, DE: Michael Glazier.

Naude, Piet. 1996. Theology with a New Voice: The Case for an Oral Theology in the Southern Context. *Journal of Theology for Southern Africa*, 96:18–31.

Neusner, Jacob. 1988. Beyond Myth, After Apocalypse: The Mishnaic Conception of History. Pages 91–106 in *The Social World of Formative Christianity and Judaism: Essays in Tribute to Howard Clark Kee*. Edited by. Jacob Neusner, et al. Philadelphia: Fortress.

———. 1989. The Absoluteness of Christianity and the Uniqueness of Judaism: Why Salvation Is Not of the Jews. *Interpretation* 43:18–31.

Njoroge, Nyambura J., and Musa W. Dube, eds. 2001. *Talitha Cum: Theologies of African Women* (Natal: Cluster Publications.

Nürnberger, Klaus. 1978. The Economics of Paul. Pages 163–71 in *Affluence, Poverty and the Word of God.:An Interdisciplinary Study Program of the Missiological Institute Mapumulo. Edited by Klaus Nürnberger. Durban: Lutheran Publishing House.

Oakman, Douglas E. 1996. The Ancient Economy. Pages 126–43 in *The Social Sciences and New Testament Interpretation*. Edited by Richard Rohrbaugh. Peabody, MA: Hendrickson.

Oduyoye, Mercy Amba. 1995. *Daughters of Anowa: African Women and Patriarchy*. Maryknoll, NY: Orbis.

Okure, Teresa. 1993. Feminist Interpretation in Africa. In *Searching the Scriptures: A Feminist Introduction*. Edited by Elisabeth Schüssler Fiorenza. New York: Crossroads.

Osiek, Carolyn. 1992. Slavery in the Second Testament World. *Biblical Theology Bulletin* 22/4:174–79.

P'bitek, Okot. 1986. *Artist, the Ruler: Essays on Art, Culture and Values*. Nairobi: East African Educational Publishers.

Pathrapankal, Joseph. 1995. Apostolic Commitment and "Remembering the Poor": A Study in Gal 2:10. Pages 1001–18 in *Texts and Contexts: Biblical Texts in Their Textual and Situational Contexts: Essays in Honor of Lars Hartman*. Edited by Tord Fornberg and David Hellholm. Oslo: Scandinavian University Press.

Patte, Daniel. 1995. *Ethics of Biblical Interpretation: A Reevaluation*. Louisville: Westminster John Knox.

———. 1999. *The Challenge of Discipleship: A Critical Study of the Sermon on the Mount as Scripture*. Harrisburg, PA: Trinity Press International.

Petersen, Norman R. 1985. *Rediscovering Paul: Philemon and the Sociology of Paul's Narrative World*. Philadelphia: Fortress.

Petersen, Robin. 1995. Time, Resistance and Reconstruction: Rethinking Kairos Theology. Ph.D. Thesis, University of Chicago.

Pobee, John S. 1985–86. Teaching the New Testament in an African Context. *Journal of Religious Thought* 42:22–39.

Ridderbos, Herman N. 1975. *Paul: An Outline of His Theology*. Trans. J. R. De Witt. London: SPCK.

Ringe, Sharon H. 1995. The New Testament and the Ethics of Cultural Compromise: *Compromiso* with the God of Life or Compromise with the Ideology of Power? Pages 232–47 in *The Bible in Ethics: The Second Sheffield Colloquium*. Edited by John W. Rogerson, Margaret Davies, and M. Daniel Carroll R. JSOT Supplement Series, Vol. 207. Sheffield: Sheffield Academic Press.

Robertson, Roland. 1987. Church-State Relations and the World System. In *Church-State Relations: Tensions and Transitions*. Edited by

Thomas Robbins and Roland Robertson. New Brunswick, NJ: Transaction Press.

———. 1992. *Globalization: Social Theory and Global Culture*. Newbury Park, CA: Sage.

Rowland, Christopher. 1995. The Gospel, the Poor and the Churches: Attitudes to Poverty in the British Churches and Biblical Exegesis. Pages 213–31 in *The Bible in Ethics: The Second Sheffield Colloquium*. Edited by John W. Rogerson, Margaret Davies, and M. Daniel Carroll R. JSOT Supplement Series, Vol. 207. Sheffield: Sheffield Academic Press.

Sanneh, Lamin. 1989. *Translating the Message. The Missionary Impact on Culture*. American Society of Missiology Series, No. 13. Maryknoll, NY: Orbis.

———. 1992. Gospel and Culture: Ramifying Effects of Scriptural Translation. Pages 1–23 in *Bible Translation and the Spread of the Church: The Last 200 Years*. Edited by P. C. Stine. Studies in Christian Mission, Vol. 2. Leiden: Brill.

Santa Ana, Julio De, ed. 1998. *Sustainability and Globalization*. Geneva: WCC.

Sassen, Saskia. 1998. *Globalization and its Discontents: Essays on the New Mobility of People and Money*. New York: New Press.

Scheffler, E. H. 1991. Reading Luke from the Perspective of Liberation. Pages 281–98 in *Text and Interpretation: New Approaches in the Criticism of the New Testament*. Edited by P. J. Hartin and J. H. Petzer. Leiden: Brill.

Schotroff, Willy, and Wolfgang Stegemann, eds. 1984. *God of the Lowly: Socio-Historical Interpretation of the Bible*. Maryknoll, NY: Orbis.

Schreiter, Robert J. 1985. *Constructing Local Theologies*. Maryknoll, NY: Orbis.

———. 1998. *The New Catholicity: Theology between the Global and the Local*. Maryknoll, NY: Orbis.

Segovia, Fernando. 1998. Biblical Criticism and Postcolonial Studies: Towards a Postcolonial Optic. Pages 49–65 in *The Postcolonial Bible, Vol. 1: Bible and Postcolonialism*. Edited by R. S. Sugirtharajah. Sheffield: Sheffield Academic Press

———. 1999. The Hermeneutics of Liberation. Unpublished paper presented to the SNTS Seminar on Hermeneutics, Johannesburg, South Africa.

Segundo, Juan Luis 1986. *The Humanist Christology of Paul*. Jesus of

Nazareth Yesterday and Today, Vol. 3. Translated by John Drury. Maryknoll, NY: Orbis.

Setiloane, Gabriel M. 1976. *The Image of God among the Sotho-Tswana*. Rotterdam: Balkema.

Sibeko, Malika, and Beverley G. Haddad. 1997. Reading the Bible 'With' Women in Poor and Marginalized Communities in South Africa (Mark 5:21-6:1). *Semeia* 78:83–92.

Sider, Ronald J. 1977. *Rich Christians in an Age of Hunger: A Biblical Study*. London: Hodder and Stoughton.

Smit, J. A. 2000. Higher Education, the African Renaissance and Higher Education's Currila. Unpublished Paper.

Smith, Theophus H. 1994. *Conjuring Culture: Biblical Formations of Black America*. Oxford and New York: Oxford University Press.

Smith-Christopher, Daniel. 1995. Introduction. In *Text and Experience: Towards a Cultural Exegesis of the Bible*. Edited by Daniel Smith-Christopher. Sheffield: Sheffield Academic Press.

Soards, Marion L. 1987. *The Apostle Paul: An Introduction to His Writings and Teaching*. Mahwah, NJ: Paulist.

Spivak, Gayatri Chakravorty. 1988. Can the Subaltern Speak? In *Marxism and the Interpretation of Culture*. Edited by Cary Nelson and Lawrence Grossberg. Urbana and Chicago: University of Illinois Press.

Stegner, W. Richard. 1993. Paul the Jew. Pages 503–11 in *Dictionary of Paul and His Letters*. Edited by Gerald F. Hawthorne, Ralph P. Martin, and Daniel G. Reid. Downers Grove, IL: InterVarsity Press.

Storey, John. 1998. *Cultural Theory and Popular Culture*. 2d Edition. Athens, GA: University of Georgia Press.

Sugirtharajah, R. S. 1998a. *Asian Biblical Hermeneutics and Postcolonialism: Contesting Interpretations*. Maryknoll, NY: Orbis.

———. 1998b. Biblical Studies after the Empire: From a Colonial to a Postcolonial Mode of Interpretation. Pages 12–22 in *The Postcolonial Bible, Vol. 1: Bible and Postcolonialism*. Edited by R. S. Sugirtharajah. Sheffield: Sheffield Academic Press.

Sundkler, Bengt. 1948. *Bantu Prophets in South Africa*. Oxford: Oxford University Press

———. 1962. *The Christian Ministry in Africa* . Liverpool: Charles Birchal.

———. 1976. *Zulu Zion and Some Swazi Zionists*. Oxford: Oxford University Press.

———, and Christopher Steed. 2000. *A History of the Church in Africa*. Cambridge: Cambridge University Press.

Tabb, William K. 1999. Progressive Globalization: Challenging the Audacity of Capital. *Monthly Review* 50/9:1–10.
Talbot, Percy A. 1923. *Life in Southern Nigeria.* London: Macmillan.
Tambasco, Anthony J. 1982. Pauline Ethics: An Application of Liberation Hermeneutics. *Biblical Theology Bulletin* 12:125–27.
Tamez, Elsa. 1993. *The Amnesty of Grace: Justification by Faith from a Latin American Perspective.* Translated by Sharon H. Ringe. Nashville: Abingdon.
Tempels, Placide. 1945. *La Philosophie Bantoe.* Paris: Présence Africaine.
———. 1956. *African Philosophy.* Paris: Présence Africaine.
Tiffin, Helen. 1991. Introduction. Pages vii–xvi in *Past the Last Post: Theorizing Post-colonialism and Post-modernism.* Edited by Ian Adam and Helen Tiffin. New York and Toronto: Harvester Wheatsheaf.
Tompkins, Jane P., ed. 1980. *Reader-Response Criticism: From Formalism to Post-structuralism.* Baltimore: John Hopkins University Press.
Tuckett, Christopher M. 1991. Paul, Tradition and Freedom. *Theologische Zeitschrift* 47/4:307–25.
Tutu, Desmond Mpilo. 1978. Whither African Theology? In *Christianity in Independent Africa.* Edited by E. W. Fashole-Luke, et al. London: Rex Collins.
———. 1983. *Hope and Suffering: Sermons and Speeches.* Johannesburg: Skotaville.
———. 1999. *No Future Without Forgiveness.* London: Rider.
Ukpong, Justin S. 1995. Rereading the Bible with African Eyes: Inculturation and Hermeneutics. *Journal of Theology for Southern Africa* 41:3–14.
———. 1999a. Models and Methods of Biblical Interpretation in Africa. *Neue Zeitschrift Fur Missionswissenschaft* 55/4:279–95.
———. 1999b. Developments in Biblical Interpretation in Modern Africa. *Missionalia* 27/3:313–29.
———. 1999c. Can African Old Testament Scholarship Escape the Historical Critical Approach? *Newsletter on African Old Testament Scholarship* [now *Bulletin for Old Testament Studies in Africa*] 7:2–5.
———. 2000. Developments in Biblical Interpretation in Africa: Historical and Hermeneutical Directions. *Journal of Theology for Southern Africa* 108:3–18.
Usry, Glenn, and Craig S. Keener. 1996. *Black Man's Religion: Can Christianity Be Afrocentric?* Downers Grove, IL: InterVarsity Press.
Vollenweider, Samuel. 1989. *Freiheit als Neue Schöpfung. Eine Untersuching zur Eleutheria bei Paulus und in Seiner Umwelt.* Göttingen: Vandenhoeck & Ruprecht.

Wallerstein, Immanuel. 1974. *The Modern World-System: Capitalist Agriculture and the Origins of the European World-Economy in the Sixteenth Century.* New York: Academy Press.

———. 1980. *Mercantilism and the Consolidation of the World-Economy, 1650–1750.* Volume 2 of *The Modern World-System.* New York: Academy Press.

———. 1989. *The Second Era of Great Expansion of the Capitalist World-Economy, 1730–1840s.* Volume 3 of *The Modern World-System.* New York: Cambridge University Press.

Walls, Andrew. 1976. Towards an Understanding of Africa's Place in Christian History. Pages 180–89 in *Religion in a Pluralistic Society*, Edited by John S. Pobee Leiden: Brill.

Wambutda, Daniel N. 1980. Hermeneutics and the Search for *Theologia Africana. Africa Theological Journal* 9/1:29–39.

Waters, Malcolm. 1995. *Globalization.* London and New York: Routledge.

Welch, Sharon D. 1985. *Communities of Resistance and Solidarity: A Feminist Theology of Liberation.* Maryknoll, NY: Orbis.

West, Gerald O. 1991. *Biblical Hermeneutics of Liberation: Modes of Reading the Bible in the South African Context.* Peitermaritzburg: Cluster.

———. 1992. Some Parameters of the Hermeneutical Debate in the South African Context. *Journal of Theology for Southern Africa* 80:3–13.

———. 1993a. *Contextual Bible Study.* Pietermaritzburg: Cluster.

———. 1993b. *The Interface between Trained Readers and Ordinary Readers in Liberation Hermeneutics: A Case Study: Mark 10:17-22.*

———. 1995. *Biblical Hermeneutics of Liberation: Modes of Reading the Bible in the South African Context.* 2d edition. Maryknoll, NY: Orbis, and Pietermaritzburg: Cluster.

———. 1995. Constructing Critical and Contextual Readings with Ordinary Readers: Mark 5:21-6:1. *Journal of Theology for South Africa* 92:60–69.

———. 1997. On the Eve of an African Biblical Studies: Trajectories and Trends. *Journal of Theology for Southern Africa* 99:99–115.

———. 1999. *The Academy of the Poor: Towards a Dialogical Reading of the Bible.* Sheffield: Sheffield Academic Press.

———. 2000. Mapping African Biblical Interpretation: A Tentative Sketch. In *The Bible in Africa: Transactions, Trends and Trajectories*, Edited by Gerald O. West and Musa W. Dube. Leiden: Brill.

———, and Musa W. Dube, eds. 2000. *The Bible in Africa: Transactions, Trajectories and Trends.* Leiden: Brill.

Wickeri, Philip L., Janice K. Wickeri, and Dayamanthi Niles. 2000.

Plurality, Power and Mission. Intercontextual Theological Explorations on the Role of Religion in the New Millennium. London: Council for World Mission.
Wilder, Amos N. 1961. Eleutheria in the New Testament and Religious Liberty. *Ecumenical Review* 13/4:409–20.
Wimbush, Vincent L. 1985–86. Biblical Historical Study as Liberation: Toward an Afro-Christian Hermeneutic. *Journal of Religious Thought* 42/2:9–21.
———. 1991. The Bible and African Americans: An Outline of an Interpretative History. Pages 81–97 in *Stony the Road We Trod: African American Biblical Interpretation.* Edited by Cain Hope Felder. Minneapolis: Fortress.
———. 1993. Reading Texts Through Worlds, Worlds Through Texts. *Semeia* 62:129–40.
———, ed. 2000. *African Americans and the Bible: Sacred Texts and Social Textures.* New York: Continuum.
Witvliet, Theo. 1985. *A Place in the Sun: Liberation Theology in the Third World.* Translated by John Bowden. London: SCM.
Wright, N. T. 1992. *The New Testament and the People of God.* Volume 1 of *Christian Origins and the Question of God.* Minneapolis: Fortress.
Wuellner, Wilhelm H., ed. 1977. *Paul's Concept of Freedom in the Context of Hellenistic Discussions about the Possibilities of Human Freedom.* Protocol of the 26th Colloquy. Berkeley, CA: The Center for Hermeneutical Studies in Hellenistic and Modern Culture.

Contributors

JUSTIN S. UKPONG is Professor of New Testament at the Catholic Institute of West Africa, Port Harcourt, Nigeria. Among his recent publications are "Tribute to Caesar, Mark 12:13-17 (Matt 22:15-22; Luke 20-26)," *Neotestamentica* 33/2 (1999); "Towards a Holistic Approach to Inculturation Theology," *Mission Studies* XVI-2/32 (1999); and "Developments in Biblical Interpretation in Modern Africa: Historical and Hermeneutical Directions," in Gerald O. West and Musa W. Dube (eds.), *The Bible in Africa: Transactions, Trajectories and Trends* (Brill, 2000).

MUSA W. DUBE is Senior Lecturer on the New Testament in the Department of Theology and Religious Studies, University of Botswana, Gaborone. Her recent publications include "Scripture, Feminism, and Postcolonial Contexts," *Concilium* 4 (1998), and *Postcolonial Feminist Interpretation of the Bible* (Chalice Press, 2000); she is the editor of *Other Ways of Reading: African Women and the Bible* (Society of Biblical Literature and WCC Publications, 2001), and (with Gerald O. West) of *The Bible in Africa: Transactions, Trajectories, and Trends* (Brill, 2000).

GERALD O. WEST is Professor of Hebrew Bible/Old Testament in the School of Theology, University of Natal, South Africa, and Director of the Institute for the Study of the Bible, a community-based project. He has recently published "On the Eve of an African Biblical Studies: Trajectories and Trends," *Journal of Theology for Southern Africa* 99 (1997), and *The Academy of the Poor: Towards a Dialogical Reading of the Bible* (Sheffield Academic Press, 1999), and edited (with Musa W. Dube) *The Bible in Africa: Transactions, Trajectories, and Trends* (Brill, 2000).

ALPHEUS MASOGA is Lecturer on Theology, African Orature, and Moral and Cultural Studies at the University of the North, Qwa Qwa Campus, South Africa. He is the author of "Towards Sacrificial-

Cleansing Ritual in South Africa: An Indigenous African View of Truth and Reconciliation," *Alteration: International Journal for the Study of Southern African Literature and Language* 6/1 (1999), and *Weeping City, Shanty Town Jesus: Introduction to Conversational Theology* (Salty Print, 2000).

NORMAN K. GOTTWALD is Adjunct Professor of Old Testament at the Pacific School of Religion and Professor Emeritus of Biblical Studies at New York Theological Seminary, and a past President of the Society of Biblical Literature. Among his major publications are *The Tribes of Yahweh* (Orbis Books, 1979; Sheffield Academic Press, reprint with new preface, 1999); *The Hebrew Bible—A Socio-Literary Introduction* (Fortress Press, 1985); *The Bible and Liberation: Political and Social Hermeneutics* (edited with Richard A. Horsley; Orbis Books, 1993); and *The Politics of Ancient Israel* (Westminster John Knox Press, 2001).

JEREMY PUNT is Lecturer in New Testament at the University of Fort Hare, Alice, South Africa. Among his recent publications are "Reading the Bible in Africa: On Strategies and Ownership," *Religion and Theology* 4/2 (1997); "The Status of the Bible in Africa: Foundational Document or Stumbling Block?" *Religion and Theology* 5/3 (1998); and "Peace, Conflict, and Religion in South Africa: Biblical Problems, Possibilities, and Prospects," *Missionalia* 27/3 (1999).

TINYIKO S. MALULEKE is Professor of African Theology and of Missiology in the Departments of Missiology and Systematic Theology, Faculty of Theology and Religious Studies, University of South Africa, Pretoria. His recent publications include "The Bible Among African Christians: A Missiological Perspective," in Teresa Okure (ed.), *To Cast Fire upon the Earth: Bible and Mission Collaborating in Today's Multicultural Global Context* (Cluster Publications, 2000); "A Historical Quest for a Black Presence That 'Walks'," in Philippe Denis (ed.), *Orality, Memory, and the Past: Listening to the Voices of Black Clergy Under Colonialism and Apartheid* (Cluster Publications, 2000); and "The Rediscovery of the Agency of Africans," *Journal of Theology for Southern Africa* 108 (2000).

VINCENT L. WIMBUSH is Professor of New Testament and Christian Origins at Union Theological Seminary, New York. In addition to numerous scholarly articles, he is the author of *Paul, The Worldly Ascetic: Response to the World and Self-Understanding According to 1 Corinthians*

7 (Mercer University Press, 1987), and the editor of *Rhetorics of Resistance: A Colloquy on Early Christianity as Rhetorical Formation* (*Semeia* 79, 1997 [1999]); *The Bible and the American Myth: A Symposium on the Bible and Constructions of Meaning* (Mercer University Press, 1999); and *African Americans and the Bible: Sacred Texts and Social Textures* (Continuum, 2000).